FINANCIAL ASPECTS OF ANNUITIES

LOMA (Life Office Management Association, Inc.) is an international association founded in 1924. LOMA is committed to a business partnership with its worldwide members in the insurance and financial services industry to improve their management and operations through quality employee development, research, information sharing, and related products and services. Among LOMA's activities is the sponsorship of the FLMI Insurance Education Program—an educational program intended primarily for home office and branch office employees.

The ***Associate, Annuity Products and Administration (AAPA) Program*** is designed for people who work with all areas of annuities—including product development, marketing/sales, administration, customer service, systems, investments, accounting, and legal/compliance—as well as regulators. To earn the AAPA designation, a student must complete all required courses as outlined in LOMA's most current *Insurance Education Catalog*. Upon successful completion of all required courses, the student receives a diploma awarded by LOMA and is entitled to use the letters *AAPA* after his/her name.

FINANCIAL ASPECTS of ANNUITIES

Susan Conant, FLMI, HIA, CEBS, PAHM

AAPA

LOMA's Associate Annuity Products and Administration Program
Atlanta, Georgia
www.loma.org

LOMA
Information that Works®

Project Team:

Author:	Susan Conant, FLMI, HIA, CEBS, PAHM
Project Managers:	Joyce Abrams Fleming, J.D., FLMI, ACS, AIRC, PAHM, AIAA, ALHC, HIA, MHP
Production/Editorial Manager:	Stephanie Philippo
Exams Editor:	Lisa Kozlowski, FLMI, ACS, AIRC, ALHC, PAHM
Manuscript Editor:	Susan Smith Jones, J.D.
Copyeditor:	Robert D. Land, FLMI, ACS
Permissions Editor:	Michon Wise
Production/Print Coordinator:	Michelle Stone Weathers, ACS
Cover Art and Design:	Score promotion+design The Project Center
Administrative Support:	Aurelia Kennedy-Hemphill

08 07 06 05 04 03 02 01 00 10 9 8 7 6 5 4 3 2 1

While a great deal of care has been taken to provide accurate, current, and authoritative information in regard to the subject matter covered in this book, the ideas, suggestions, general principles, conclusions, and any other information presented here are for general educational purposes only. This text is sold with the understanding that it is neither designed nor intended to provide the reader with legal, accounting, investment, marketing, or other types of professional business management advice. If legal advice or other expert assistance is required, the services of a competent professional should be sought.

Statement of Purpose: LOMA Educational Programs Testing and Designations.
Examinations described in the LOMA Insurance Education Catalog are designed solely to measure whether students have successfully completed the relevant assigned curriculum, and the attainment of the FLMI and other LOMA designations indicates only that all examinations in the given curriculum have been successfully completed. In no way shall a student's completion of a given LOMA course or attainment of the FLMI or other LOMA designation be construed to mean that LOMA in any way certifies that student's competence, training, or ability to perform any given task. LOMA's examinations are to be used solely for general educational purposes, and no other use of the examinations or programs is authorized or intended by LOMA. Furthermore, it is in no way the intention of the LOMA curriculum and examinations staff to describe the standard of appropriate conduct in any field of the insurance and financial services industry, and LOMA expressly repudiates any attempt to so use the curriculum and examinations. Any such assessment of student competence or industry standards of conduct should instead be based on independent professional inquiry and the advice of competent professional counsel.

Library of Congress Cataloging-in-Publication Data

Conant, Susan
Financial aspects of annuities / Susan Conant
p. cm.
Includes index.
ISBN 1-57974-046-4 (pbk.)
1. Annuities. I. Title.
HG8790 .C64 2000
368.3'7—dc21 99-054029

ISBN 1-57974-046-4

Printed in the United States of America

CONTENTS

PREFACE

The purposes of *Financial Aspects of Annuities* are to describe the technical elements of individual nonqualified annuity products in the United States and Canada and to provide a broad overview of related financial concepts. This book has been designed for students who are preparing for LOMA's AAPA 313 examination in the Associate, Annuity Products and Administration (AAPA) designation program. Several features have been included in each chapter to help you organize your studies, reinforce your understanding of the materials, and prepare for the examination. As we describe each of these features, we give you suggestions for studying the material. The examination is based exclusively on the assigned textual materials, including information in the body of the text and in the figures in each chapter. *To ensure that you are studying from the correct texts, check the current LOMA* Insurance Education Catalog *for a description of the texts assigned for the examination for which you are preparing.*

Learning Objectives. The first page of each chapter contains a list of learning objectives to help you focus your studies. Before reading each chapter, review these learning objectives. Then, as you read the chapter, look for material that will help you meet the learning objectives.

Key Terms. This text assumes that you have a basic knowledge of the key terms and concepts associated with annuity principles and products. These basic terms and concepts are reviewed and explained in this text. All of the important terminology introduced in this text is defined or explained when it is first used. Important terminology is highlighted with bold italic type when the term is first defined and is included in a list of key terms at the end of the chapter. All key terms also appear in a comprehensive glossary at the end of the book. As you read each chapter, pay special attention to these key terms.

Figures. Figures appear throughout the text and are designed to illustrate or give examples of the text's discussions of selected important topics. Note that figures may contain information that is tested on the AAPA 313 examination.

Insights. Insights appear throughout the text and are designed to amplify the text's descriptions of certain topics. These insights should help you get a better feel for the operation of annuity products in life and health insurance companies.

CD-ROM. This textbook includes a CD-ROM on the inside back cover. This CD contains additional reference materials that we believe will help you to interpret financial aspects of annuity products. The CD includes (1) *ExecuView* software, (2) an *ExecuView* User's Guide, (3) an *ExecuView* Help file, (4) a sample of a single premium deferred annuity contract, (5) a sample single premium immediate annuity contract, and (6) interest factor tables.

ExecuView: An Asset Share Analysis/Product Profitability Model, Version 2.1, illustrates the financial design and valuation of annuity contracts and life insurance products. *ExecuView 2.1* allows the user to test the profitability of two annuity products under various assumptions affecting interest margins, lapse rates, mortality rates, and expenses. Moreover, *ExecuView* permits users to combine four product models into various product mixes in order to test the effects of different product mixes on an insurance company's overall profitability. *ExecuView* approximates the kind of software actuaries use for modeling annuity products. Version 2.1 of *ExecuView* runs on any computer using Microsoft Windows Version 3.1 [95] or higher. Although using *ExecuView* can considerably enhance a student's learning experience, using *ExecuView* is not a requirement for understanding the textual narrative. In this textbook, instructions for *ExecuView* users will be marked by the symbol EV.

Test Preparation Guide. In addition to this book, LOMA's *Test Preparation Guide for Financial Aspects of Annuities* (Sean Schaeffer Gilley, FLMI, ACS, AIAA, ALHC, HIA, CEBS, PAHM, and Robert H. Hartley, FLMI, ALHC, ACS, CLU, ChFC, RHU, PAHM, is assigned reading for students preparing for the AAPA 313 examination. Used along with this textbook, the test preparation guide (TPG) will help you master the course material. The TPG includes practice exam questions, a full-scale sample examination in both paper and electronic format, and answers to every question in the TPG.

LOMA recommends that you use all of the study aids available for this course. **Studies indicate that students who use LOMA study aids consistently perform significantly better on LOMA examinations than other students.**

ACKNOWLEDGMENTS

No matter how much work an author puts into developing a book, many other individuals always provide valuable expertise and assistance that makes the book possible. The idea for this book and the designation Associate, Annuity Products and Administration originated with LOMA's Education Council, comprised of industry volunteers acting on behalf of the LOMA membership, who identify the membership's most urgent needs in the area of education and direct the LOMA staff to meet those needs. Developing *Financial Aspects of Annuities* required the combined efforts of many highly qualified experts in annuity products, pensions, and insurance. On behalf of LOMA and its membership, we would like to express appreciation to those individuals who generously gave their time and energy and shared their considerable expertise for the development of this textbook.

Textbook Development Panel

Our foremost thanks go to the members of the textbook development panel who reviewed the outline of the entire book and each chapter as it was completed. These individuals have overseen the entire project from beginning to end and have made countless valuable contributions. These people contributed personal time, shared their many years of professional experience and education, provided valuable real-world examples of concepts to bring the material to life for students, suggested wording changes to several drafts of the manuscript, and guided the book's focus toward the most important information for students to learn. In short, this textbook would have been a very different product without their participation. Their critical judgment, diligence, patience, and technical expertise were essential to the book's accuracy and completeness. The members of the textbook development panel include

Robert M. Ahlschwede, FLMI, CLU
Compliance Manager, Investment Products Business Unit
CNA Life Companies

Barry Black, FSA, MAAA, CLU, FLMI
Vice-President, Product Design
Teachers Insurance and Annuity Association–College Retirement Equities Fund

Warren A. Carter, ASA, MAAA
Teachers Insurance and Annuity Association–College Retirement Equities Fund (retired)
Recipient, 1991 FLMI Insurance Education Award

William L. Evans, FLMI, CLU, ChFC
Marketing Consultant
The Principal Financial Group

Francois J. Genest, FSA, FCIA, MAAA, FLMI
Senior Vice-President, Product Management
Fortis Family Life Insurance Company

Eric Henderson, FSA, MAAA
Product Officer—Individual Variable Annuities
Nationwide Financial

David Herder, FLMI, CLU, ChFC
Senior Filing Analyst
North American Company for Life and Health Insurance

Terry Huff, FSA, CLU, ChFC, FLMI
Vice-President
State Farm Life Insurance Company

JoAnn Rumelhart, FSA, MAAA
Vice President—Life Operations
FBL Financial Group

Additional Expert Reviewers

In addition to the members of the textbook development review panel, many other individuals contributed their considerable expertise to ensuring the accuracy and reliability of various specialized aspects of the book. This category includes industry experts who reviewed one or more chapters in the early stages of the text's development. For this effort, we owe a debt of gratitude to the following individuals:

Patricia L. Allison, FSA, CFA, FLMI
Executive Director, Annuity Product Development
USAA Life Insurance Company

Jason A. Bickler, FSA, MAAA
Actuary and Director
Allstate Life Insurance Company

Kevin Borie, FSA, MAAA
Vice-President and Senior Actuary, Investment Products
Protective Life Insurance Company

Charlene N. Butz, EA, MAAA, APA, FLMI
Associate Pension Actuary, Diversified Retirement Services
The Principal Financial Group

Mei-Ying Chao, FSA, MAAA
Associate Actuary, Actuarial—Individual Annuity
The Principal Financial Group

Tom Howell, FLMI
Participant Conservation/Asset Conservation Specialist
American United Life Insurance Company

The author would also like to thank Janice Conort and Mike Suwalski for their contributions to this project.

LOMA Staff

All textbooks developed by LOMA are team projects. The following individuals deserve special mention for the work they performed on this text. Joyce Abrams Fleming, J.D., FLMI, ACS, AIRC, PAHM, AIAA, ALHC, HIA, MHP, Director, Insurance & Financial Services Programs, served as project manager for the entire text. Susan Smith Jones, J.D, and Kenneth L. Huggins, FLMI/M, ACS, served as manuscript editors for the entire text. Lisa Kozlowski, FLMI, ACS, AIRC, ALHC, AIAA, PAHM, Senior Associate, Examinations Department, reviewed the entire manuscript and made many helpful suggestions. Cynthia Mathis Henry, FLMI, ACS, ALHC, PAHM, Senior Associate, Examinations Department, and Mary C. Bickley, J.D.,

FLMI, AIRC, ACS, AIAA, PAHM, Associate, Insurance & Financial Services Programs, reviewed portions of the manuscript and made valuable suggestions. Sean Schaeffer Gilley, FLMI, ACS, AIAA, ALHC, HIA, CEBS, PAHM, MHP, Senior Associate, Examinations Department, and Nicholas L. Desoutter, FLMI, ACS, PAHM, Senior Associate, Educational Programs, performed research that established a valuable foundation for several chapters. Kristen L. Falk, FLMI, ACS, AIAA, Associate, Insurance & Financial Services Programs, reviewed all chapters and made many helpful suggestions. Aurelia Kennedy Hemphill, Administrative Assistant II, Insurance & Financial Services Programs, provided administrative support. Michelle Stone Weathers, ACS, Production/Print Coordinator, Production Department, prepared graphics and performed typesetting. Michon Wise, Editorial/Permissions Coordinator, Production Department, obtained permissions for use of copyrighted material, read the entire manuscript, and made many valuable suggestions. Iris F. Hartley, FLMI, ACS, CLU, drafted the glossary, read the entire manuscript, and made many valuable suggestions. Robert D. Land, FLMI, ACS, copyedited the entire manuscript and drafted the index. Audrey Hiers, Business Coordinator, Production Department, provided business support for the project. From LOMA's Information Center, Olivia Blakemore, ACS, Technical Assistant, Information Center, along with Mallory Eldridge, Writer/Analyst, and Janet Smith, Information Center Researcher, assisted with the research for the project. David A. Lewis, FLMI, ACS, Senior Associate, Examinations Department, Keith Hesser, Senior Programmer/Analyst, Information Systems, and Amy Souwan, Production Coordinator, provided technical support for revisions to the *ExecuView* software and assisted with development of the CD-ROM. The author would like to thank Jeffrey L. Hasty, FLMI, ACS, Vice-President, Management Services, E. Scott Cass, FLMI, General Manager, Banking and Investment Services, and James R. Huffman, FLMI, ACS, Assistant Vice President, Management Services, for providing liaison with LOMA's membership.

We would also like to thank William H. Rabel, Ph.D., FLMI, CLU, Senior Vice President, Education Division, and Dennis W. Goodwin, FLMI, ACS, HIA, Second Vice President, Insurance & Financial Services Programs, for their encouragement and support throughout the text's development. And finally, special thanks to Stephanie Philippo, Director, Production Department, who designed the inside of the text, coordinated the entire production process, made many helpful suggestions, and worked tirelessly to move the project through typesetting.

Susan Conant, FLMI, HIA, CEBS, PAHM
Atlanta, Georgia
2000

CHAPTER 1

Annuity Products and How Insurance Companies Develop Them

After studying this chapter, you should be able to

- Recognize the significance of the annuity contract's owner, annuitant, payee, and beneficiary
- Recognize and distinguish among the features of three popular annuity products: the single premium immediate annuity (SPIA), the single premium deferred annuity (SPDA), and the flexible premium deferred annuity (FPDA)
- Distinguish between fixed and variable annuity contracts
- Recognize the purposes of a market analysis, product design objectives, and feasibility studies for new products

Insurance companies are in business because they offer insurance and annuity products that consumers find valuable. Otherwise, consumers would not purchase these products. Traditionally, under federal law, only life insurance companies were allowed to issue annuity contracts. Accordingly, in this book we frequently discuss the concerns of life insurers as issuers of annuity products. Customers spend vast amounts of money on insurance and annuity products, and so entrust these funds to insurance companies. In 1997, assets under management of the U.S. life insurance industry were approximately $2.6 trillion.[1] Reserves for annuity contracts and pension plans comprised 67.3 percent of the 1997 reserves of life insurance and annuity issuers.[2] Figure 1-1 shows the distribution of reserves by products for life insurance companies in 1997.

PLAN OF THIS TEXTBOOK

Our goal in this textbook is to explore how insurance companies construct annuities so as to benefit all parties involved. We first look at how

FIGURE 1.1

Reserves for Annuity and Insurance Contracts.

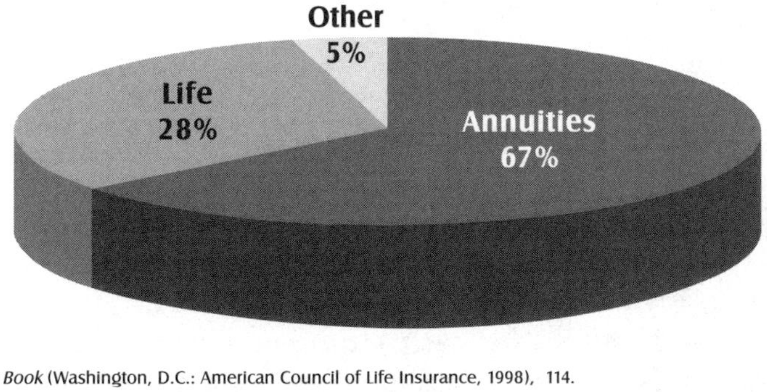

Source: ACLI, *1998 Life Insurance Fact Book* (Washington, D.C.: American Council of Life Insurance, 1998), 114.

insurers develop a new annuity product. Chapter 1 shows the organizational process that insurers employ for decisions concerning new annuity products. Chapter 2 provides a foundation for this textbook's later discussions of technical aspects of insurance companies' annuity products. In Chapter 3, to understand how money grows when invested at interest, we will consider the time value of money. Also in Chapter 3, we will discuss insurance company investment activities.

In Chapters 4 and 5, we will explore some basic financial concepts related to investing, risk, and return. In Chapters 5 and 6, we will cover calculations of the time value of money and discuss how these calculations apply to annuity products. In Chapters 7 and 8, we will discuss how an insurer tests a product design to carefully evaluate whether it will support a product that is profitable for the company. Our attention will then turn to important financial concepts affecting annuity products. Chapter 9 discusses company expense structures, Chapter 10 covers mortality, and Chapter 11 covers reserves. Finally, in Chapter 12, we will address pensions, a group form of retirement plan, and discuss how insurance companies participate in providing pensions for employers and other pension plan sponsors.

In Chapter 1, we begin our discussion of the financial aspects of annuities with an overview of product development and technical product design.

About Annuity Products

In the financial services industry, an ***annuity contract*** is a legally enforceable written agreement under which an insurance company promises to make a series of periodic payments to a named person, starting on a specified date, in exchange for a premium or series of premiums paid to the insurer. To understand an annuity contract, you need to become familiar with a range of specialized terms and concepts. Therefore, before reading further in this chapter, review Figures 1-2 and 1-3. Many terms that are fundamental to annuity contracts are defined in Figure 1-2, while Figure 1-3 identifies and defines various features of different annuity contracts.

Popular Types of Annuities

Despite the many potential varieties of annuities, three types of annuities are particularly popular in the United States. Thus, most of the discussion in this text will refer to these types of annuities.

- **Single premium immediate annuity.** Single premium annuity contracts can be immediate or deferred. A ***single premium immediate annuity (SPIA) contract*** is an immediate annuity contract that is purchased with a lump-sum premium payment on the contract's issue date. As shown in Figure 1-2, an immediate annuity contract begins making periodic income payments one period after

FIGURE 1.2

Annuity Contract Definitions.

annuitant	The ***annuitant*** is the person whose lifetime is used in determining the benefits payable under an annuity contract.
contract owner	The ***contract owner*** of an annuity contract is the person who exercises all rights and privileges in the contract during the lifetime of the annuitant. The contract owner may be someone other than the annuitant. The annuitant is automatically made the contract owner, however, unless the applicant specifically requests to name another party as owner.
payee	The ***payee*** of an annuity contract is the person designated to receive all periodic income payments. Although the payee may be someone other than the contract owner or the annuitant, the owner is automatically made the payee unless there is a specific request to name another party as payee.
periodic income payment	The ***periodic income payment*** of an annuity contract is the monthly, quarterly, semiannual, or yearly payment made to the payee throughout the contract's payout period.
beneficiary	The ***beneficiary*** of an annuity contract is the person named in the contract application to receive any proceeds payable after the annuitant's death.
proceeds	The annuity contract's ***proceeds*** are any death benefit payable upon the death of the annuitant; proceeds usually are in the amount of the contract's accumulation value.
accumulation value	The ***accumulation value*** of a deferred annuity contract is the amount paid for the annuity plus interest earned, less the amount of any withdrawals or fees.
deferred annuity contract	For a ***deferred annuity contract***, periodic income payments generally are scheduled to begin more than one period after the contract's issue date. Only deferred annuity contracts typically can be purchased with multiple premium payments. Any annuity contract purchased with the payment of multiple premiums is a type of deferred annuity.
immediate annuity contract	For an ***immediate annuity contract***, periodic income payments generally are scheduled to begin one period after the contract's issue date; contract issue is typically initiated by a single premium payment.
accumulation period	The ***accumulation period*** of a deferred annuity contract is the time period between the issue date and either the date that the contract's payout period begins or the date that the contract's surrender value is paid; during the accumulation period, the accumulation value of the annuity account grows.
payout period	During the ***payout period***, also known as the *annuitization period*, of an annuity contract, periodic income benefits are payable to the contract's payee.

the single premium payment. Immediate annuity contracts are typically purchased with a single premium payment, and SPIA contracts have a payout period, but no accumulation period. For example, Steve Reuters, at age 65, might use his retirement savings of $75,000 to purchase an immediate annuity that will provide monthly income payments beginning one month after the contract is purchased.

FIGURE 1.3

Features of Annuity Contracts.

Number of Lives Covered	
None	An ***annuity certain*** is a type of annuity contract that has no life contingencies—that is, periodic income benefits are payable under such an annuity whether the annuitant lives or dies.
One	Many annuities cover just one life. A ***life annuity*** is a type of annuity contract under which benefits are payable for only so long as the annuitant lives.
More than one	A ***joint and survivor annuity*** is a type of annuity contract that covers more than one life; under such an annuity, benefits are payable until both covered people die.
	A ***joint life annuity*** is a type of annuity contract that covers more than one life; under such an annuity, benefits are payable until one of the covered people dies.
Premium Payments	
Single	A ***single premium annuity*** is a type of annuity contract that is purchased by the payment of one lump-sum premium.
Periodic	An ***installment premium annuity*** is a type of annuity contract that is paid for in installments.
Level	A ***level premium annuity*** is a type of annuity contract that is paid for in equal installments.
Flexible	A ***flexible premium annuity*** is a type of annuity contract that is paid for in installments that may vary in timing and amount.
Date Periodic Income Payments Begin	
Immediate	The first periodic income payment from an *immediate* annuity is scheduled to take place no later than one period after purchase.
Deferred	The first periodic income payment from a *deferred* annuity is scheduled to take place more than one period after purchase.
Guarantee Affecting Continuation of Periodic Income Payments	
Life annuity only	A ***straight life annuity*** is a type of annuity contract that pays the promised annuity income for so long as the covered person lives, regardless of how long that is. Once the annuitant dies, no further benefit is payable.
Specified period only	A ***period certain annuity*** is a type of annuity contract that promises to make benefit payments for a specific number of periods, regardless of whether the covered person lives.
Later of life or specified period	A ***life with period certain annuity*** is a type of annuity contract that promises to make benefit payments either until the death of the annuitant or until the end of a specified period, whichever is later.
Earlier of life or specified period	A ***temporary life annuity*** is a type of annuity contract that promises to make benefit payments either until the end of a specified period or until the death of the annuitant, whichever is first. No benefits are payable after death or after the temporary period expires.
Refund	A ***refund annuity*** is a type of annuity contract that promises a return of premiums paid if the covered person dies before recovering all premiums paid.
Guaranteed minimum amount or number of payments	A ***guaranteed minimum payout annuity*** is a type of annuity contract that promises to pay a specified minimum dollar amount or a specified minimum number of payments. The minimum payout can take the form of a lump sum or installments.

Figure 1.3 Features of Annuity Contracts. ***continued***

Periodic Income Payment Amount	
Stated and fixed amount per period	For example, $45,000 per year.
Stated and fixed number of annuity units, variable amount of benefit payout per period	The value of annuity units is determined at each payment date by a specified standard, such as the investment performance of a separate account. Example: 400 annuity units, each unit valued at each periodic income payment date according to the performance of a separate account.
Variable number of annuity units, variable amount of benefit payout per period	Value and number of annuity units determined by formula or by another specified standard.
Contract Owners	
Individual owner	The individual contract owner purchases the annuity.
Group (pension) owner	Employers, labor unions, associations, and other groups sponsor pension plans that cover their constituents.

- **Single premium deferred annuity.** Deferred annuities can be purchased with a single premium payment or several premium payments. A deferred annuity contract that is purchased with a single premium payment is a ***single premium deferred annuity (SPDA) contract***. Under an SPDA, the insurer holds the single premium payment at interest until a date specified by the contract owner for benefit payments to begin. During the first contract year of an SPDA, most insurers will accept additional premiums, known as ***window premiums***. Unlike immediate annuities, all deferred annuities have an accumulation period, and benefit payments do not begin within the first period after the annuity purchase.

  Consider the following example. Lucy Paz, upon changing jobs at age 45, might use a lump-sum distribution from a retirement plan as a single premium to purchase a deferred annuity that would not begin making payments until she retires. If Ms. Paz retires at age 65, her annuity contract would have a 20-year accumulation period.

- **Flexible premium deferred annuity.** Under a ***flexible premium deferred annuity (FPDA) contract***, the contract owner typically must pay an initial premium of some minimum amount, such as $1,000, and then may make additional payments at any future times, usually subject to some smaller minimum amount, such as $25. The contract owner can choose not to pay any premium in a given year; the only requirement is that any premium amount paid each year must meet the stated minimum. Figure 1-4 shows an example of contract language describing the premium payment requirements under an FPDA.

FIGURE 1.4

FPDA Premium Provision.

Premium

Premiums may be paid during the lifetime of the Annuitant, and prior to the Retirement Date. Each premium after the first is payable at our Home Office or to our authorized agent. Upon request, a receipt signed by our President or Secretary will be given for any premium payment. Premium payments may be made as frequently or infrequently as is desired. They may be discontinued at any time. We reserve the right to refuse a payment of less than $50. In addition, we reserve the right to refuse all or part of any premium payment in excess of $10,000.00 in any contract year unless this contract is part of a Qualified Plan under the Internal Revenue Code and such larger contribution is allowed under such plan.

All types of deferred and immediate annuity contracts can be classified as either variable or fixed annuities. The distinction hinges upon the presence or absence of guarantees concerning the contract's (1) investment earnings and its (2) investment principal, which for annuities is the amount of premiums paid.

- **Variable annuities.** Under a ***variable annuity contract***, for investment purposes, the contract owner allocates the premiums paid among several pools of investments, known as subaccounts. The subaccounts may be portfolios of stocks, bonds, or other mutual funds designed for insurance and annuity products. The variable annuity contract may offer one fixed interest subaccount, but, under most of the subaccounts offered, the investment results are variable. During the accumulation period, the rate of investment return and the value of the variable subaccounts will fluctuate in accordance with the performance of the subaccounts. During the payout period, the contract owner typically has the option of receiving a periodic income payment that is fixed in amount, or periodic income payments that fluctuate according to the underlying variable subaccounts. Variable annuities offer only limited guarantees as to investment return and only limited guarantees as to cash value or death benefit.
- **Fixed annuities.** A ***fixed annuity contract*** typically guarantees the annuity contract owner that the contract's accumulation value will experience no loss of the investment principal and further, that the contract's accumulation value will earn interest at a current rate

no lower than the minimum interest rate guaranteed in the contract. The fixed annuity contract provides for the insurance company to elect to declare a current interest rate that exceeds the minimum guaranteed interest rate. The amount by which the current interest rate exceeds the minimum guaranteed interest rate is known as excess interest.

The CD-ROM that accompanies this textbook contains sample annuity contracts for a flexible premium deferred annuity (FPDA) and a single premium immediate annuity (SPIA). You may wish to refer to these contracts as you review the material in this book.

Overview of Annuity Product Development

Although a variety of financial institutions may sell annuity products, only insurance companies can develop and issue an annuity product. The activity of creating new annuity products involves employees from all functional areas in an insurance company. We begin this section by considering the usual responsibilities assigned to various organizational units. As you read this section, keep in mind that the names companies give to their organizational units can vary considerably.

Actuarial Services

The actuarial function is responsible for performing a variety of calculations relating to product design, risk, mortality, expenses, and investments. An ***actuary*** is an expert in the mathematics of insurance, annuities, and financial instruments. In insurance companies, actuaries are responsible for ensuring that products are financially sound. An actuary specializing in designing new products is known as a ***product actuary***. In addition to designing new products, actuaries also perform many other mathematical calculations needed in the insurance business. For example, actuaries calculate crediting rates for fixed annuity contracts, establish values for reserves, and create mathematical models of the expected future net cash flows. An actuary specializing in rendering a professional opinion as to proper values for an insurance company's assets and liabilities is known as a ***valuation actuary***. Investment actuaries specialize in performing calculations related to investments, and marketing actuaries specialize in performing calculations related to marketing. The actuarial function is usually headed by a senior company executive who is qualified as an actuary, typically with the title of Chief Actuary.

Accounting

The accounting function is responsible for keeping records of all company transactions. The accounting function of an insurance company must keep several sets of records for different purposes, including internal management information, reporting to company owners, regulatory reporting, and tax reporting.

Compliance

The compliance function in a life insurance company is responsible for ensuring that an insurer's products and operations conform to all standards set by law or regulation. These duties include product and market compliance, contract language, product filings with various state or federal regulators, and review of advertising. The company executive heading the compliance function may have a title such as Chief Compliance Officer.

Contract Administration

The contract administration function is responsible for administering and paying contractual benefits to customers. A company executive, often with the title of Vice-President, Annuity Administration, usually heads the contract administration function.

Customer Service

The customer service function is responsible for all contact with internal and external customers of the company. These customers include contract owners, marketers, and sometimes the owners of shares in the company. (A separate investor relations office usually handles contact with company stockholders.) A senior company executive, with a title such as Chief Administrative Officer, usually heads the customer service function.

Information Systems

The information systems (IS) function is responsible for all information storage, retrieval, and communication systems, especially computerized information systems. The IS function maintains software, hardware, and data, and advises on how information should be captured and stored. The IS function is usually headed by a senior company executive, often with the title of Chief Information Officer.

Investments

The investments function of a life insurance company is responsible for all purchases and sales of assets for the insurance company's investment activities. A senior company executive, with a title such as Chief Investment Officer, typically heads the investment function.

Legal Services

The legal services function in an insurance company is responsible for performing all legal work connected with the company's activities and contracts and participating in legal actions affecting the company. The legal function is headed by a senior company executive who is typically a qualified attorney. A typical title for the executive in charge of legal services is General Counsel.

Marketing

The marketing function is responsible for all product and market planning, market development, marketing strategy, promotion, advertising, direct marketing campaigns, sales training, distribution channels, and distribution systems. In marketing, ***distribution*** refers to the activities involved in making products available for sale to consumers. Thus, a ***distribution system***, also known as a *marketing channel*, is the network of organizations or individuals that performs all of the marketing activities needed to complete a marketing exchange process. In conjunction with the compliance function, the marketing function is responsible for all market conduct compliance. The marketing function is usually headed by a senior company executive, often with the title of Executive Vice President, Marketing.

Cross-Functional Assignments

Each of the functional areas we have described uses distinctive technical terms. Thus, during product development activities, all parties involved need to know how to communicate with others outside of their technical field. For example, product development activities are often guided by a committee or team with membership from different functional areas. The ***marketing committee*** is a senior management group whose primary role is to (1) provide overall guidance and control of the product development process; (2) review new product designs; and (3) approve the further development of each new product design, reject it, or call for product redesign. Hands-on product development is usually undertaken by a group of professionals forming a specific type of project team known as a ***product development team***. A ***project team*** is a group of individuals who are assembled on a temporary basis for the purpose of completing a specified complex task or project. An insurance company's product development team is assembled for the purpose of developing a specific type of new product, perhaps a new variable annuity contract. This product development team would likely have representation from the company's marketing, actuarial, underwriting, contract administration, investments, information systems, customer service, legal, and accounting areas.

Stages in Product Development

Throughout the product development process, an insurance company's staff must continually ensure that a developing product (1) meets the needs of the company's various customers, (2) complies with legal and regulatory requirements, and (3) conforms to the company's financial standards for risk taking and profitability. Although the terminology used to describe the product development process varies from company to company, development of individual annuity products usually includes the following cycle of activities:[3]

- ***Idea generation.*** The insurer must first gather ideas for new product concepts that will meet the needs of the company and of specific segments of the market for annuities. Insurers tend to look continuously for new product ideas through market research, special projects, and monitoring competing products.
- ***Idea screening.*** During idea screening, new product ideas are evaluated quickly and inexpensively. The purpose of idea screening is to select those ideas that deserve further investigation.
- ***Comprehensive business analysis.*** As part of the comprehensive business analysis, the insurer prepares a number of studies designed to thoroughly analyze the feasibility of each product idea. The insurer also identifies the investment strategy that optimizes results and evaluates whether the proposed product can meet all legal and regulatory requirements.
- ***Technical product design.*** The major activities of technical product design include designing a contract form, setting a technical product design, and making sure that procedures and staffing are available to support all aspects of the product. Also during technical design, actuaries and other team members conduct studies to ensure that the product will be financially sound and profitable for the company.
- ***New product implementation.*** The insurer files the contract form and related documents with the appropriate regulatory authorities—usually state insurance departments—and obtains any required approvals of the product. Systems support and administrative processes are put in place to accept the new contracts. The insurer makes plans to advertise and promote the product and designs training materials for its sales producers and employees. The compliance and legal departments review advertisements and training materials to ensure compliance with applicable laws and regulations. In some cases, advertisements and training materials are filed along with the contract form. The sales force is trained to sell the product, and finally, the product is actually offered for sale.
- ***Product evaluation.*** Throughout product development and beyond, the product development team must ensure that new products will meet the company's financial goals and will comply with applicable laws and regulations. After contracts are issued to consumers, the company must continue to monitor the product's performance relative to the performance expectations built into the product's structure. If results are not satisfactory, the new product can be adjusted slightly, or it can be abandoned and possibly replaced with an improved product. Information gathered from monitoring recent products is a stimulus to the idea generation process that begins the product development cycle, which is illustrated in Figure 1-5.

In the remainder of this chapter we will take a closer look at the activities of comprehensive business analysis. The remaining phases of the product development cycle will be discussed in Chapter 2.

FIGURE 1.5

The Product Development Cycle.

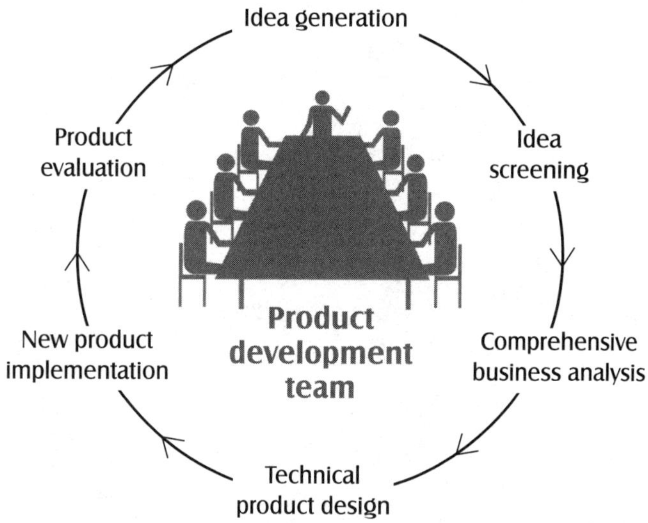

Comprehensive Business Analysis

Before insurance companies commit their resources to developing and introducing a new annuity product, they may conduct considerable research. This preparatory research activity is generally referred to as the comprehensive business analysis phase of product development. Comprehensive business analysis includes five elements that deserve our examination:

1. Market analysis
2. Product design objectives
3. Feasibility studies
4. Marketing plan
5. Forecasts

Market Analysis

A ***market analysis*** is a study of all factors that might affect sales. In essence, it represents the company's effort to learn whether customers want a proposed product. In many cases, staff can prepare a market analysis for a new product using information already gathered during ongoing marketing research activities or while preparing market analyses for similar new product ideas. For a product type that is totally new to the company, however, staff must undertake a complete research process. Figure 1-6 presents some of the topics that typically would be included in a market analysis.

FIGURE 1.6
Contents of a Market Analysis.

Issue	Investigative Focus
Needs to Be Met by the Product	The needs can be the company's needs, consumers' needs, or sales channel needs.
Product and Company Fit	Does the product fit the company's mission and objectives? Can existing systems support the product?
Appeal to Agents	Will this product be easier or more difficult to sell than comparable products? Will agents be enthusiastic about selling it? Will new distribution channels need to be created?
Appeal to Customers	What attributes differentiate this product from those offered by competitors? What attributes make this product unique? What attributes make this product attractive to customers? These attributes must be recognizable, credible, important enough, and relatively easy to communicate to prospects.
Company's Product Mix	Will the new product supplement, complement, or replace current products?
Target Market	How large is the target market? How entrenched are the current competitors in this market? Is the target market compatible with overall company objectives? What level of market penetration can we assume? Will current distribution systems reach the target market?
Product's Competitiveness	How competitive are the annuity product's features? Which key products will be the main competitors? How do we expect our competitors to respond?
Economic Outlook	What are current projections for market interest rates? Unemployment?
Product's Tax Features	Does the product have any special tax advantages for consumers? What about tax problems?
Compliance Issues	Can the product be legally produced and sold? Could the product develop any negative reputation among regulators or consumer advocacy groups?

As a product idea progresses through the product development cycle, the product development team makes progressively more detailed product design decisions. Although the team conceptualizes many aspects of a new product before performing a market analysis, the market analysis provides a foundation for a set of product design objectives.

Product Design Objectives

Product design objectives for a proposed annuity product specify the product's basic characteristics, benefits, limits on the contract amount, age limits for an annuitant, any special features, commission range, and the manner in which the insurer will provide annuity income payments. These specifications then serve as guidelines during the technical design of the product. It is important for the company to obtain the distribution channel's acceptance of the new product during this phase. Figure 1-7 illustrates annuity product design objectives.

FIGURE 1.7

Annuity Product Design Objectives.

Design Characteristics	Areas in Which Design Objectives Are Set
Basic Product Features	· Asset-based fees · Transaction charges · Interest guarantees · Interest crediting frequency and formula · Withdrawal and surrender benefits · Death benefits · Annuity payout benefits · Supplementary benefits · Funds (subaccounts offered for variable annuities)
Technical Product Design	· Premium pattern assumptions (single, multiple, level, decreasing, increasing) · Competitive positioning of product · Minimum premium · Surrender charge schedule · Assumptions as to investment earnings, persistency, average contract size, and expense loading · Premium taxes
Marketing Expenses	· Distribution system, marketing channels · Commission rates · Marketing overhead expense rate · Promotion and advertising expense allocation · Field expenses, if any
Miscellaneous Risks	· Investment risks assumed · Interest-rate risk · Legal and regulatory risks · Persistency risk, including assumptions as to loans and withdrawals
Underwriting	· Any minimum age, maximum age for annuitants · Any dollar limit · Any medical questionnaire required above certain initial premium amount

Feasibility Study

Once product design objectives are established, the company proceeds to investigate the operational and technical feasibility of the new product. To accomplish this step in the product development process, the staff studies whether (a) the product can be structured to be competitive and profitable and (b) the insurer's operating and distribution systems can accommodate the product. A ***feasibility study*** evaluates whether the company has the capability to take the product to market. A feasibility study can include either a review of the results of another company's introduction of a similar product or a discussion with key agents and other market experts to determine if the product will appeal to consumers and marketers. It is also important to gain an understanding of how implementation of this product will compete for resources with other company initiatives and how this affects the time span required to take the product to market.

Marketing Plan

An insurer prepares a ***marketing plan*** primarily to define the product, price, distribution, and promotion strategies that a company will follow in order to reach potential customers and meet their needs. Marketing plans establish the steps required for accomplishing the company's day-to-day marketing activities. Most marketing plans specify marketing objectives, budgets, and a plan for evaluating progress toward objectives. Although there is not one best way to structure a marketing plan, the content of a marketing plan relies heavily on the information collected for market analysis.

Forecasts

A ***forecast*** is a projection or prediction of future values, events, or conditions. A forecast specifies an expected or a most likely value—rather than a best-case value or a worst-case value—for an unknown future value. The expected values set in forecasts are *not* the same as the assumed values that actuaries use in technical product design.

After developing a marketing plan, the product development team can make rough preliminary forecasts of future sales volume, sales revenues, expenses, and profit. ***Sales volume*** is defined as the number of units of product sold. ***Sales revenue*** is the total dollar volume of sales. Sales revenue is calculated by multiplying the sales volume by the average contract size. For the purpose of forecasting important sales figures, marketing forecasters define expenses as the administrative costs the company incurs to support a product, plus the periodic income payments, cash surrenders, and other benefits paid out. Later in the text, we see that product actuaries normally consider benefit costs separately from the administrative expenses associated with a product. For an annuity product, the ***profit***, also known as the *profit margin*, the *margin*, or the *spread*, is the amount by which the product's revenues exceed its expenses. Forecasts of these values at this early stage of annuity product development provide useful data for product design, but data from early forecasts contain a great deal of uncertainty. Accordingly, the values are revised as better information becomes available.

Research completed as part of comprehensive business analysis serves as a foundation for the activities that follow it. For example, after a product idea is approved for proceeding with technical product design, the product design objectives can serve as an overall guide for the design, profit testing, and introduction of the product. Similarly, the marketing plan later will guide the marketing of the product. After the research is completed in the comprehensive business analysis phase, the product development team proceeds with technical product design.

Key Terms and Concepts

annuity contract
annuitant
contract owner
payee
periodic income payment
beneficiary
proceeds
accumulation value
deferred annuity contract
immediate annuity contract
accumulation period
payout period
annuity certain
life annuity
joint and survivor annuity
joint life annuity
single premium annuity
installment premium annuity
level premium annuity
flexible premium annuity
straight life annuity
period certain annuity
life with period certain annuity
temporary life annuity
refund annuity
guaranteed minimum payout annuity
single premium immediate annuity (SPIA) contract
single premium deferred annuity (SPDA) contract
window premium
flexible premium deferred annuity (FPDA) contract
variable annuity contract
fixed annuity contract
actuary
product actuary
valuation actuary
distribution
distribution system
marketing committee
product development team
project team
idea generation
idea screening
comprehensive business analysis
technical product design
new product implementation
product evaluation

market analysis
product design objective
feasibility study
marketing plan
forecast
sales volume
sales revenue
profit

ENDNOTES

1. ACLI, *1998 Life Insurance Fact Book* (Washington, D.C.: The American Council of Life Insurance, 1998), 91.
2. Ibid., 114.
3. William R. Keller, VALIC, "Product Management for Annuities," *LOMA Activity Report*, EPAC Committee Meeting, March 5–8, 1996.

CHAPTER 2

Technical Design of Annuity Products

After studying this chapter, you should be able to

- Describe important contractual provisions found in annuity contracts
- Identify various product design assumptions that actuaries use in establishing an annuity product design
- Identify the similarities and differences between annuity product design in the accumulation period and the payout period
- Identify types of documentation in a typical filing package for a contract form
- Recognize the purposes of product evaluation
- Identify examples of favorable and adverse deviations

In Chapter 1, we discussed the product development cycle and then looked in detail at the product development phase of comprehensive business analysis. Here in Chapter 2, we continue to discuss details of the product development process for annuities. In particular, we examine the important activities of technical product design: developing a contract form, setting the product's financial structure, and scheduling and budgeting for the future of the new product.

Developing a Contract Form

For each new individual annuity product it develops, a life insurer develops a standard contract form and the application form that will be completed by applicants for the new product. The ***contract form*** is a document that describes the contractual agreement between the insurance company and the contract owner. The insurer then adapts the standard contract form to meet all regulatory requirements of each state in which the policy will be issued.

When the insurer issues a contract to a customer, it tailors the appropriate contract form by adding a schedule that identifies the contract owner, the annuitant, and the benefits provided. The customized contract represents the contractual agreement between the insurer and a contract owner.

Contractual Provisions

In developing a contract form, an insurer must meet regulatory requirements concerning certain required, optional, and prohibited contractual provisions and the readability of the language used in the contract. A ***contractual provision*** is a written statement in the contract that specifies the rights and duties of the parties to the contract. Contracts typically include several different provisions. The drafting of contractual provisions is an important part of product design. In the next few pages we discuss some important contractual provisions found in annuity contracts.

Entire Contract Provision

The ***entire contract provision*** in an annuity contract specifies that only documents attached to or appearing in the contract are part of the contract. After issue, the insurer cannot modify any part of the contract without the contract owner's consent. The entire contract provision means that changes to the contract can be made only in writing and only by a designated officer of the insurance company. The entire contract provision may stipulate that any oral statements made by any party to the contract—including the sales producer—are not part of the contract.

Incontestability Provision

An ***incontestability provision*** is an annuity contract provision that limits the time, typically to two years, in which the issuer may contest the validity of the contract on the ground of a material misrepresentation in the application. The incontestability provision does not apply to basic annuity income benefits. In an annuity contract, the incontestability provision typically applies to supplementary benefits—such as the waiver of surrender charge for disability—which require evidence of insurability at the time of application. In connection with an annuity's incontestability provision, the ***misstatement of age or sex provision*** typically states that if the annuitant's age or sex was misstated, then the affected benefits will be adjusted to the appropriate level for the correct age or sex, given the premium amount paid. The ***adjustment methods provision*** describes the adjustment methods the insurer will use to correct any material misstatement of age or sex.

Assignment Provision

An ***assignment provision*** in an annuity contract grants the contract owner the right to temporarily or permanently transfer ownership of the contract. Some annuity contracts, however, do not allow assignment of the contract.

Nonforfeiture Provision

As required in individual fixed deferred annuity contracts, a ***nonforfeiture provision***, also known as a *surrender provision*, is a contract provision which states that, if the contract owner terminates the contract, an annuity benefit will still be payable based on the amount of premiums already paid. If an annuity contract provides for a lump-sum settlement, the contract must also provide that, on surrender of the contract during the accumulation period, the insurer will provide a lump-sum payment to the contract owner in settlement of the contract.

A ***surrender charge***, sometimes called a *back-end load, back load*, or *withdrawal charge*, is a fee charged at the time of a withdrawal from an annuity account, and the amount of the charge is usually expressed as a percentage of the account value. The nonforfeiture provisions in some fixed deferred annuities set a schedule of surrender charges for surrenders or withdrawals of funds under specified circumstances. However, such contracts often also provide for waivers of the surrender charges under specified circumstances.

- A ***waiver of surrender charge provision*** states that the insurer will not impose a surrender charge on withdrawals under specified conditions. The usual circumstances under which the insurer will waive surrender charges include the death of the contract owner or annuitant, disability or poor medical condition of the contract owner, unemployment of the contract owner, and confinement of the contract owner in a nursing home or hospital. The company also sometimes waives surrender charges if a deferred annuity contract owner annuitizes the contract.

- A ***bailout provision***, sometimes known as an *escape clause* or *cash-out provision*, enables the contract owner to surrender the annuity contract, usually without a surrender charge, if renewal interest rates on a fixed annuity fall below a pre-established level—typically one percent below the initial interest rate.

Other contractual provisions that protect the contract owner's access to money in the contract are the withdrawal privilege and any loan provision.

- ***Withdrawal privilege.*** The owner of a deferred annuity typically has the right during the annuity's accumulation period to withdraw a portion of the contract's accumulated value at any time. Many contracts impose a charge on each withdrawal and limit the number of withdrawals allowed in any one year. Many contracts also specify a ***free withdrawal amount***, which permits a partial withdrawal of the annuity account value free of charge.

- ***Loan provision.*** Most nonqualified individual annuity contracts do not allow the contract owner to obtain a loan against the annuity balance. However, many qualified individual annuities include a contract provision allowing the contract owner to obtain a loan. An important distinction exists between a loan and a withdrawal. Annuity loans are not withdrawals, because the contract owner must pay interest that is then credited to the annuity account value. In contrast to a loan, a withdrawal is a permanent reduction. Loans and withdrawals are treated differently for tax purposes.

Death Benefit Provisions

Annuity contracts typically include ***death benefit provisions*** that describe how benefits will be paid upon the death of the contract owner or the annuitant. During the accumulation period of a fixed annuity contract, the death benefit typically equals the value of the annuity account as of the date the insurer receives the proof of death. During the payout period of a fixed or variable annuity contract, any death benefit depends upon the type of payout option specified in the annuity contract. As a death benefit, any guaranteed periodic income payments sometimes can be continued to the beneficiary, or are sometimes payable as a lump sum at a discounted value. By definition, periodic income payments under a life annuity cease upon death.

Variable annuities usually include a minimum death benefit guarantee during the accumulation period. This ***minimum death benefit guarantee*** states that, if the contract owner dies before the annuity payments begin, the named beneficiary will receive a benefit equal to the greater of (1) the total amount of premium payments made for the annuity, less any withdrawals made, or (2) some enhanced value established as of the time of the contract owner's death. Examples of the enhanced values paid as death benefits are either (a) the maximum previous anniversary values plus subsequent premium payments less subsequent withdrawals or (b) premium payments less withdrawals accumulated at a specified rate of interest. The death benefit guarantee ensures that the beneficiary will receive at least the amount that the contract owner deposited into the variable annuity contract, less any withdrawals, even if poor investment performance causes the contract's accumulation value to be less than the premiums paid.

Payout Option Provision

The ***payout option provision***, also known as the *settlement option provision*, describes the payout options the insurer offers under the annuity contract. For an immediate annuity, the applicant chooses a payout option when applying for the annuity. For a deferred annuity, the contract owner chooses a payout option just prior to the beginning of the payout period. Annuity contract payout arrangements differ for fixed and variable annuity contracts.

- Fixed annuity contracts automatically provide for a ***fixed payout***, which means that periodic income benefit payments are guaranteed to remain the same throughout the payout period.
- A variable contract offers the choice of (1) a fixed payout option; (2) a ***variable payout option***, which means that the payments vary in amount based on the performance of the underlying subaccounts; or (3) a combination of fixed and variable payout arrangements.

Technical Product Design

During the technical design phase of product development, product actuaries establish the product's structure. To establish a product design, actuaries employ a quantitative model of the product, sometimes in the form of a computerized spreadsheet, usually provided as part of a sophisticated software package. Into the quantitative model, actuaries enter a set of assumed values for the important elements of product design, including the product's assumed investment earnings, assumed costs of providing benefits, and various assumed values for company expenses.

These assumed values used in product design are known as ***actuarial assumptions***. Product actuaries are free to use whatever values seem appropriate for actuarial assumptions, so long as the company is willing to assume the risk implied in those assumptions. The following product design assumptions are important for the accumulation stage of a fixed annuity contract.

- **Interest margin.** The ***interest margin*** represents the investment earnings on the company's assets less the interest credited to the annuity accumulation value.
- **Accumulation rate.** An annuity contract design must specify the expected future growth in a contract's accumulation value.
- **Crediting rate formula.** The ***crediting rate*** is the interest rate applied to the customer's accumulation value. Insurers typically employ one of two methods of crediting interest:
  1. **Portfolio method.** Under the ***portfolio method***, all money in the customer's annuity account is credited with one specified current rate of interest, regardless of when the money was placed in the account.
  2. **New money method.** Under the ***new money method***, different interest rates are credited to various portions of the money in an annuity account; a current interest rate is in effect at the time of each premium payment; the interest terms and guarantees for a given premium payment remain attached to the amount of that payment.
- **Schedule of surrender charges.** Usually, the highest surrender charge applies in the first year, and then the charge diminishes until it disappears after the contract has been in force for a number of years. Whenever surrender charges apply, an annuity contract's surrender value differs from its accumulation value. An annuity contract's ***surrender value*** equals the accumulation value minus any applicable surrender charges.
- **Mortality basis**. A ***mortality table*** is a chart that shows the expected death rates among a particular group of people at given ages—that is, the percentage of people in each age group who are expected to die in a particular year. A ***mortality rate*** is the percentage rate at which death occurs among a defined group of people of a specified age and sometimes of a specified gender. The company must specify a mortality table for use in setting the actuarial assumptions for mortality rates relating to any death benefits. These actuarial assumptions are called the mortality basis of the contract.
- **Lapse rates.** A ***lapse rate*** is a measure of the percentage of contracts that are surrendered in a given year. A ***lapse-rate assumption*** is a value assigned to the percentage of contracts that will be surrendered in a specified future year. Product actuaries set a series of annual lapse rates to reflect product lapses.
- **Commissions.** The ***commission*** is an amount paid to compensate a sales producer. A ***commission rate*** is the percentage of premium or

annuity account value specified for calculating the amount of a commission. A commission may apply to the initial premium only, or it may also apply to the account value. A ***trail commission*** is a commission amount calculated on the basis of an annuity contract's accumulation value, after an initial commission was paid at the inception of the contract. When multiple premiums are paid, multiple initial commissions are paid. But, only one trail is paid at a time on the contract's accumulation value created by all of the premiums.

- **Expenses.** Product assumptions specify an amount for the insurer's expenses of issuing and supporting the product, including administrative expenses, but excluding the cost of providing benefits and investment expenses.
- **Expense charges.** ***Expense charges*** are the portion of a product's structure designed to reimburse the insurer for its operating expenses—specifically, commissions, premium taxes, and general operating expenses. Note that these operating expenses do not include investment expenses or the cost of providing benefits.
- **Reserve basis.** A ***reserve*** is a liability amount representing the insurer's expected financial obligation under its contracts. This liability represents the amount of money the insurer estimates will be needed, together with premiums and investment earnings, to pay obligations to contract owners as the obligations come due. Insurance laws impose a variety of reserve requirements on insurance companies and their products. Accumulation period reserves for many annuities are assumed to be equal to a contract's surrender value.

Financial Elements of Annuity Products

Product actuaries consider a variety of factors when designing an annuity, including

- Cost of benefits
- Company expenses
- Investment earnings

The factors taken into account differ when designing for an annuity's accumulation period and payout period. In addition, certain features of annuity contract design can vary depending on whether an annuity is fixed or variable.

Cost of Benefits

When actuaries design annuity products, one of their first steps is to estimate the cost of benefits. For product design, a product's ***cost of benefits*** is the value of benefits the product promises to pay. The cost of benefits equals all of the insurer's potential payments of benefit obligations to customers times the expected probability that each benefit will be payable. The insurance company's benefit obligations under annuity contracts differ between the accumulation period and the payout period.

Company Expenses

The amount of company expenses in a product design is based on an estimate of the costs—other than the cost of benefits—associated with supporting the product. These expenses include operating expenses and product distribution expenses, occasionally with an additional amount to provide a cushion against unexpected expenses.

Investment Earnings

An insurance company invests the premium dollars it collects from annuity customers. Insurance companies invest in many different assets, including corporate bonds, government bonds, mortgages, corporate stocks, and real estate. For products that are in force for several years, these investments can grow substantially. For annuity products, the treatment of investment earnings depends upon whether a product is fixed or variable. For fixed annuity products and for the fixed subaccounts of variable annuity products, the customers receive a guaranteed crediting rate. For variable subaccounts of variable annuity products, all of the actual investment results, whether increases or decreases, are borne by the customer.

ANNUITY DESIGN FOR THE ACCUMULATION PERIOD

During the accumulation period, insurers must focus on designing products to provide customers with the product features they seek. Thus, the financial design of annuity products for the accumulation period follows a competition-based approach. The insurance company first adopts a set of product features known to have consumer appeal, then specifies other product features that are calculated to enable the insurer to financially support the product design's competitive features. To be successful, a new deferred annuity product must offer potential customers a structure of benefits and costs comparable to or better than those available in products already on the market. Accordingly, insurers offer many different annuity product designs to potential customers. Figure 2-1 profiles four different deferred variable annuity product designs. Most features of these designs are also offered as features of fixed annuity products.

FIGURE 2.1 **Deferred Annuity Designs.**

Here we see four variations of deferred variable annuity designs commonly available through brokers:

1. A ***back-load annuity***. This product imposes surrender charges from the outset and for several years thereafter. The product also has a relatively low minimum initial premium requirement.
2. A ***no-load annuity***. This product has no front load and no surrender charges, but requires a relatively large initial premium amount of around $25,000.
3. A ***front-credit annuity***. This product awards a bonus to the customer for signing on, but also imposes relatively high surrender charges from the outset and for several years thereafter.
4. A ***front-load annuity.*** This contract imposes a significant load charge to the customer upon signing on, but has no surrender charges thereafter.

The table below shows typical financial specifications for these four variable deferred annuity designs. The bottom row of the table shows the projected result of each product design to a customer, in terms of how the same initial premium would grow for the customer over the course of 20 years, with no withdrawals, if all funds grew annually at 10 percent.

	Back-Load	No-Load	Front-Credit	Front-Load
• Surrender charge period	5–7 years	None	8–9 years	None
• Front-end credit/load	None	None	3.00%–5.00% credit	1.00%–6.00% load
• Minimum initial premium	$1,000–$5,000	$25,000	$10,000	$1,000–$5,000
• M&E charges	1.25%–1.50%	1.50%–1.65%	1.50%–1.65%	0.75%–0.90%
• Fund charge	0.70%–1.00%	0.70%–1.00%	0.70%–1.00%	0.70%–1.00%
• Commission, Year 1	5.00%–6.00%	1.00%	4.00%	0.50%–1.00% less than load
Commission trail	0.25%	1.00%	0.25%	0.25%
Approximate value of $100,000 after 20 years	$521,000	$507,000	$527,000	$553,000

Source: Product designs from a presentation by Kevin Borie, Protective Life, March 27, 1999, The Annuity Conference.

Fixed Annuity Design for the Accumulation Period

For the accumulation period, the financial success of a fixed annuity product design depends primarily upon how the company sets the product's interest crediting rate and expense charges. Later in this text, in Chapter 3, we describe the interest crediting rate for fixed deferred annuities. Charges for fixed deferred annuities may be stated or unstated. The insurer may apply the following types of expense charges to the customer's fixed annuity account, among others:

- An ***annual administration charge***—a stated charge in a flat dollar amount, automatically deducted from the customer's annuity account value each year
- A surrender charge
- An ***investment management charge***—an unstated charge for the expenses of investing. (We see later that a similar stated charge applies to variable annuities.)

The insurer's expenses for fixed and variable annuities in the accumulation period also include sales commissions, costs of contract issue, ongoing administrative expenses, and persistency as measured by lapse (surrender) rates. These costs must be taken into account in the financial design of a product.

Potential benefit payments for fixed and variable annuities in the accumulation period include

- Cash surrender value
- Survivor benefit upon death of the owner or annuitant
- Periodic annuity income payments calculated as of the scheduled maturity date
- Periodic annuity income payments calculated as of a date earlier than the scheduled maturity date
- Partial withdrawals of the account balance prior to the scheduled maturity date

Variable Annuity Design for the Accumulation Period

Unlike fixed annuities, variable annuities do not have an interest margin, except for any guaranteed subaccounts. All investment results of variable investment subaccounts flow directly to the customer. The insurer bears none of the investment risk and earns no investment margin related to the variable subaccounts.

Variable annuities, like fixed deferred annuities, often incorporate annual administration charges, surrender charges, and investment management fees. Variable subaccounts impose expense charges known as M&E charges and administrative charges. The ***mortality and expense risk charge (M&E charge)*** and the ***administrative charge*** are specified percentages of the assets deducted on periodic valuation dates from the assets in the investment subaccounts. Most contracts specify a *maximum* M&E charge and a *current* M&E charge, but no minimum M&E charge. The current M&E charge may be adjusted after policy issue. Each variable annuity subaccount is also subject to investment advisory fees and other charges for investment expenses.

Variable annuity products commonly incorporate the following features:

- A guaranteed minimum death benefit applied to values in variable subaccounts
- ***Transfer fees*** for administrative processing of asset transfers between subaccounts when a customer's number of transfers within a given period exceeds the contract's maximum

Fixed Annuity Design for the Payout Period

Important design components for annuity products in the payout period include all of the components that were important in the accumulation period. Potential benefit payments in the payout period include

- Payment of a contract's periodic income benefits
- Any permitted withdrawals of account values granted under the contract
- Supplementary death benefits or other supplementary contractual benefits

As part of the product design for an annuity's payout period, the insurer must develop tables indicating the amount of annuity benefit provided for a given premium amount. Different insurers have different ways of expressing this information. For single premium purchases of immediate annuities, this information may be expressed as a table of annuity purchase costs. For annuitization of deferred annuities, two common forms for this information are tables of (1) annuity conversion costs or (2) periodic annuity payment factors.

- ***Annuity conversion costs*** for deferred annuities—or ***annuity purchase costs*** for immediate annuities—are the costs to the contract owner to obtain a specified dollar amount of periodic income payment. Tables of these costs show the actuarial present value of periodic income payments of a specified amount per period for an annuitant of a specified age and sometimes of a specified gender. Generally, annuity conversion costs do not contain any provision for loading, whereas annuity purchase costs must provide for loading to cover company expenses. Annuity purchase costs and annuity conversion costs are discussed again in Chapter 9.
- ***Periodic annuity payment factors*** show the periodic income payment amount for the annuitant's life that a contract owner can purchase for a given dollar amount of single premium applied. The periodic payment interval might be a monthly, a quarterly, a semi-annual, or an annual interval. Monthly annuity payment factors are illustrated in Figure 2-2.

FIGURE 2.2

Monthly Annuity Payment Factors.

In the table below, the monthly annuity payment factor for males at each age represents the monthly payment amount for the annuitant's life that a contract owner can purchase for each $1,000 of single premium applied.

Monthly income payment per $1,000 applied	
Exact Age	**Male**
50	$4.34
55	$4.70
60	$5.17
65	$5.82
70	$6.73
75	$8.01
80	$9.80

For example, Lucas Moschierri, a man aged 70, has a deferred annuity accumulation value of $500,000. Mr. Moschierri wishes to convert his accumulation value to a monthly annuity for life. The above table of minimum values appears in his deferred annuity contract. This table shows monthly income payments per $1,000 of deferred annuity value converted to a life annuity income. Mr. Moschierri is planning to pay a single premium of $500,000, and not just $1,000. Thus, to find the amount of monthly benefit he can obtain, we must multiply the tabular cost for men his age by 500, as follows:

$6.73 per month × 500 = $3,365.00 per month

This result indicates that Mr. Moschierri's deferred annuity contract guarantees that he can convert the account value of $500,000 to at least a monthly income payment of $3,365 for his lifetime.

Annuity costs for the payout period are developed using a cost-plus approach to product design. Under a ***cost-plus approach*** to product design, an insurer calculates the costs of developing, offering, and supporting a given product, then adds a small margin for error or profit, and thus calculates the annuity purchase cost or conversion cost charged to buyers. As described earlier in this chapter, a contrasting competition-based approach to annuity product design is typically employed for the accumulation phase.

Modeling and Testing New Annuity Designs

After the product development team develops an initial product design, that design must be tested to ensure that it can support a sound annuity product. If the initial testing produces unsatisfactory results, the company can change some of the assumed values entered into the product testing model—provided the new values are realistic and actuarially sound. To improve a product's financial soundness, the company can either increase the assumed investment earnings or decrease the assumed expenses. The insurer could increase charges, and in so doing could limit the product's attractiveness to consumers. While designing a product, the product development team obtains feedback from the company's marketing experts to make sure that the product meets the needs of the marketplace.

Creating a new annuity product involves modeling and testing the product. Each product model represents the operating results of the new product over a selected period of years for an identified group of annuitants. Within the limitations of a given model and a given set of product design assumptions, these operating results show the product's profitability over the time period modeled. The foundation for the product model usually is a computerized spreadsheet provided within a complete actuarial software package. In product models, the spreadsheet often focuses on showing an annuity product's assumed profits. The product testing process used during product design is similar to the product testing process used to monitor a product after it is in force.

The product models used for product testing can take a variety of basic formats. Two formats commonly employed in this context are the financial statements known as (1) a balance sheet and (2) an earnings (income) statement.

A Balance Sheet Format

One popular product testing model, the asset share model, takes the form of a basic financial statement known as a balance sheet. A balance sheet takes its form from an equation known as the ***basic accounting equation***, which states that assets equal the sum of liabilities and owners' equity. Let's look at the components of the basic accounting equation for an insurance company:

- ***Assets*** are all things of value owned by the insurance company, such as cash, stocks, bonds, mortgages, real estate, office buildings, and equipment.
- ***Liabilities*** are the company's debts and future obligations. The liabilities of insurance companies tend to consist of limited debts and vast reserves for future contractual obligations.
- ***Owners' equity*** represents the owners' financial interest in the company. For insurance companies, owners' equity is often called *capital and surplus* or simply *surplus*.

A product testing model that takes the form of a balance sheet represents the components of an asset share model as follows:

Assets	*equal the sum of*	**Liabilities**	*plus*	**Owners' Equity**
Asset share	=	Product reserve	+	Product surplus

We discuss asset share models in greater detail in later chapters of this textbook.

An Earnings Statement Format

A product can also be thought of in terms of another basic form of financial statement: an ***earnings statement***, also called an *income statement*. In a basic earnings statement, earnings equal the difference between revenues and expenses. For an annuity product, earnings can be viewed as the amount that the product adds to a company's owners' equity in a given period. A product testing model can take the format of an earnings statement, as shown:

Revenues	*minus*	**Expenses**	*equal*	**Earnings**
• Premiums • Other fees from customers • Investment earnings	–	• Operating expenses • Contractual benefits • Reserve increases (reserve reductions)	=	Profit (also known as *spread* or *margin*)

BUDGETING AND SCHEDULING

The final activity of technical product design, the budgeting and scheduling process, consists of (1) preparing a budget for the human, financial, and computer resources needed to implement the product and (2) developing a project schedule. The ***budget*** is a document that shows the costs associated with each activity and the anticipated revenue for the new product. The ***project schedule*** is a document that shows the time frames required for the completion of the activities and the interrelationships among these activities. Figure 2-3 shows an excerpt from a project schedule for an annuity product.

After preparing the project schedule and budget, the product development team then presents the product design to the insurance company's marketing committee for review and approval. After the technical design of the new product is finalized, the insurer is ready to implement the product and prepare to sell the product to customers.

FIGURE 2.3 Project Schedule.

This figure presents an actual product development schedule that has been abbreviated for educational purposes.

Variable Annuity Product Development Schedule

This schedule is based on estimates of the time the Securities and Exchange Commission (SEC) staff will take to respond to our filings—a factor beyond our control. We generally recommend allowing 5 or 6 months from the initial filing for the product to be declared effective. However, we have had annuities clear the SEC in 3½ months, including sophisticated, complicated products. This development schedule allows 5 months. Tentative dates shown are only approximate dates.

This schedule does not cover the organization or registration of the investment fund or its investment advisor.

This schedule also assumes that any fixed subaccount option offered under the annuity would not have to be registered as a security.

This schedule employs the following notation:

- Schedule **Day X** represents the initial filing with the SEC.
- Schedule **Day X−30** indicates that the designated task should be completed 30 days before the initial filing with the SEC.
- Schedule **Day X+30** indicates that the task is scheduled for completion 30 days after the initial filing with the SEC.

		Scheduled	
Item No.	**Task**	**Day**	**Date**
1	Initial product specifications	X−90	05/01
2	System development or acquisition	—	——
3	First draft of policy form	X−70	05/15
	(Items omitted)		
6	First draft of policy riders	X−55	06/05
7	Draft resolution establishing variable account and authorizing filings, etc.	X−50	06/10
8	First draft of Form N-4 Registration Statement	X−45	06/15
	(Items omitted)		
11	First steps of exemptive application	X−35	06/25
12	Prepare policy application	X−30	06/30
	(Items omitted)		
16	File policy and riders with insurance department in domiciliary state	X−10	07/20
17	First draft of two required memoranda on M&E charge	X−5	07/25
	(Items omitted)		
23	Assemble final Form N-4	X−2	07/29
24	Assemble exhibits for initial filing	X−2	07/29
	• Separate account resolution		
	• Policy form		
	• Riders		
	• Certificate of incorporation		
	• By-laws of insurance company		
25	Obtain 2 checks for SEC filing fees (1 certified)	X−2	07/29
26	Initial SEC filing	X	07/31
27	File policy and rider with other insurance departments	X+15	08/15
28	First draft of distribution agreement	X+20	08/20
29	First draft of agreement with sales agents	X+20	08/20
	(Items omitted)		
52	SEC declares registration statement effective, issues exemptive order	X+135	12/15
53	Print final prospectus	X+140	12/20
54	SEC effective order and exemptive order received	X+140	12/20
55	File final prospectus with SEC	X+145	12/27
56	Begin selling contracts	X+150	01/01

IMPLEMENTING A NEW PRODUCT

At the product implementation stage, the insurance company establishes all of the administrative structures and processes necessary to take the product to market. Before taking the product to market, however, the staff first must

- Obtain legal approval for the product from all appropriate jurisdictions
- Design promotional and training materials to support sales activities
- Develop and put in place all information systems and all administrative systems necessary to market and administer the product

Meeting Regulatory Requirements

Before an insurer can market and sell an annuity product, the company must meet all requirements of the states in which the company intends to market the product. Typically, to meet these requirements, the insurer must file a finished contract form and any other required documents with the insurance departments in those jurisdictions in which the product will be issued and sold. Figure 2-4 lists materials included in a contract form filing package.

FIGURE 2.4

Materials in a Contract Form Filing Package.

- ✓ A transmittal (submission) letter
- ✓ Copy of the contract form and any other documents that will be issued along with the contract form, including the annuity application and any endorsements or riders
- ✓ Any required filing fee
- ✓ Any required certification forms from actuaries or attorneys
- ✓ The contract form's score on a readability test, if required
- ✓ Premium rate structures and actuarial memoranda, as required

Most insurers establish a minimum number of jurisdictions in which a new contract form must be approved before the company will introduce the product in any jurisdiction. Some jurisdictions do not require the insurer to obtain their approval of the contract form, and the contract form is filed for the insurance department's information only. In Canada, only the contract forms for variable contracts usually require approval by provincial insurance departments. In most U.S. states, however, the insurance department must approve a contract form before the contract can be introduced there. For U.S. states, an insurer from another state must first obtain contract approval in the company's home state before filing for approval in another state.

The specific filing requirements that a company must meet to obtain insurance department approval of a new contract form vary among states. Many states require a readability certification attesting that the contract is written in direct, comprehensible language. State readability requirements are designed to require insurers to limit the amount of technical language included in annuity contracts. A state insurance department may require a company to change contractual language.

Insurers may be required to file various types of actuarial reports with regulators. Many states require contract form filings to include an ***actuarial memorandum***, which is a report showing that the contract in question complies with all state insurance laws and regulations that apply to the actuarial (mathematical) soundness of the contract. These required reports are prepared by the insurer's actuaries and signed by the appointed actuary. A company's ***appointed actuary*** is an actuary who (1) has been duly appointed by a corporation's board of directors to render an official *Actuarial Opinion and Memorandum* as to the insurance company's financial condition and (2) possesses the professional qualifications necessary for the appointment. State laws and regulations often specify that an actuary must have certain professional qualifications to sign and submit such certifications.

In both Canada and the United States, products with variable contract values are subject to requirements imposed by additional regulatory authorities. Under securities laws in the United States, variable annuities are subject to federal securities laws and the jurisdiction of the Securities and Exchange Commission (SEC). In the United States, variable contracts and the sales materials to be used with them must be filed with the SEC. Figure 2-5 shows the variety and detail required for a filing using Form N-4 for a variable annuity. Form N-4 imposes slightly different requirements in different situations. We describe only the requirements applied to a variable annuity issued by a very large insurer for sale in most states.

Designing Promotional and Training Materials

While contract form filing continues, the marketing department's promotion and training units begin their share of product implementation activities. These activities could include designing sales materials and information kits for sales agents, customer service staff, and external customers; creating product-specific advertisements, often with the assistance of an outside advertising agency; and placing advertising and publicity materials about the product in appropriate advertising media.

Companies that use a personal selling distribution system may develop special sales programs to encourage agents to sell a new product. If agents

FIGURE 2.5 Form N-4 Filing Requirements.

Form N-4 is the SEC filing form required for filings of variable annuity contracts. In the language of Form N-4, the Registrant and the Depositor are the insurance company issuing the new variable annuity product. Form N-4 primarily consists of three sections labeled Parts A, B, and C, as shown in the table below. Finally, on its last three pages, Form N-4 requires

- A copy of the information contained on the prospectus cover
- An Independent Auditor's Consent statement
- A signature page for the Registrant's officers and directors

Part A	***Product Prospectus.***
	A ***prospectus*** is a document that offers a security for sale and that must contain most of the information presented in the security's registration statement.
Part B	***Statement of Additional Information.***
	Further explains calculations for fund performance. The *Statement of Additional Information* displays year-end financial statements for the separate account and the Registrant. Unlike Part A, Part B must be provided to customers only upon request.
Part C	***Other Information.***
	Contains information labeled by item numbers. Some of this information concerns officers and directors of the Registrant and subsidiary and affiliated companies of the Registrant. In addition, Part C contains exhibits and other required information, listed below.

Item		
24 (a)	Cross-references information contained in the prospectus and in the *Statement of Additional Information.*	
24 (b)	Lists the required Exhibit filings for Form N-4.	
	Exhibit	
	1	Resolution of Depositor's Board of Directors authorizing the establishment of the Registrant.
	3	Form of the Underwriting or Distribution contracts between the Registrant and the Principal Underwriter.
	4	The variable annuity contract form.
	5	The variable annuity application form.
	6	Articles of Incorporation of the Depositor.
	9	Opinion of Counsel.
	13	Computation of Performance Quotations.
25	Identifies directors and officers of the Depositor.	
26	Identifies persons controlled by or under common control with the Depositor and the Registrant. This item includes an organizational chart.	
27	Lists the number of contract owners as of a specific date.	
28	Indemnification plans.	
29 (a)	Identifies the principal underwriter.	
29 (b)	Identifies the officers and directors of the principal underwriter.	
30	Specifies the location of the accounts and records.	
31	Identifies management services.	
32	Lists all the Registrant's undertakings, which include any representations on the reasonableness of prices for products contained in the registration statement.	

are not properly educated about the new product, they may not be enthusiastic or effective in selling it. Thus, an insurer generally offers training about new products to its sales forces.

For products employing a direct response distribution system, promotion consists primarily of developing and testing advertising materials, because no agent is involved in the selling process. In such cases, the promotion unit is often assisted by outside advertising agencies.

Product Introduction

During the product introduction phase of product development, the insurer advertises the new product and begins to distribute it to customers according to the marketing plan the insurer adopted for the product. In personal selling distribution systems, insurers are responsible for overseeing sales producers to ensure they comply with applicable laws and regulations. Insurers also are responsible for keeping records related to sales of their products.

PRODUCT EVALUATION

Insurers are constantly entering new product ideas into the product development cycle, and the ideas that emerge must be reevaluated in an ongoing feedback process. In particular, product evaluation continues after a product has been introduced. This evaluation and feedback process may result in minor refinements to existing products or in major innovations in product design. Existing products must be evaluated in terms of their impact on the company's financial performance, the performance of agents and other product distributors, and the marketplace reactions of consumers and competitors.

As described earlier, a product's structure reflects a set of actuarial assumptions about relevant earnings and costs. Once a product is in force and the company accumulates experience with the product, the insurer can compare the actual values from experience against the actuarial assumptions used in product design. In comparisons of actual values to assumed values, a difference between the values is known as a deviation. Deviations can be favorable or adverse.

A ***favorable deviation*** is a difference between actual and assumed product values that produces an increase in actual product profitability relative to assumed product profitability. A favorable deviation arises whenever an actual product value differs from its actuarial assumptions so that, relative to the assumptions for these factors, any of the following conditions arises:

- Company revenue is *higher* than assumed
- Benefit payments are *decreased*
- Company expenses are *decreased*

An ***adverse deviation*** produces a decrease in actual product profitability relative to assumed product profitability. An adverse deviation arises whenever an actual product value differs from assumptions so that, relative to the assumptions for these factors, any of the following conditions arises:

- Company revenue is *lower* than assumed
- Benefit payments are *increased*
- Company expenses are *increased*

If large deviations occur, then the insurer must try to identify reasons for them and, if possible, take corrective action, such as cutting operating expenses.

KEY TERMS AND CONCEPTS

contract form
contractual provision
entire contract provision
incontestability provision
misstatement of age or sex provision
adjustment methods provision
assignment provision
nonforfeiture provision
surrender charge
waiver of surrender charge provision
bailout provision
withdrawal privilege
free withdrawal amount
loan provision
death benefit provision
minimum death benefit guarantee
payout option provision
fixed payout
variable payout option
actuarial assumption
interest margin
crediting rate
portfolio method
new money method
surrender value
mortality table
mortality rate
lapse rate
lapse-rate assumption
commission
commission rate
trail commission

expense charge
reserve
cost of benefits
back-load annuity
no-load annuity
front-credit annuity
front-load annuity
annual administration charge
investment management charge
mortality and expense risk charge (M&E charge)
administrative charge
transfer fee
annuity conversion cost
annuity purchase cost
periodic annuity payment factor
cost-plus approach
basic accounting equation
assets
liabilities
owners' equity
earnings statement
budget
project schedule
actuarial memorandum
appointed actuary
prospectus
favorable deviation
adverse deviation

Chapter 3

Investments for Annuity Products

After studying this chapter, you should be able to

- Calculate an interest rate
- Calculate interest earnings on an investment
- Distinguish between an insurer's general account and separate accounts
- Distinguish among bonds, stocks, mortgages, real estate, and other asset types

Almost all of an insurance company's assets are invested for the benefit of policyowners, and investment earnings are an important part of the company's total earnings, as illustrated in Figure 3-1. In fact, an insurance company's investment earnings—the money that the insurer earns by investing premium dollars—are a major factor in annuity benefits.

Because deferred annuity contracts are usually in force for some time before benefits become payable, the premium dollars are available for the insurer to invest. For accumulation products such as deferred annuities, higher investment earnings for the insurer mean larger accumulations for contract owners and possibly a larger investment margin (spread) for the insurer. For annuities in the payout period, the earnings from

FIGURE 3.1

Premiums and Investment Earnings.

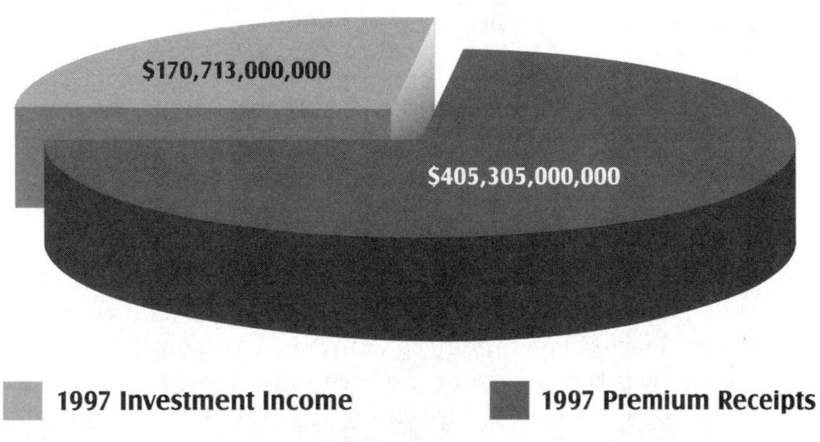

Source: ACLI, *1998 Life Insurance Fact Book* (Washington, D.C.: American Council of Life Insurance, 1998), 64.

company investments provide funds that make it possible for insurance companies to provide higher benefit payments. Figure 3-2 explains how insurers use investment earnings to increase fund accumulations for annuity contract owners.

FIGURE 3.2

Investment Earnings and Annuity Contract Growth.

In the accumulation phase of annuity contracts, the effects of the insurer's investment earnings differ according to whether the annuity contract is fixed or variable.

Fixed Annuity Contracts

A fixed annuity contract typically specifies two interest rates: (1) a minimum guaranteed interest rate and (2) a current interest crediting rate, also known as an excess interest crediting rate. The minimum guaranteed interest rate is guaranteed for the life of the contract. However, the current interest crediting rate is declared by the company at specified intervals and applies to a specified period, such as one year.

Variable Annuity Contracts

Variable annuity contracts offer the contract owner the options of both (1) fixed and guaranteed interest earnings and (2) variable investment earnings. The variable annuity contract owner chooses between these options by allocating funds to either the contract's guaranteed subaccount or one or more of the contract's variable subaccounts. The manner in which investment earnings are credited to these accounts differs as follows:

- **Guaranteed subaccount.** The interest credits to the guaranteed subaccount function in virtually the same manner as the interest credits to a fixed annuity contract.
- **Variable subaccount.** The credits of investment earnings to shares in a variable subaccount function so that the annuity contract owner is awarded a rate of investment return exactly equal to the rate of net investment earnings on the subaccount portfolio.

In Chapter 3, we look at how investments create earnings for annuity products. We begin by examining the mechanics of interest rates and the interest earnings on an investment. Then we introduce the time value of money and discuss how investment earnings grow over time. In this chapter, we also cover the essential vocabulary of investing, reviewing the types of assets insurers purchase for their investment programs and the types of earnings that different assets provide.

HOW INVESTMENTS GROW

Interest is a fee an institution or an individual pays for the use of someone else's money.[1] The ***time value of money*** is the concept that the value of a sum of money will change over time as the result of the effect of interest. Thus, a sum of money invested today, such as $1.00, has a present value that is generally less than its future value. The ***present value (PV)*** of a future amount of money is defined as the amount that, if invested at a specified interest rate on a given date, called the valuation date, would grow to equal that future amount of money. The present value is often called the *discounted value*. If that amount of money is loaned at interest or invested in an interest-bearing account, that money also has a future value representing the original investment plus interest earnings over a specified period of time. The ***future value (FV)***, sometimes known as the *accumulated value* or *compound value*, of a sum of money is the amount that the sum is expected to be worth at a specified future date, given a stated rate of interest. Thus, future value concepts allow the contract owner of a deferred annuity contract to calculate the future growth of a present-day retirement fund.

A sum of money originally invested is called the ***principal***. Principal can also be defined as the amount upon which the interest is calculated. (In this context, principal is another term for present value.) If you save your money in a savings account at a bank, the bank pays you a specified percentage of that investment as interest in return for the use of your money. The bank, in turn, lends that money to someone else and receives interest in return for the borrower's use of the money. That borrower, in turn, may lend the borrowed money to someone else and receive interest. The entire financial services industry relies heavily upon the concept of the time value of money. The concept of interest is the key to understanding the time value of money.

Calculating Interest Earned

Interest is measured in percentages. An ***interest rate*** is the percentage by which an amount of money is multiplied to derive the amount that is paid for the use of that money. Interest rates are usually expressed in decimal form because interest rates are used in calculations. For example, a 5 percent interest rate is expressed as either 5% or 0.05. Similarly, a 2½ percent interest rate is expressed as 2.5% or 0.025, and a 10 percent interest rate as 10% or 0.10.

To find the interest to be paid on a principal amount of $100 invested at 5 percent simple interest for a year, you would multiply the principal by the interest rate expressed in decimal form:

Principal × Interest rate = Interest earned

or

$$\$100 \times 0.05 = \$5$$

Suppose an investor puts $5,200 in an account paying 6 percent interest per year. To find how much interest he will earn in a year, using our formula for deriving the amount of interest earned, we would multiply the principal, $5,200, by the interest rate in decimal form, as follows:

$$\$5{,}200 \times 0.06 = \$312$$

Calculating an Interest Rate

Suppose you know the amount of the principal, and you know the amount of interest you will earn at the end of a period, but you do not know the interest rate. Because the interest amount divided by principal equals the interest rate, you can calculate the interest rate as

Interest amount ÷ Principal = Interest rate

For example, suppose you are considering a one-year investment. If you invest $1,250, this particular investment will provide you with a total of $1,350 after a year. What is the interest rate? In this case, the interest is $100, found by taking the $1,350 you will receive in one year and subtracting your $1,250 investment, which is the principal. The interest rate, then, is

$100 ÷ $1,250 = 0.08 = 8 percent

Types of Interest

Interest can be simple or compound, and it can be nominal or effective.

Simple Interest

The examples and problems we have discussed thus far represent ***simple interest***, the type of interest that is calculated only on the principal invested. The principal is multiplied by the interest rate to derive the amount of interest earned. In the concept of simple interest, none of the interest earned is credited with interest. For each interest period—in our examples, one year—the same principal is multiplied by the interest rate to determine the interest earned.

For example, suppose you invested $1,000 for five years at 5 percent annual simple interest, without making any withdrawals. How much interest would you have earned at the end of five years? What would the principal plus interest be worth? The following table shows the solution:

Year	**Beginning Balance**	*plus*	**(Principal × 5% Interest Rate)**	*equals*	**Year-End Balance**
1	$1,000.00		$50.00		$1,050.00
2	$1,050.00		$50.00		$1,100.00
3	$1,100.00		$50.00		$1,150.00
4	$1,150.00		$50.00		$1,200.00
5	$1,200.00		$50.00		$1,250.00

Each year, the $1,000 principal would earn $50 in interest, calculated as $1,000 × 0.05. At the end of five years, the account would have $250 in interest earnings, calculated as $50 annual interest × 5 years. The principal plus interest would be $1,250 after five years, because your $1,000 would have earned $250 in interest.

Compound Interest

Compound interest is interest earned paid on both the principal *and* the accumulated interest. In most situations, the interest on loans and other investments is compound interest rather than simple interest. When interest is compounded, first the interest earned at the end of an investment period is added to the initial principal. The interest rate is then applied to the sum.

Suppose you invest $1,000 in an account that pays 5 percent interest compounded annually. How much interest would the investment be worth at the end of five years? We can use a table to develop the solution:

Year	Beginning Balance	*plus*	(Balance × 5% Interest Rate)	*equals*	Account Total
1	$1,000.00		$50.00		$1,050.00
2	$1,050.00		$52.50		$1,102.50
3	$1,102.50		$55.13		$1,157.63
4	$1,157.63		$57.88		$1,215.51
5	$1,215.51		$60.78		$1,276.29

The investment would be worth $1,276.29 at the end of the five-year period. With compound interest, you would earn $276.29 in interest over those five years. Recall that you would earn only $250 under simple interest.

Compound interest is a powerful force over time. The longer the time period, the greater the power of compound interest. As an example, suppose that 200 years ago an ancestor had bequeathed you $5.00. At an annual rate of 6 percent simple interest, today the bequest would be worth $65.00, calculated as the $5.00 principal plus the result of multiplying 30 cents per year times 200 years. But if the interest payable were 6 percent compound interest, the value of the $5.00 bequest after 200 years would grow to $575,629.53! The huge difference in value is because, over a long time, more and more interest builds as a result of compounding.[2] In our example, only $60.00 of the final amount is attributable to interest on the principal alone. The rest is attributable to the compounding of interest. For an illustration of the effects of compounding more frequently than annually, see Insight 3-1.

INSIGHT 3.1

Frequency of Compounding.

The more frequently the same interest rate is compounded for a given term, the greater the interest amount and the corresponding effective interest rate. To see how the frequency of compounding influences the effective annual interest rate, assume a 10 percent interest rate compounded for various periods:

Compounding Period	Times Compounded in One Year	Effective Interest Rate
Year	1	10.00000%
Quarter	4	10.38129
Month	12	10.47131
Week	52	10.50648
Day	365	10.51558
Hour	8,760	10.51703
Minute	525,600	10.51709

Daily compounding, for example, results in an effective interest rate that is more than half a percentage point greater than the effective interest rate for annual compounding. If you borrowed $5,000 for one year at 10 percent interest compounded daily, for example, you would pay $25.78 more in interest than if you borrowed the same sum at 10 percent interest compounded annually.

Source: Ernest L. Martin, *Intro to the Time Value of Money* (Atlanta: LOMA, 1999), 16. Reprinted with permission of the publisher.

Effective Interest

The interest rates we have discussed so far to demonstrate interest rate calculations have been ***nominal interest rates***, also known as *stated interest rates,* which can be defined as interest rates that are quoted without the effects of compounding. *Nominal* means in name only.

The interest rate that includes the effects of compounding is known as the ***effective interest rate***, as shown in the table in Insight 3-1. The effective interest rate is greater than the nominal interest rate because of the effects of compounding. For the rest of this text, when we refer to a given percentage rate, we mean a nominal rate, unless otherwise noted.

INTRODUCTION TO INVESTMENTS AND INVESTING

Insurance companies invest premium dollars in many different types of assets. In fact, insurance companies can place money in any secure investment that has the potential for good earnings and is not prohibited by regulation. Assets such as bonds, stocks, mortgages, policy loans, and real estate produce an important part of an insurance company's investment earnings.

Before we discuss the assets insurers manage, we will first examine the terminology of investing. Investment professionals use many terms and concepts that are not part of everyday language. ***Investing*** refers to employing a principal sum of money to generate earnings. In a financial sense, investing usually involves using a principal sum of money to purchase assets or placing a sum on deposit. The expectation is that the principal sum will increase in value by generating earnings. An investment ***portfolio*** is a collection of various assets usually assembled for the purpose of meeting a defined set of investment goals. Investment goals usually focus on factors such as investment returns, risks, and patterns of cash flow. In investing, a ***return*** is the reward an investor hopes to receive for taking a risk, and a ***risk*** is the possibility that an investor will fail to earn an expected return or will lose all or part of an investment. ***Liquidity*** is the ease with which an asset can be converted into cash for an approximation of its true value.

We discussed assets briefly in Chapter 2. For our purposes in discussing investments, assets are items of value that a company or other legal entity owns. Assets are recognized for accounting purposes in the assets portion of a balance sheet. Assets may be tangible (real) or intangible (nonphysical). *Tangible* means having physical form. Accordingly, a ***tangible asset*** generally is an asset that has physical form. However, accounting rules may seem to arbitrarily classify some assets as tangible and others as intangible. Examples of tangible assets include cash, real estate, automobiles, collectibles, equipment, and machinery. *Intangible* means nonphysical. Accordingly, an ***intangible asset*** is an asset that represents ownership of a legal right or another nonphysical resource. Important examples of intangible assets are securities, patents, copyrights, computer software, leases, and licenses. ***Securities*** are financial agreements representing evidence of the right to collect repayment of a loan, ownership of an asset, or the legal right to purchase or sell ownership of an asset. Examples of securities include common stock and bonds. We discuss several types of securities in the next section of this chapter.

Property is an asset that can be owned or possessed. Property can be classified as real property or personal property. *Real property*, also known as ***real estate***, is land or anything attached to the land. Examples of real estate are a parcel of land, a home, or a commercial building. ***Personal property*** is any property that is not real estate. Some examples of tangible personal property are automobiles, computers, furniture, appliances, fine art, gold, jewelry, and antiques.

Insurers purchase assets for their general account and one or more separate accounts. For insurers, the ***general account*** is the portfolio of assets backing guaranteed products, such as traditional fixed-rate annuities. A ***separate account*** is a portfolio set apart from the general account and used to support contracts such as variable annuities, in which the consumer shares or assumes the investment risk. In Canada, the equivalent of a separate account is a segregated account. For invested assets of all U.S. insurers, roughly 71 percent are general account assets and the other 29 percent are separate account assets. In the United States, the provisions of the *NAIC Investments of Insurers Model Act* restrict investments for the general account. Investments on behalf of separate accounts are not covered by the Act.

The assets in a portfolio can be classified according to whether they represent debt, equity, or derivatives. Insurance companies hold a much greater monetary share of their assets in debt than in equities or derivatives.

- ***Debt*** represents the investor's loan of funds to the debt issuer in return for the promised repayment of principal and payment of interest. Important examples of debt securities are bonds and mortgages.
- ***Equity*** represents the investor's ownership or share of ownership in an asset such as a business or property. Common stock is an important example of an equity asset.
- ***Derivatives*** are financial securities that derive their value from another security. For example, stock options are derivative securities.

ASSETS HELD BY LIFE INSURERS

Life insurance companies invest in a variety of asset types, but the greatest portion of their overall investing is in bonds. By purchasing bonds of good quality, insurers can be reasonably certain of earning the investment returns they need in order to meet their future annuity obligations. Bond investments appeal to annuity issuers because bonds generally offer the payment of interest on a regular schedule and the repayment of principal at a predictable date. In order of importance in the industry, the assets in life insurance company investment portfolios include bonds, common stocks, mortgages, policy loans, and real estate. Figure 3-3 shows the relative distribution of assets held by insurance companies.

Bonds

A ***bond*** is a debt certificate issued by a borrower. In a bond certificate, the issuer promises to (1) repay the borrowed sum, which is specified as the ***face value*** of the bond; (2) pay interest at a rate specified on the bond according to a specified schedule; and (3) repay the debt by a specified maturity date. Bonds produce income to the investor in the form of payments of interest and principal. A bond owner can also realize a profit from the sale of a bond, if the bond is sold for a price higher than its purchase price. The date on which the borrower must repay the amount originally borrowed is the ***maturity date***. A bond has a fixed maturity period, which generally extends from 2 to 30 years after the issue date. In general, life insurers concentrate their investing in intermediate- and long-

FIGURE 3.3

Investments of Life Insurance Companies.

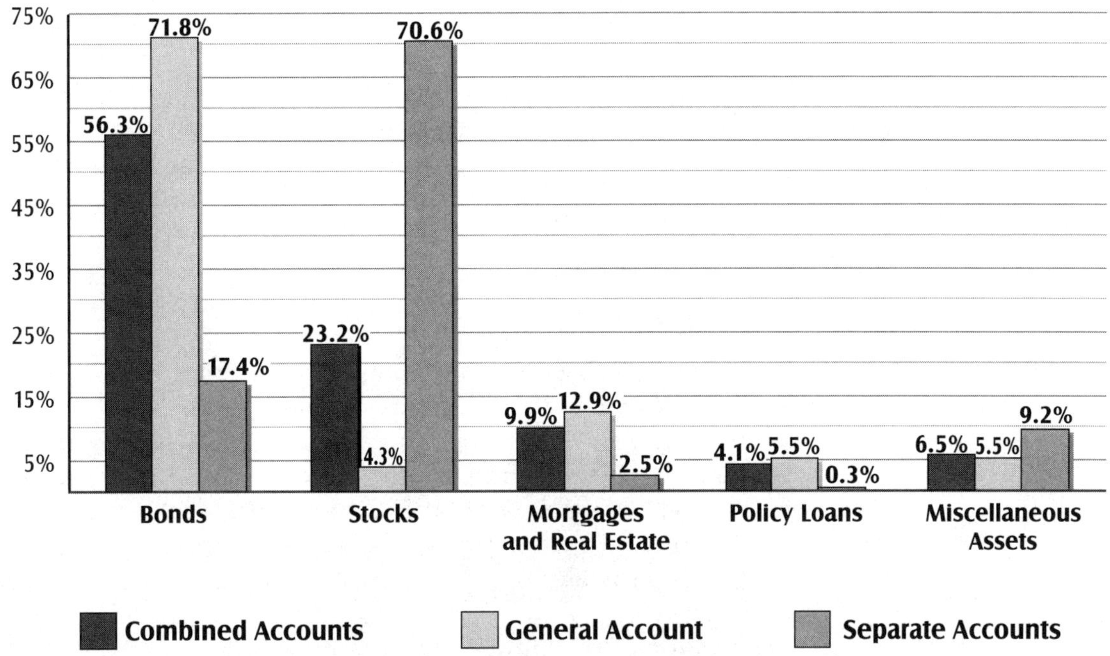

Source: ACLI, *1998 Life Insurance Fact Book* (Washington, D.C.: American Council of Life Insurance, 1998), 100–101

term debt securities. For investments in the United States, a ***short term*** is defined as covering less than 1 year, an ***intermediate term*** may be defined as covering from 1 to 10 years, and a ***long term*** may be defined as any period greater than 10 years. You will find that usage differs somewhat within the United States concerning the length of the intermediate term and the long term but that the short term is consistently viewed as being less than one year. Also, usage differs in Canada, where a short term is consistently defined as covering from 0 to 6 years, an intermediate term is consistently defined as covering from more than 6 years to 10 years, and a long term is consistently defined as any period greater than 10 years.

Most bonds are issued with a stated face amount, known as the par value, which is also the principal amount of the loan. ***Par value*** for any security is the security's nominal or face value. A bond's par value is also known as the *face value, maturity value,* or *principal.* A bond's par value generally is set in increments of $1,000. However, a bond's market price does not necessarily equal the par value. When a bond's market price is greater than the bond's par value, the excess of the price over the par value is termed a ***premium***. When a bond's market price is less than the bond's par value, the difference between the market value and the par value is a ***discount***. When a bond is first sold, a market price is established for the bond, and the bond's price fluctuates thereafter according to competitive market forces. Fluctuations in a bond's price are inversely related to fluctuations in market interest rates. In other words, if market interest rates rise, a bond's price will fall. If market interest rates fall, a bond's price will rise.

The inverse relationship between the market value for bonds and the level of market interest rates results from competitive forces in the market for bonds. Suppose an Acme Corporation bond was issued at $1,000 with a stated interest rate of 5 percent. If market interest rates later were to fall to 3 percent, Acme, as the bond issuer, would still be obligated to pay interest at a rate of 5 percent. Further suppose that the Frieze Insurance Company owns a block of these Acme 5 percent bonds. With market interest rates at 3 percent, if Frieze wished to sell these bonds, Frieze would then demand a bond price higher than $1,000, because the Acme bond's high stated rate of interest would make it a premium buy in a market where bonds of comparable quality no longer offered a 5 percent interest rate. Thus, Frieze would demand a bond price higher than the bond's par value. Conversely, if interest rates were later to rise to 8 percent, then Frieze, as the bond's owner, would face a market bond price lower than the bond's par value. Market forces ensure that the market price and the stated interest rate will produce a rate of investment return equal to the current market interest rate on bonds of similar quality.

Bonds may be secured or unsecured. Under a secured bond, the borrower pledges specified assets as security to guarantee the safety of the investment. Assets pledged as security for a debt obligation are known as ***collateral***. If a borrower fails to honor the terms of a secured bond instrument, the investor is entitled to take ownership of the pledged assets. Under an unsecured bond, the borrower does not pledge any security for the debt. An unsecured corporate bond is called a ***debenture***.

When an investor buys a bond, the investor cannot be certain that the bond issuer will repay the obligation of interest and principal as promised. Thus, the investor risks losing the money invested in the bond. The level of risk varies from one bond issuer to another, depending upon the issuer's financial stability. For this reason, a bond issuer with a poor credit rating must offer a higher rate of interest to investors than would a bond issuer with a better credit rating. As the level of risk increases, the level of promised return increases.

Bonds are usually issued by corporations or governments. Bonds issued by corporations are called ***corporate bonds***, whereas those issued by governments—including federal, state, county, city, and other local governments—are called ***government bonds***. By far the largest category of life insurance company assets is corporate bonds, but insurance companies also invest a considerable amount of money in government bonds.

Mortgages

For our purposes, a ***mortgage*** is a loan secured by a pledge of specified real property. If the borrower fails to honor the terms of the loan, the lender is entitled to follow procedures necessary to take the property. All mortgages represent debt secured by real estate.

Most insurers today invest in mortgages primarily through mortgage-backed bonds, known as ***collateralized mortgage obligations (CMOs)***, which are secured by a pool of residential mortgage loans. Mortgages and CMOs are appealing to insurers because these securities (1) offer monthly debt repayment schedules, thus providing a predictable stream of cash flows; (2) offer the insurer a minimum—and sometimes a fixed—rate of return; and (3) are secured debt instruments.

Stocks

Stocks are equity securities that represent ownership in a business. Stock is sold in shares. Any owner of stock shares is known as a ***shareholder*** or *stockholder* of a company. Stock can be common or preferred. Our discussion here is confined to common stock. An owner of common stock expects to earn returns in the form of increases in the price of the stock shares and income from dividends. Increases in the price of the stock shares are known as ***price appreciation*** or *capital gains*. A ***dividend*** on common stock is a share of earnings that the company pays to owners of the stock. A dividend on common stock is not guaranteed. Dividends on common stock are declared and paid by the issuing company's board of directors. Because common stock does not represent a loan, interest is not paid on common stock. As shown in Figure 3-3, insurers hold common stock mainly in their separate account portfolios, where they hold the funds used to support variable annuities and other variable products.

Policy Loans

When insurance company customers take a loan against their contract's cash value, the loan is accounted for as an investment of the insurer. Many annuity contracts do not permit loans, but the insurance company still must invest in any policy loans that it makes under other contracts that permit such loans. Even for a loan against an annuity contract, the investment is classified as a policy loan. Although most annuity contracts do not permit loans, any policy loan on the books of an insurer is considered a policy loan. Policy loans earn a relatively low rate of interest for the insurance company. A higher-than-expected level of policy loans can limit the insurance company's overall portfolio investment return.

Real Estate

Insurance companies often own the buildings where their home offices are located. Insurers also sometimes directly own other commercial real estate.

Earnings associated with real estate ownership generally take the form of rental income and a profit upon the sale of the property at a price higher than the purchase price. Commercial real estate—and commercial mortgages—generally constitute a relatively small percentage of life insurance company investments. Insurers frequently gain ownership of real estate after a mortgage goes into default, and ownership of the property is settlement for the mortgage. Figure 3-4 illustrates typical classifications of insurers' assets.

FIGURE 3.4

Classifications of Insurers' Assets.

	Asset Classifications					
Asset Type	Short-Term	Long-Term	Tangible	Intangible	Debt	Equity
Common Stocks	No	Yes	No	Yes	No	Yes
Bonds	No	Yes	No	Yes	Yes	No
Mortgages	No	Yes	No	Yes	Yes	No
Policy Loans	No	No	No	Yes	Yes	No
Real Estate	No	Yes	Yes	No	No	Yes
Cash	Yes	No	Yes	No	No	Yes

INVESTMENT RETURNS OTHER THAN INTEREST

For the sake of simplicity, we have illustrated investment returns only in terms of an interest rate earned on loans, deposits, or bonds. However, when we discussed different asset types, we saw that earnings on an asset can additionally take the form of (a) gains upon the sale of the asset, (b) rent, or (c) dividends, as illustrated in Figure 3-5.

FIGURE 3.5

Forms of Earnings.

	Potential Forms of Earnings			
Asset type	Price Appreciation (Gain on Sale)	Interest	Dividend	Rent
Common Stocks	Yes	No	Yes	No
Bonds	Yes	Yes	No	No
Mortgages	Yes	Yes	No	No
Policy Loans	No	Yes	No	No
Real Estate	Yes	No	No	Yes

If an asset generates more than one type of earnings, the total return on the asset would be the sum of the earnings from various sources. Any form of investment earnings, however, can be expressed as a percentage of the principal invested. When a return is expressed as a percentage relative to the invested principal, it is called a ***rate of return***. We can illustrate this concept with several examples.

- Insurance companies purchase and hold stock in other corporations. An insurance company holding stock will probably earn dividends on that stock. In addition, the insurer might be able to sell the stock for more than it paid for the stock, thus allowing it to earn a gain upon the sale of the stock. The insurer's total earnings on the stock—dividend earnings and gains upon sale—can be expressed in terms of a percentage of the stock's purchase price.
- When an insurance company evaluates the earnings on its general account assets for a given period, it sums the investment returns for that period and then expresses the total returns for the period as a percentage of the value of the general account portfolio at the beginning of the period.
- When an insurance company evaluates the investment earnings on a customer's variable annuity contract for a given period, the insurer first sums the contract's gains and any losses on all of its investment subaccounts and then expresses this sum as a percentage of the account's value at the beginning of the period.

Many factors enter into an insurance company's calculations concerning the rate of return on various assets. In this text, however, we will not go into greater detail regarding the insurer's calculations of returns on its investment portfolios.

Key Terms and Concepts

interest
time value of money
present value (PV)
future value (FV)
principal
interest rate
simple interest
compound interest
nominal interest rate
effective interest rate
investing
portfolio
return
risk
liquidity

tangible asset
intangible asset
security
property
real estate
personal property
general account
separate account
debt
equity
derivative
bond
face value
maturity date
short term
intermediate term
long term
par value
premium
discount
collateral
debenture
corporate bond
government bond
mortgage
collateralized mortgage obligation (CMO)
stock
shareholder
price appreciation
dividend
rate of return

ENDNOTES

1. Much of the treatment of interest rates and time value of money concepts was adapted with permission of the publisher from Ernest L. Martin, *Intro to the Time Value of Money* (Atlanta: LOMA, 1999), 2–7.
2. Adapted from Stephen A. Ross, Randolph W. Westerfield, and Bradford D. Jordan, *Fundamentals of Corporate Finance*, 3rd ed. (New York: McGraw-Hill Companies, 1995). Used with permission of the publisher.

Chapter 4

Risks Insurers Face

After studying this chapter, you should be able to

- Describe general approaches to risk management
- Recognize and interpret the risk-return tradeoff
- Identify various sources of risk to investors and to insurance companies
- Characterize the effects on insurers when market interest rates change

In Chapter 3, we looked at how investments create earnings for annuity products. However, the investments that insurers make to support annuity products are not risk-free. Here in Chapter 4, we turn our discussion to the topic of risks. Risk in supporting annuity products is not limited to the risks of investing. Insurers face many different risks, which they manage with a variety of techniques. In this chapter, we introduce you to some general approaches to risk management, and then go on to the concept of the risk-return tradeoff. Then we discuss investment risks and liability risks, and finally conclude the chapter by describing asset/liability management.

General Approaches to Risk Management

Risk is simply the possibility of suffering a loss. Risk management provides a set of principles for dealing with financial risk. The practice of ***risk management*** involves identifying, assessing, and dealing with risk. In order to eliminate or reduce exposure to financial risk, insurers can choose any of at least four options: (1) avoiding risk, (2) controlling risk, (3) accepting risk, and (4) transferring risk.

Avoiding Risk

One method of managing risk is to avoid risk altogether. Individuals can avoid the risk of financial loss in the stock market by not investing in it. Insurance companies can avoid some liability risks by rejecting applications for insurance. Often, however, avoiding risk is not an effective option for insurance companies.

Controlling Risk

We can take steps to prevent or reduce losses. For instance, many annuity contracts sold in the 1980s and early 1990s had guaranteed interest rates of 4 percent or more. In recent years, many insurers have developed new annuity contracts with lower guaranteed rates of 3 or 3½ percent in an attempt to help control interest-rate risk. Most deferred annuity contracts impose a surrender charge for the first several years, which helps control the risk of early withdrawals.

Accepting Risk

A third method of managing risk is to accept, or *retain*, risk. Simply stated, to accept a risk is to assume all financial responsibility for that risk. Some people and businesses consciously choose to accept significant risks. Another option is to accept only part of a risk. For instance, an employer can partially insure a medical expense benefit plan by paying its employees' medical expenses up to a stated amount and buying insurance to cover all expenses in excess of that stated amount.

Transferring Risk

Transferring risk is another method of risk management. When you transfer risk to another party, you are shifting the financial responsibility for that risk to the other party, generally in exchange for a fee.

The most common way for most individuals and businesses to transfer risk is to purchase insurance coverage. Insurers also transfer their risks when they issue coverage under insurance and annuity contracts and then reduce the possibility of catastrophic losses by transferring some or all of the risks to another insurer. ***Reinsurance*** is a type of insurance that one insurance company, known as the ***ceding company***, purchases from another insurance company, known as the ***reinsurer***. To ***cede*** insurance business, such as annuity business, is to obtain reinsurance on that business by transferring all or part of the risk to a reinsurer. With fixed annuities, insurers sometimes reinsure some of the interest-rate risk. With variable annuities that promise at least a return of premiums upon the death of the annuitant, insurers often obtain reinsurance for guaranteed minimum death benefits.

THE RISK-RETURN TRADEOFF[1]

Financial experts recognize a direct relationship between the amount of potential return from an investment opportunity and the amount of risk connected with investing in that opportunity. In Chapter 3, we saw that, in investments, a risk is the possibility that an investor will fail to earn an expected return or will lose all or part of an investment. Generally, though, a risk is a potential loss. On the other hand, a return is the reward an investor hopes to receive for taking a risk. Investors generally seek returns. However, most investors want to seek returns while avoiding risk. These two goals—avoiding risk and seeking returns—inevitably come into conflict because earning an adequate return requires taking some amount of risk. Investors, including insurers, must decide how much risk they are willing to take and how much return they require as a reward for taking that risk.

Generally, the higher the potential return from an investment, the greater the potential risk associated with making that investment. This relationship is known as the ***risk-return tradeoff***. The relationship between risk and return affects any investment decision. The investor in a bond must weigh the expected return from the bond against the risk incurred by investing in the bond. When an investor buys a bond, the investor risks losing the amount invested in the bond. The level of risk varies from issuer to issuer, depending on the issuer's financial stability. For this reason, a bond issuer having poor credit must pay a higher interest rate to investors than would a bond issuer with a better credit rating. As the level of risk increases, the level of return also must increase. As risk decreases, the level of return decreases. The risk-return tradeoff applies to virtually all business decisions.

For example, when a bank reviews a loan application, the bank consults a credit rating agency to find the applicant's credit report. The bank will use the credit report in evaluating the borrower's ability to repay a loan. If the bank decides to make the loan, it will charge a higher interest rate to a borrower having a poor credit rating than it would to a borrower with a spotless credit history. The high interest rate compensates the bank for the additional risk of making the loan. Similarly, the bank would probably specify a lower interest rate on a loan to an applicant with an excellent credit history, because such a loan would pose a lower level of risk for the bank.

The same principle holds true in insurance company investments. An insurance company can choose between investing in so-called risk-free U.S. government bonds or the risky type of corporate bonds known as junk bonds. The U.S. government bonds pay a low rate of return to the investor, but these bonds represent little or no risk to an investor. So, safe U.S. government bonds return a lower rate than do risky junk bonds. Junk bonds represent a high level of investment risk and thus must offer high rates of return to compensate the investor for the investment risk taken.

Specific investment risks and the economic environment are both sources of risk for the investor. These elements can serve either to decrease or increase both risk and potential return. The chart in Figure 4-1 shows how these elements typically influence an investor's risk and return on any given investment decision or transaction.

FIGURE 4.1

Risk and Return in Investment Decisions.

Lower Risks That Require *Lower* Potential Return	Higher Risks That Require *Higher* Potential Return
A short-term investment	A long-term investment
A borrower with a good credit rating	A borrower with a poor credit rating
An investment with good liquidity or marketability—one that is easy to sell	An investment with poor liquidity or poor marketability—one that is difficult to sell
A loan that is secured by collateral	A loan that is unsecured by collateral
A new product that has low initial costs	A new product that has high initial costs
The selling of a new product in a familiar market	The selling of a new product in an unfamiliar market
A loan that is repaid on a specified due date	A loan that can be repaid any time
A loan that specifies a variable interest rate	A loan that specifies a fixed interest rate

Insurance companies do not have the option of taking high risk in the hope of earning high investment returns. For insurance companies, the goal of generating returns must always be balanced against the need to protect the company's financial soundness. Insurance companies must place as much emphasis on safety as they do on returns. An important factor in the appeal of financial products and services is the consumer's perception of the financial institution's safety. For financial institutions, successful financial performance consists of an appropriate balance between achieving good returns for the company's owners and customers and maintaining appropriate safety.

Investment Risks

An investment opportunity is riskier than most others if its range of possible returns is broader than the range for most investment opportunities. The financial risks any investor faces in investing are (1) the risk of losing some or all of the original investment and (2) the risk of failing to earn some or all of an expected return. Investors may encounter the following types of financial risks: interest-rate risk, credit risk, market risk, and currency risk.

- ***Interest-rate risk*** is the uncertainty arising from fluctuations in market interest rates. Suppose an individual investor put $10,000 in a certificate of deposit (CD) paying 6 percent annual interest, and the investor cannot withdraw the money for two years without incurring a major financial penalty. Then, three months after the investor purchases the certificate, market interest rates begin to rise rapidly, so that new certificates of deposit offer 10 percent interest. In this case, the investor will have incurred the effects of interest-rate risk. If the investor had purchased a three-month CD and then had reinvested in another CD, he could have earned a higher rate of interest.
- ***Credit risk*** can be defined as the possibility of poor financial performance on the part of a business and the possibility that it could be late with payments or could entirely fail to pay its obligations. A failure to meet a financial obligation is known as a ***default***. Accordingly, credit risk is sometimes called *default risk*.
- ***Market risk*** is the risk arising from movements in the direction of an entire market, such as the stock market, the bond market, or the real estate market. For example, the stock market in general may lose value due to such influences as loss in investor confidence; the bond markets may lose value due to an increase in interest rates; or a market for commercial buildings may lose value due to overbuilding. A related form of risk is ***inflation risk***, the risk that the overall level of prices in the economy will increase. Inflation risk arises from the possibility that the returns from an investment might not keep pace with losses in the purchasing

power of currency. Deflation risk is the possibility that assets could lose value along with a decrease in the overall level of prices in the economy.

- ***Currency risk*** is the risk arising from changes in currency exchange rates. Insurers have a limited exposure to currency risk, because they limit their investments in assets denominated in foreign currency.

Contingency Risks for Insurers[2]

The investments of a financial institution must be safe and must adequately support the institution's obligations to its customers. Financial institutions face risks similar to those of individual investors plus additional risks that individual investors don't face. In order to ensure their financial strength, insurance companies must also focus their attention on a few crucial areas of risk that the actuarial profession has identified as being vital. Overexposure to these *contingency risks*, usually known as ***C risks***, can cause financial distress for insurers. Actuaries have developed a classification system that officially recognizes four different C risks—C-1, C-2, C-3, and C-4.

- ***C-1 risk (asset risk)*** is the risk that the insurer will lose money on its investments in stocks, bonds, mortgages, and real estate. Insurers can control C-1 risk by evaluating investment risks realistically, investing a large share of their assets in high-quality securities, and maintaining sound investment practices.
- ***C-2 risk (pricing risk)*** is the risk that the insurer's experience with mortality or expenses will differ significantly from expectations, causing the insurer to lose money on its products. Insurers can control C-2 risk by evaluating insurance risks conservatively, maintaining sound actuarial practices and reinsurance programs, controlling their expenses, and designing products sensibly.
- ***C-3 risk (interest-rate risk)*** is the risk that market interest rates might shift, causing the insurer's assets to lose value or its liabilities to gain value. Insurers attempt to control C-3 risk through asset/liability management (ALM) programs, which we cover later in this chapter.
- ***C-4 risk (general management risk)*** is the risk of losses resulting from the insurer's ineffective general business practices or from the need to pay a special assessment to cover another insurer's unsound business practices. Practices that combat C-4 risk include sound managerial judgment, ethical behavior, prevention of internal dishonesty, and control of operating costs. Emphasizing an ethical organizational culture supports an insurer's valuable reputation and goodwill and guards against the need to pay costly legal settlements.

Examples of the officially recognized C risks appear in Figure 4-2.

FIGURE 4.2

Examples of C Risks for Life Insurance Companies.

C Risk	Examples
C-1 Asset risk	• Loss in market value of assets, except if caused by interest-rate movements • Borrower's default in payment of interest • Borrower's default in payment of principal
C-2 Pricing risk	• Adverse change in mortality experience; for annuities, an adverse change in mortality would mean an increase in life expectancy • Increase in administrative costs
C-3 Interest-rate risk	• Loss of assets' value because of interest-rate increases; loss on forced sale of assets when market interest rates rise • Withdrawals by customers when interest rates rise • Loss on bond prepayments and mortgage prepayments when interest rates fall • Losses due to asset/liability mismatches
C-4 General management risk	• Market risk from expansion into new lines of business, geographic expansion • Changes in laws affecting the business • Fraud by employees or customers; embezzlement • Mismanagement of any sort • Regulatory assessments to cover the obligations of failed insurers • Withdrawals by customers driven by fears of insolvency

The large investment portfolios held by financial institutions are the focus of advanced investment management techniques. Important investment management techniques include

- Seeking a targeted rate of return for a portfolio
- Monitoring the liquidity and marketability of assets
- Managing the timing of asset maturity dates
- Diversification of assets and liabilities, as discussed below

One way to distinguish among types of risks is to determine whether a risk can in theory be controlled under a risk management method called diversification. ***Diversification*** is a technique for spreading risk by investing in different assets having different risk profiles. Diversification can be used to control nonsystematic risk, but not systematic risk. ***Nonsystematic risk***—also known as *diversifiable risk* and *specific risk*—is risk that is specific to an individual asset. Credit risk is an example of a nonsystematic risk. To diversify their investments, insurers carefully spread their investment selections among the securities of different industries, different geographic regions, and different issuers. ***Systematic risks***, on the other hand, are risks that affect all assets in our economic system, and thus are considered nondiversifiable. Inflation risk is an example of a systematic risk.

Insurers apply the principle of diversification to their product offerings as well as to their investments. To achieve product diversification, insurers (1) issue different product types—for example, life insurance products and annuity products; (2) issue annuity contracts to customers in a variety of geographic regions; and (3) issue contracts to customers having a variety of demographic characteristics.

OVERVIEW OF ASSET/LIABILITY MANAGEMENT

For a life and annuity insurance company, the ***asset portfolio*** is the company's investment portfolio, in which the insurer holds securities and other assets. The ***liability portfolio*** is the insurance company's collection of products, which represent obligations to customers. Insurers must respond to the risk-return tradeoff by balancing the risks and returns in their asset and liability portfolios. Insurers and other financial institutions attempt to do this through a management process called asset/liability management (ALM). Primary responsibility for asset/liability management is usually shared between an insurer's actuarial staff and investment staff.

Recall from Chapter 3 that invested assets produce earnings in the form of interest, income, dividends, capital gains, and rent. Insurers use the earnings from invested assets to support the payment of future contractual benefits to customers. ***Asset/liability management (ALM)*** is the activity that coordinates the administration of the insurer's obligations to customers with the administration of the insurer's investment portfolios so as to achieve the best possible financial effects. Figure 4-3 illustrates the balances that insurers must maintain through ALM.

FIGURE 4.3

The ALM Balancing Act.

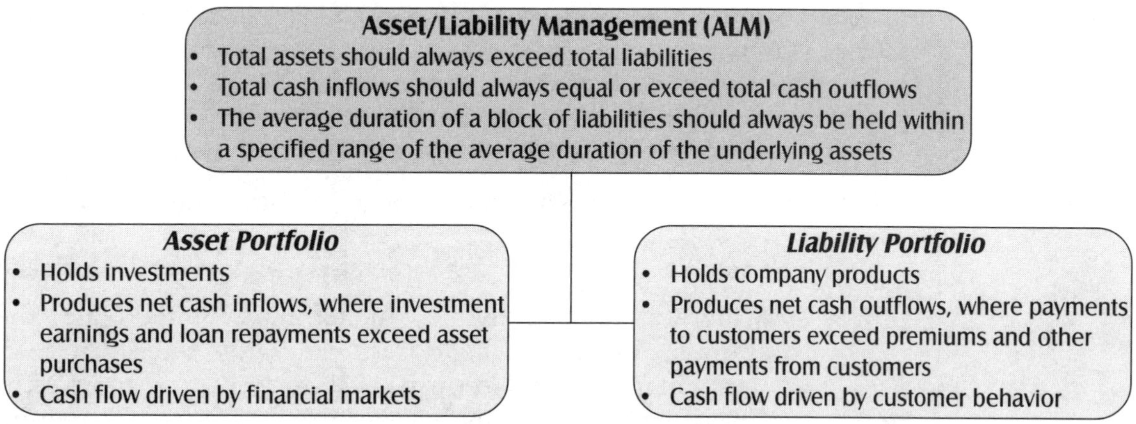

ALM focuses on appropriately matching the characteristics of the company's investments with the characteristics of its contractual liabilities. The goal of ALM is to produce a pattern, in timing and amount, of net cash earnings from investments to match the expected pattern of net cash payments required under the company's annuity products and other contracts with customers. ALM helps to ensure that the value of the company's assets always exceeds the value of the company's liabilities.

An example illustrates the need to match the cash flows. The Archer Insurance Company anticipates now that in the year 2015 it will need to pay out in cash $2.5 million per month in annuity benefits. In this context, Archer's awareness that it will need to pay out $2.5 million at a specified future date identifies this amount as an expected cash outflow. To meet that future need for cash, Archer could invest today in bonds and other securities that are expected to produce in the year 2015 cash payments to Archer that meet Archer's need for $2.5 million per month. In this example, Archer's expectation of investment earnings of $2.5 million per month in 2015 is an expected cash inflow.

The Challenge of Interest-Rate Changes[3]

As we have seen in Chapters 2 and 3, insurance companies use the concept of interest rates for a variety of financial purposes. For example, insurers use market interest rates to determine the crediting rate they offer on their annuity products and the margin they expect to earn on those products. Unfortunately, market interest rates are constantly in motion, so the rate that seemed the right choice for a crediting rate one year may turn out to be inadequate a year later or five years later. Changes in market interest rates translate into operating gains or losses for insurers, and these operating gains or losses in turn affect the insurers' overall financial position. Moreover, market interest rates represent a systematic risk; they are beyond the control of insurers and other financial institutions. Therefore, the most crucial challenge for ALM is to limit the negative effects of interest-rate changes on a company's asset and liability portfolios.

In order to understand more precisely how changes in market interest rates affect insurers, we will examine the possible effects of (1) *increases* in interest rates and (2) *decreases* in interest rates.

Effects of Interest-Rate Increases on Fixed-Rate Deferred Annuities

When market interest rates are *rising*, the following conditions may occur:

- The value of bonds and other interest-bearing securities goes down.
- New investments earn the new higher market rate. Money that is being invested at the new higher rate comes from three main sources: (1) premium income and fees from customers, (2) current investment earnings from assets held in the insurer's portfolio, and (3) maturities or prepayments of debt securities.

- Customers of annuities using the portfolio method of interest crediting are more likely to withdraw their money and place it in higher-rate investments. As mentioned in Chapter 2, the portfolio method does not show a quick response to changes in market interest rates. Customers can withdraw their funds by (1) surrendering their contracts, (2) taking loans, or (3) withdrawing money from various accumulation products, such as deferred annuities. If excessive withdrawals occur, insurers may need to sell assets unexpectedly or borrow short-term funds. When interest rates are high, asset prices are depressed.
- In order to attract new premiums and keep funds already under management, the insurance company may need to credit the higher current market interest rate to customers. In order to support the increased interest credits, the insurer in turn will need to earn a greater return on investments.
- Insurers may experience spread compression. Here, *spread* refers to a difference between the interest rates the insurer is earning on its total portfolio and the interest rates the insurer must pay to customers. ***Spread compression*** occurs when insurers are forced to take a smaller profit because customers immediately demand the higher market interest rate. At the same time, the average rate of return on the insurer's investment portfolio rises only slowly, because older assets continue to earn the lower interest rates available in the financial markets when the older assets were purchased.

  If the rise in interest rates is very large, happens fairly suddenly, and is expected to continue, spread could actually turn negative. Spread compression does not occur automatically, because an insurer can choose to keep its margin constant. In this situation, however, when choosing to keep the margin constant, the insurer must be prepared to face a higher lapse rate and a drop in sales. The insurer must decide which choice incurs less disadvantage.

Effects of Interest-Rate Decreases on Fixed-Rate Deferred Annuities

Insurers generally can expect to have excess cash available for investment only when interest rates are low. When market interest rates are *decreasing*, the following conditions arise:

- Bonds held in the insurer's investment portfolio, if purchased during periods of higher market interest rates, gain market value.
- The insurer's liabilities under its fixed interest annuity and insurance contracts, if issued during periods of higher interest rates, become more valuable to policyholders because the policyholders' annuities continue to earn high rates of interest while the market is offering lower rates. Therefore, policyholders are less likely to allow their contracts to lapse, and the insurer's persistency should

improve. On the other hand, this situation may create a mismatch between the characteristics of assets and liabilities.

- An insurer can lower its crediting rates immediately to the new lower market rate.
- Because the average rate of return on insurers' investment portfolios declines only slowly in annuities that use the portfolio method of interest crediting, insurers may experience spread expansion in connection with the affected products. ***Spread expansion*** is the widening of an insurer's spread that occurs when market interest rates fall and the insurer reduces crediting rates to the new market level while it continues to earn a higher overall rate of return on investments. Like spread compression, spread expansion does not occur automatically, because an insurer can choose to keep its margin constant.
- Issuers of an insurance company's bond and mortgage investments, if these securities are paying older and higher interest rates, may choose to ***refinance***—repay the debt before repayment is due. Those same borrowers can usually make new borrowing arrangements at the new lower prevailing interest rates. The insurer thus would lose the higher-yielding older investments. This would actually cause spread compression on products with long-term guarantees. For this reason, insurers typically match their products having long-term guarantees with assets that are unlikely to be refinanced.
- New investments will earn only the new lower interest rate, reflecting current market conditions.
- If market interest rates fall below the minimum interest-rate guarantees, such as the three percent specified in some deferred annuity contracts, insurers will experience spread compression on those contracts. For recent sales of contracts using the old minimum rate guarantees, spread compression appears immediately. For contracts already on the books, spread compression appears slowly.

Insight 4-1 discusses how the problem of low interest rates creates spread compression.

Important Asset/Liability Management Reports[4]

Asset/liability management (ALM) reports are designed to communicate the results of technical analysis to decision makers who are not technical experts. Important ALM reports include the investment activity report, crediting rate declarations, and the portfolio performance review. The titles of these reports could vary from one company to another.

The Investment Activity Report

The investment activity report is a detailed weekly report showing all portfolio activity during the week, including the following activities:

- Purchases of new assets, showing each new asset's rate of return, term to maturity, and its quality rating, if applicable
- Removals of assets from the portfolio through sales, prepayments, or repayment of securities upon maturity

INSIGHT 4.1

The Problem of Low Interest Rates.

Low interest rates can be at least as harmful to insurers as high interest rates. Why would low interest rates pose a problem for insurers? The short answer is that, in a prolonged environment of low interest rates, assets will *shorten* and liabilities will *lengthen*. When assets shorten and liabilities lengthen, the combined outcome is known as spread compression. To better understand these effects of low interest rates, we need to examine what is meant by some potentially new expressions:

- Assets shorten
- Liabilities lengthen
- Spread compression

Assets Shorten

Saying that assets will shorten means that assets such as fixed interest rate bonds and mortgages will be repaid faster than expected. To the extent possible, corporations will repay their bond debt early and homeowners will refinance their mortgages to take advantage of lower interest rates.

Liabilities Lengthen

Saying that liabilities will lengthen means that an insurer's obligations to customers—its products—will remain in effect for longer than the insurer expected when it issued the products. In an environment of low interest rates, customers keep their existing contracts to take advantage of guaranteed interest crediting rates that are higher than current market rates.

For example, a typical flexible premium annuity contract might provide that the policyholder can receive a guaranteed interest crediting rate of 6 percent while new contracts offer only 4 percent. Some contracts also allow contract owners to deposit additional premiums at the guaranteed interest crediting rate for the lifetime of the contract—which could be a long time. Contract owners may even arbitrage a contract by borrowing from it or against it at low rates to make additional investments that earn a higher rate. Thus contract owners keep their contracts for a longer time.

When assets shorten and liabilities lengthen, insurers are forced to reinvest asset proceeds at interest rates much lower than the previous ones—and over shorter periods—while their liabilities are extending over longer periods.

Spread Compression

The combined effect of shortened assets and lengthened liabilities is spread compression—a squeeze on profits. In spread compression, the insurer earns lower returns on its investments at a time when contractual guarantees force it to credit more interest than it can otherwise afford. Policyholders further exacerbate the negative effects of spread compression by adding more money to existing contracts and keeping their contracts longer.

This risk is further exacerbated by such factors as the "*USA Today* effect"—that is, a front-page newspaper story that, in essence, tells homeowners to refinance their mortgages and policyholders how to take advantage of an option that the insurance company awarded at issue. This effect could greatly increase the number of policyholders taking advantage of the guaranteed options.

Annuities and long-term care products provide for payments to customers over long periods of time. At the same time, the insurer faces shortening assets which force the insurer to make more and earlier reinvestments. The investment earnings rate can fall below what was originally priced, and profitability becomes a concern. If these long-tailed liabilities were the primary products a company sold and interest rates were to drop and remain low, an insurer's solvency might be threatened.

Source: Max J. Rudolph, "Low Interest Rates: A Solvency Threat?" *Resource* (April 1999): 24–26. Article adapted by Francois I. Genest, Senior Vice President, U.S. Fortis Family, with permission of the publisher.

Crediting-Rate Declarations

To insurance companies, a ***crediting-rate declaration*** is the insurance company's formal declaration of the crediting of a specified current interest rate on a specified product. When adopted, crediting-rate declarations represent a formal commitment as to the rate of interest that the insurer will award on money held in fixed deferred annuities and other interest-sensitive products. Many contracts provide that current interest rates are credited at the discretion of the company, subject to a resolution by the board of directors. Figure 4-4 shows a crediting-rate declaration.

FIGURE 4.4 **Dividend and Interest Declarations.**

Jupiter Life Insurance Company

It is necessary that dividends and excess interest payable be declared by our Board of Directors. It is recommended that the following resolutions be adopted:

RESOLVED, that effective October 1, 1997, through September 30, 1998, excess interest at a rate equal to the difference between the Total Interest Rate from the following table and the guaranteed interest rate be declared on the outstanding balances of various previously issued individual annuity policies as specified in the following table:

Individual Annuity Contract Type	Total Interest Rate
Non-deferred, qualified—HR10, TSA, IRA	5.50%
Non-deferred, non-qualified	5.50%
Non-qualified single premium deferred annuities	4.05%

BE IT FURTHER RESOLVED, that effective October 1, 1997, through September 30, 1998, excess interest at a rate equal to the difference between the Total Interest Rate from the following table and the guaranteed interest rate be declared on the cash value of paid-up additions held on various previously issued Flexible Premium Retirement annuities as specified in the following table:

Flexible Premium Retirement Annuity Type	Total Interest Rate
Non-qualified—7.45% loan interest	5.30%
Non-qualified—6.00% loan interest	4.05%
Non-qualified—5.00% loan interest	3.55%
Qualified—HR10, TSA, IRA	5.50%

BE IT FURTHER RESOLVED, that effective October 1, 1997, through September 30, 1998, excess interest at a rate equal to the difference between the Total Interest Rate from the following table and the guaranteed interest rate be declared on the outstanding balances of various previously issued individual annuity policies as specified in the following table by premium provision:

Premium Provision	Total Interest Rate
Single premium	5.95%
Annual premium	5.95%
Flexible premium	6.45%

Investment Portfolio Performance Review

The investment portfolio performance review is probably the most comprehensive type of ALM report. However, it is not detailed, because it presents information in summary form, highlighting the following aspects of investment performance:

- Overall investment growth, including asset growth and income growth; analysis of changes in the market value of assets
- Summary of investment purchases and sales by asset type
- Summary of distribution of assets; comparison of the company's asset distribution to the asset distribution of the industry as a whole
- Summary explanations of key events in the external environment and discussion of strategic responses to those events
- Reports on special topics, such as problem assets and investments in unusual asset types

RISKS IN THE LIABILITY PORTFOLIO

Insurance and annuity products contractually transfer a specified risk from the consumer to the insurance company. The risks the company undertakes to manage in connection with a product such as an annuity can include some or all of the following:

- The risk that the insurer's administrative costs could be greater than assumed in product pricing
- The risk that the insurer's costs of providing benefits could be greater than assumed in product design, including the risks that (1) annuitants could live longer than expected or that (2) lapses could be higher than assumed in product design
- The risk, in deferred variable annuities, where investment revenue comes primarily from the stock market, that prolonged downturns in the stock market may occur
- The risk, in deferred variable annuities, that mortality could be worse than expected when the stock market is down, because most deferred variable contracts guarantee at least a return of premium upon death prior to annuitization
- The risk that investment results could be less favorable than assumed in product design, including the risks that (1) actual investment returns could fail to match required investment returns, or (2) invested funds could suffer losses of principal

KEY TERMS AND CONCEPTS

risk management
reinsurance
ceding company
reinsurer
cede
risk-return tradeoff
interest-rate risk

credit risk
default
market risk
inflation risk
currency risk
C risk (contingency risk)
C-1 risk (asset risk)
C-2 risk (pricing risk)
C-3 risk (interest-rate risk)
C-4 risk (general management risk)
diversification
nonsystematic risk
systematic risk
asset portfolio
liability portfolio
asset/liability management (ALM)
spread compression
spread expansion
refinance
crediting-rate declaration

ENDNOTES

1. Adapted from Susan Conant et al., *Managing for Solvency and Profitability in Life and Health Insurance Companies* (Atlanta: LOMA, 1996), 35–38. Used with permission of the publisher.
2. Ibid., 43–45.
3. Ibid., 536–39.
4. Ibid., 581–83.

Chapter 5

Finding Future Values

After studying this chapter, you should be able to

- Recognize the use of time value of money concepts in annuity product design
- Calculate the future value of a single sum
- Differentiate between an ordinary annuity and an annuity due
- Calculate the future value of an ordinary annuity and an annuity due
- Apply future value techniques to annuity product values

As we saw in Chapter 3, both future value and present value views of the time value of money are central to the operation of annuity contracts. An important application of future value concepts in annuity contracts is the growth of the accumulation value under a deferred annuity contract. When a deferred annuity contract is issued, an annuity purchaser is interested in the future value of money she is now investing in the annuity, because the accumulated value of the deferred annuity contract might be used to purchase a series of periodic income payments. In turn, when an annuity contract's payout period begins, the contract owner is interested in the present value of a series of future periodic income payments. The accumulation value and several other elements can influence the size of the periodic income payments during the payout period of an annuity contract.

Applying a basic application of the time value of money, we will now consider how four elements influence the size of the periodic income payments from an annuity contract:

- **Accumulation value.** Periodic income payments under an annuity contract can be purchased using the accumulation value of a deferred annuity contract. However, a lump sum from any source can be used to purchase an immediate annuity contract. If all other factors are equal, a larger accumulation value—or other single premium amount—purchases a larger size of periodic income payments. The sum of money required to purchase a given size of future periodic income payments roughly corresponds to the present value of that series of future payments.
- **Accumulation period.** The length of an accumulation period corresponds to the number of interest compounding periods in a future value calculation. If all other factors are equal, increasing the length of an accumulation period produces a larger accumulation value for use in purchasing a stream of periodic income payments. In this sense, all other factors being equal, a longer accumulation period produces a larger size of periodic income payment.
- **Interest rate or other rate of investment return.** We know that investment earnings cause a principal sum of money

to grow, and even more investment earnings will cause a sum of money to grow even more. If all other factors are equal, an increase in the rate of investment return during the accumulation period produces a larger accumulation value. In turn, if all other factors are equal, a larger accumulation value purchases a larger size of periodic income payments. Thus, during the accumulation period, if all other factors are equal, a higher rate of investment return provides a larger accumulation value for the purchase of a larger size of periodic income payment.

- **Number of periodic income payments.** If all other factors are equal, increasing the number of periodic income payments decreases the size of each periodic income payment.

These elements and their effects are summarized in Figure 5-1.

FIGURE 5.1

Factors Affecting the Amount of Periodic Income Payments.

If all other factors remain unchanged, then upon an **increase** in an annuity contract's...	...The amount of **periodic income payments** will
Accumulation value available	Increase
Accumulation period	Increase
Interest rate (Rate of investment earnings)	Increase
Number of periodic income payments	Decrease

Consider a brief example to illustrate how these elements operate. The following information describes retirement planning for Morton Avery:

- At age 55, Mr. Avery used his retirement savings of $50,000 to purchase a single premium deferred annuity (SPDA) with an investment return of 5 percent.
- The SPDA matured upon Mr. Avery's 65th birthday, when Mr. Avery annuitized the contract. Upon annuitization, the contract began paying monthly income payments. Under the SPDA, the annuity conversion factor for age 65 was $5.60 a year for each $1,000 of accumulation value.
- Over the course of 10 years, the accumulation value of Mr. Avery's SPDA grew to more than $80,000. For this value, Mr. Avery was able to purchase a lifetime annual income payment of approximately $15,000.

We can apply our knowledge of elements affecting the size of periodic income payments to analyze Mr. Avery's situation.

- Mr. Avery's annuity contract would have paid a larger annual income payment if the SPDA had grown at an interest rate of 6 percent instead of 5 percent, while all other elements of his situation remained unchanged.
- Mr. Avery's annuity contract would have paid a larger annual income payment if, at age 55, Mr. Avery had purchased his SPDA with retirement savings of $60,000 instead of $50,000 while all other elements of his situation remained the same.
- Mr. Avery's annuity contract would have paid a larger annual income payment if, while all other elements of his situation remained the same, Mr. Avery had waited until age 75 to annuitize the contract. By waiting to annuitize, Mr. Avery would have simultaneously (1) increased the accumulation period of his SPDA and (2) decreased the number of lifetime annual income payments expected under the SPDA.

As we mentioned in Chapter 3, when money is invested at interest, the value of a sum of money at a given date will, as a result of interest earnings, be different from its value at another date. Although all businesses use the concept of the time value of money, an insurance company depends to an unusual degree on accurate calculations of future value and present value. Insurance, after all, involves a legal promise of a financial benefit in the future in exchange for a customer's payment of a premium. Insurers use time value of money concepts in determining annuity cost factors to charge a customer for periodic income payments. Once a single premium contract is sold, the insurer does not get a second chance to change the premium. As we saw in Chapter 2, one way to express the price of periodic income benefits is an annuity cost factor or an annuity conversion factor. For single-premium immediate annuities, an annuity cost factor is applied once to determine the amount of periodic income payments; then a contract is issued, and the contract cannot be cancelled by the insurance company. If the insurer has structured a contract that the company cannot support, one action it can take is to increase expense charges for future contracts. However, an insurer can never restructure existing annuity contracts.

The time value of money affects many of the functions of a life and health insurance company. For example, the time value of money is applied to such decisions as whether to support a new insurance product, lease equipment, purchase real estate, or invest in financial assets. In this chapter, we look at important calculations of the time value of money and also how to calculate future values. Before we start these discussions, read Insight 5-1 for some tips on how to work with numbers effectively. You may find these tips useful as you study this textbook and as you perform any work that requires the use of numbers.

FUTURE VALUE IN INSURANCE COMPANIES

Life insurance companies typically offer annuity products in many forms and plans. Life insurance companies determine the financial structure of these products by considering entire blocks of contracts of the same type. In designing an annuity product, an insurer must calculate the present value of a stream of annuity payments it will begin making at some date in the future. These payments may not start until 20, 30, 40, or even 50 years after the issue of the annuity. Insurers charge a specified amount of money in return for the promise of providing periodic income payments starting on a specified date or upon the occurrence of a specified event. Typically, the date or event that signals the start of the income payments is the annuitant's (a) attainment of a particular age or (b) retirement.

The factors that a life insurance company must consider in designing a deferred annuity product include the time remaining until the contract matures, investment earnings, company expenses, and a reasonable profit margin for the company.

INSIGHT 5.1

Tips for Using Numbers Effectively.

Approach your search for data in an organized manner. Decide what data will help you understand the business situation you are studying. Then determine if the data is available and where you can find it. Find out if you have colleagues who can help you in locating the proper data and in analyzing it.

Choose which statistical measures will most help you analyze the data and the situation.

Identify the types of calculations you will need to do and the units of measure—time, dollars, policies, claims, etc.—in which the calculations must be made.

Proceed with your calculations slowly. Whether you are doing calculations manually, on a calculator, or on a computer, don't rush.

Don't take shortcuts. Do all calculations step by step, and write down your calculations as you go along. Spreadsheet software offers the convenience of keeping a record of your data. These spreadsheet files can be used both as rough worksheets and as final reports of calculations.

Label your data and your calculations. Even with spreadsheets, you must be careful to identify all your data. Otherwise, you risk the danger of returning to a spreadsheet file only to find that the columns of numbers that you created in the file have become just that—merely columns of numbers for which you have forgotten the meaning and significance.

Once you complete a calculation, write down in narrative form what the results of that calculation mean to you. Otherwise, you run the risk of forgetting some of the insights derived from your analysis.

When you can, draw a picture. When dealing with present value factors especially, drawing a time line and indicating on the time line when payments are received can help you determine what formula you need to use.

Experience is a great help in understanding the results of statistical calculations. As you become experienced in your work or in a given business, you develop a sense of what is normal in different situations. Sometimes these *norms* or *standards* are recorded and are well-known throughout an industry. Some norms are informal, however, and are more like rules of thumb. Nonetheless, norms help you judge the results of your statistical analysis. Numbers have meaning only when you compare them with other numbers, particularly standard numbers. Are your results above the norm or below the norm? Do the values of your results seem reasonable or typical?

Source: Susan Conant et al., *Managing for Solvency and Profitability in Life and Health Insurance Companies* (Atlanta: LOMA, 1996), 140. Adapted with permission of the publisher.

Estimating Future Investment Earnings

As part of technical product design, an insurance company estimates the total earnings it can achieve by investing an annuity product's premiums before periodic income payments begin. To construct such an estimate, the company must (1) estimate the amount of time remaining until periodic income payments begin, (2) estimate a rate of return from investments, (3) calculate the future value of invested assets, and (4) calculate the present value of invested assets.

Estimating Future Operating Expenses

An annuity product design includes a charge to cover the company's operating expenses such as staff salaries, office costs, commissions, taxes, and other costs of doing business related to the product. As part of designing annuities, the insurance company estimates these expenses and incorporates them into an annuity product's structure. Thus, as part of the product design process, the insurance company finds the present value of the estimated future expenses, discounted at an assumed interest rate.

Estimating Future Profits

In designing an annuity product, the insurer provides for earning a profit or covering adverse contingencies related to the product. Sometimes in product design, the insurance company's provision for a profit or for adverse contingencies is stated clearly to the customer. Other times, this charge, sometimes called a risk charge or a risk premium, is combined with various other charges. Thus, as part of the product design process, the insurance company finds the present value of the estimated future profits, discounted at an assumed interest rate.

Additionally, popular measures of product profitability incorporate time value of money concepts. One popular measure of product profitability is the profit margin. We will discuss calculating the profit margin in greater detail after we cover present value calculations in Chapter 6. The insurer finds the ***profit margin*** by calculating the ratio of the present value of profits to the present value of premiums.

$$\textbf{Profit margin} = \frac{\textbf{Present value of profits}}{\textbf{Present value of premiums}}$$

Other popular measures of profitability that use present value concepts are (1) the net present value (NPV) and (2) the internal rate of return (IRR). Calculating the NPV involves finding the present value of all cash flows associated with an asset (or other investment project) over a future period, usually the entire life of the asset. We focus on NPV and IRR in Chapter 6 and later chapters of this book.

Investing Assets on Hand

An insurer's investment specialists use the principles of the time value of money to determine a theoretically correct price for investment alternatives. In turn, the investment staff uses this information to set purchase values and reported values for assets. Again, NPV and IRR are employed in measuring asset values.

Setting Reserve Amounts

Life insurance companies are required by law to set aside funds to pay future benefits. You'll recall from Chapter 2 that the funds set aside for this purpose are called reserves. Actuaries use time value of money concepts to calculate contractual reserves. To set annuity contract reserves, insurance companies generally apply present value concepts to potential future benefits. We discuss reserves extensively in Chapter 11 of this book.

TIME VALUE OF MONEY CALCULATIONS[1]

As we mentioned in Chapter 3, the time value of money suggests that an amount of money invested at interest will, over time, grow to a larger amount. Thus, any amount of money can be said to have a future value equal to the amount that it is presently worth, plus accumulated interest. Similarly, any amount of money promised to be paid in the future can be said to have a present value, which is the amount of money that would have to be invested on a specified date (usually today) at a specified interest rate to accumulate to that future amount. An important concept affecting all financial decisions is that the timing of cash flows affects their value. Present value and future value are mathematically linked. Present value can be used to calculate future value, and future value can be used to calculate present value.

A common way to illustrate a financial transaction is to use a line diagram of the transaction's cash flows. A ***time line***, or *line diagram*, is a visual device that shows the essential elements of a particular financial transaction. A line diagram displays the end of each compounding period, the frequency and amount of each cash flow, and the timing of the valuation date. As we discussed in Chapter 3, the process of setting a value for an asset or a transaction is known as valuation. The ***valuation date*** is the date as of which a value is determined. An example of a financial transaction can illustrate how to interpret a time line.

An investor has $1,000 that she can invest today so that it will be worth $1,200 in a year's time. The $1,000 she has today is the present value of the $1,200 she will have in a year. Also, the $1,200 she will have next year is the future value of the $1,000 she has today. Figure 5-2 shows a basic time line.

FIGURE 5.2 **Present and Future Value Time Line.**

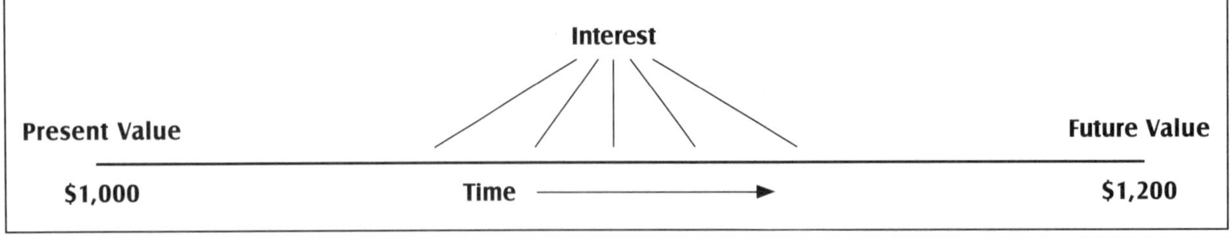

A given present value can have any number of future values. Similarly, a given future value can have any number of present values. Two factors—(1) the interest rate and (2) the length of time between the present and future dates—determine the present or future value of a sum of money. In practice, insurance companies generally perform present and future value calculations quickly and easily by using computers. Our discussion of the time value of money will rely on financial tables, but will also present the mathematics behind present and future value calculations so that you can understand these concepts.

Several mathematical equations will appear in our discussion. We will use a special style of notation to represent the various interest factors we will discuss. This style of notation, commonly used by financial analysts, is designed to help you remember and understand the concepts underlying the interest factors. The notation we use is summarized in Figure 5-3. Right now, you might not recognize the items displayed in Figure 5-3. However, we'll explain each item. By the end of Chapter 6, you'll know what all of these terms mean.

FIGURE 5.3

Time Value of Money Notation.

i = interest rate
n = number of compounding periods or discounting periods
PP = periodic payment of an annuity

Future Value Notation		Present Value Notation	
FV	= future value of a single amount	***PV***	= present value of a single amount
FVA	= future value of an ordinary annuity	***PVA***	= present value of an ordinary annuity
FVAd	= future value of an annuity due	***PVAd***	= present value of an annuity due
FVIF	= future value interest factor	***PVIF***	= present value interest factor
FVIFA	= future value interest factor for an annuity	***PVIFA***	= present value interest factor for an annuity

Actuaries use a different style of notation. Figure 5-4 compares the financial style of notation used in this chapter with the equivalent traditional actuarial notation.

FIGURE 5.4

Two Styles of Notation.

	Our Notation	Actuarial Notation
Future value interest factor	*FVIF* (*n*, *i*)	$(1 + i)^n$
Future value interest factor for an annuity	*FVIFA* (*n*, *i*)	$s_{\overline{n}\rceil i}$
Present value interest factor	*PVIF* (*n*, *i*)	v^n
Present value interest factor for an annuity	*PVIFA* (*n*, *i*)	$a_{\overline{n}\rceil i}$

In the next section, we explain ways of calculating the future value of a single amount and the future value of a series of payments. These concepts will help you to understand how annuity products provide benefits to customers as well as how insurers design the financial structure of annuity products.

CALCULATING FUTURE VALUE

As we have discussed in Chapter 3, the future value (*FV*) of a sum of money is the amount that the sum is expected to be worth at a certain point in the future, given a stated rate of interest. The terms accumulated value and compound value are sometimes used to refer to future value.

Future Value of a Single Amount

When calculating future values, we can substitute the term *present value* for *principal* because, like principal, present value refers to an amount of money before it is affected by interest. When *PV* represents present value and the interest rate is represented by i, then the formula for interest earned on a one-year investment can be expressed as follows:

$$\textbf{Interest earned} = \boldsymbol{PV \times i}$$

To find the future value, we need to add the interest earned to the present value. Because our example takes into account only one period, interest is not compounded, and we do not specify any value for n. Thus, we can calculate the future value of a one-year investment by adding the interest earnings to the original sum of money, using the following equation:

$$\begin{aligned} \textbf{Future value} &= \textbf{Present value + Interest earned} \\ \boldsymbol{FV} &= \boldsymbol{PV + (PV \times i)} \\ &= \boldsymbol{PV \times (1 + i)} \end{aligned}$$

We can then calculate the future value of a one-year investment of \$100 earning 2 percent interest as follows:

$$\begin{aligned} FV &= \$100 + (100 \times 0.02) \\ &= \$100 \times (1 + 0.02) \\ &= \$100\ (1.02) \\ &= \$102 \end{aligned}$$

When we calculate the future value of an investment earning interest at a fixed interest rate for more than one year, the interest is compounded, and the present value is multiplied by one plus the interest rate $(1 + i)$ once for each period that interest is applied to the investment. In future value calculations, each period that interest is applied is called a compounding period; in present value calculations, each period is called a discounting period. In the example discussed above, if the \$100 were invested for five years, the formula could be expressed as

$$\begin{aligned} FV &= \$100 \times [(1.02)(1.02)(1.02)(1.02)(1.02)] \\ &= \$100 \times (1.02)^5 \end{aligned}$$

The expression $(1.02)^5$ is read "1.02 to the fifth power," and it is equal to the result of (1.02)(1.02)(1.02)(1.02)(1.02). No matter how the expression is written, the result of the calculation is the same. The expression $(1 + i)^n$ is read "$(1 + i)$ to the nth power." The superscript numbers in the expressions $(1 + i)^n$ and $(1.02)^5$ are referred to as exponents. An exponent n raises a base number such as 1.02 to the nth power.

$$
\begin{aligned}
FV &= \$100 \times (1.02)^5 \\
&= \$100 \times (1.10408), \text{ which can be rounded to} \\
&= \$110.41
\end{aligned}
$$

We can use this example to derive a general formula for finding the future value of an investment earning interest for more than one year—that is, compound interest. In Figure 5-3, we saw that n represents the number of periods for compounding or discounting. If the future value after five years is found by multiplying the present value by $(1 + i)$ five times, then the future value after n years is found by multiplying the present value by $(1 + i)$ n times. Thus, the general equation for finding the future value of a single amount for n periods can be expressed as

$$\boldsymbol{FV = PV \times (1 + i)^n}$$

Future Value Interest Factors

Using the method we have just seen for calculating the value of $(1 + i)^n$ can become tedious, especially when the number of compounding periods is as high as 5, 10, or 100. As you might suspect, these calculations are not often performed manually. Computers and financial calculators can make such calculations quickly and easily. To help with manual calculations, another approach to the calculations is available. This approach makes use of tables showing the future value of $1.00 for numerous interest rates and numbers of compounding periods. The future value of $1.00 at a given rate of interest for a stated number of periods is generally referred to as the ***future value interest factor (*FVIF*)*** or the *compound value interest factor*. A table that lists the values of future value interest factors for a variety of interest rates and compounding periods is called a ***future value interest factors table***.

The *FVIF* can be used to replace $(1 + i)^n$ in the future value equation, so that the formula for finding *FV* using an FVIF is written as

$$\boldsymbol{FV = PV \times FVIF\,(n, i)}$$

In this expression *FVIF* is *not* being multiplied by n and i. The n and i show the number of compounding periods and interest rate, and also indicate where the *FVIF* can be found in the *FVIF* table. The *FVIF* table is divided into rows and columns. The *FVIF* table shows $(1 + i)^n$ values where $(1 + i)^n$ is at the intersection of row n and column i. The notation (n, i) indicates the row and column coordinates for a cell in an *FVIF* table. Figure 5-5 presents a portion of an *FVIF* table. To use the *FVIF* table, find the row for the appropriate number of compounding periods (n), and then find the column with the appropriate interest rate (i). The cell (n, i) that represents the intersection of row n and column i is the correct *FVIF* to use. This *FVIF* represents the value of $1 accumulated at i interest for n periods, or $(1 + i)^n \times \$1$.

FIGURE 5.5

***FVIF* Table.**

Future value of $1 at the end of *n* periods, earning interest rate *i*, that is, $\$1(1 + i)^n$.

Period (n)	Interest Rate (i)			
	1%	2%	5%	10%
1	1.010	1.020	1.050	1.100
2	1.020	1.040	1.103	1.210
3	1.030	1.061	1.158	1.331
4	1.041	1.082	1.216	1.464
5	1.051	1.104	1.276	1.611

Whether for future values or present values, all interest factor tables have the same format: (1) the interest rates shown in the columns represent the interest rates per period, and (2) the periods shown in the rows represent the number of compounding periods. In Figure 5-5, the number 1.464 is at the row and column intersection of 4 periods and 10 percent interest per period. This could be written *FVIF* (4,10%), and the number 1.464 is equivalent to $(1.10)^4$. If you have a calculator, you can try raising 1.10 to the fourth power. The result of this calculation is actually 1.4641, but our table shows only three decimal places, and so the result is rounded to 1.464. Because n is the number of compounding periods and i is the interest rate per period, *FVIF* (4,10%) is the correct future value for a four-year investment of $1 that pays 10 percent interest compounded annually.

The future value of $5,000 invested for five years at 5 percent interest compounded annually can be calculated using the *FVIF* table. First, substitute the specific data relating to this problem into the future value equation, as shown:

$$FV = \$5{,}000 \times FVIF\ (5,\ 5\%)$$

Next, find the appropriate *FVIF (n, i)* from the table. In this example, the proper *FVIF* is *FVIF* (5, 5%). Now, substitute this factor into the equation, and compute the result, as shown.

$$\begin{aligned} FV &= \$5{,}000 \times 1.276 \\ &= \$6{,}380 \end{aligned}$$

Thus, the future value of $5,000 invested at 5 percent interest compounded annually for five years is $6,380.

So far we have assumed that all interest is compounded annually. Alternatively, interest can be compounded quarterly, monthly, weekly, daily, or even continuously. See Insight 5-2 to see how the *FV* calculation must be adjusted to account for compounding periods shorter than one year.

INSIGHT 5.2

Compounding Interest More Often Than Annually.

To find the interest rate (*i*) per compounding period (*n*) when the compounding period is less than a year, you need to divide the stated annual interest rate by the number of compounding periods per year. In such situations, *n* refers to the number of compounding periods, and *i* is the interest rate per compounding period. For example, if the stated interest rate is 10 percent compounded semiannually, then in our future value formula, the interest rate *i* for half a year is 5 percent, found as follows:

$$\frac{\text{10 percent}}{\text{2 compounding periods}} = \text{5 percent}$$

Also, the value of *n* is calculated by multiplying the number of years over which money accumulates by the number of compounding periods per year. For example, for a 20-year investment with quarterly compounding, *n* would equal 80, found as follows:

$$\text{20 years} \times \text{4 compounding periods per year} = 80$$

The future value of $100 invested for one year at 10 percent interest, compounded semiannually, will accumulate as shown in the calculation below:

$$\begin{aligned} FV &= PV \times (1 + i)^n \\ &= \$100(1.05)^2 \\ &= \$100(1.103) \\ &= \$110.30 \end{aligned}$$

This example also shows that 10 percent compounded semiannually adds up to more than 10 percent—in this case 10.3 percent. Here, the effective interest rate is 10.3 percent.

Characteristics of All *FVIFs*

If you look at any *FVIF* table, you'll notice three facts about *FVIFs*:

- Values of *FVIFs* are always greater than 1.0.
- At a given interest rate (*i*), the values of *FVIFs* increase as the number of compounding periods (*n*) increases.
- At a given number of compounding periods (*n*), the values of *FVIFs* increase as the interest rate (*i*) increases.

Future Value of an Annuity

Insurance companies often must calculate the future value of a series of payments, rather than the future value of a single amount. For purposes of the mathematics used in finance, an ***annuity*** is any series of equal payments made over equally spaced time periods. Examples of this type of annuity can include a series of salary payments, rental payments, periodic premium payments, bond interest payments, or mortgage payments. The formulas used in the mathematics of finance—and the ones that we use in this book for calculating future and present values of annuities—are designed for general application to any series of payments that are equally spaced and equal in amount. Our discussion of the formulas for an annuity applies both to a series of payments *received* and to a series of payments *paid out*. These formulas are valid without any specific application to the annuity contracts issued by insurance companies.

Up until this point in this book, we have frequently made reference to the annuity contracts issued by insurance companies. However, the type of annuity described by future and present value annuity formulas is not necessarily a contract at all. Now, the reason that we are discussing these annuity formulas is that they often apply to forms or features of the annuity contracts issued by insurers. Annuity contracts typically involve a series of periodic payments from the insurer to the annuity payees, or from the contract owner to the insurance company. For instance, a series of level premiums for a deferred annuity contract fits the mathematical formula for an annuity. However, a series of premiums paid for a flexible premium annuity contract does not, because flexible premium payments are not necessarily equal in amount nor are they necessarily equally spaced. Similarly, when the insurer pays a series of annuity income payments under a fixed annuity contract, the series of payments fits our mathematical formulas, whereas a series of unequal annuity income payments under a variable annuity contract does not. For purposes of applying these formulas, you should not consider flexible premium payments or variable annuity periodic income payments as examples of an annuity.

Stream of payments related to annuity products	Amount of payments
Fixed premiums	Equal
Flexible premiums	Not equal
Periodic income payments from a fixed annuity	Equal
Periodic income payments from a variable annuity	Not equal

The ***future value of an annuity*** at a given future date is the amount that a series of equal payments earning compound interest will accumulate by that date. Before we begin to explain how the future value of an annuity is calculated, we first discuss two different types of annuities, the ordinary annuity and the annuity due. The ordinary annuity and the annuity due relate to any equally spaced series of equal payments, regardless of any contractual context for the payments. The difference between an ordinary annuity and an annuity due centers on the timing of the first payment—whether it occurs at the end of the compounding period (ordinary annuity) or at the beginning of the compounding period (annuity due). Read Figure 5-6 to see the differences between the ordinary annuity and the annuity due.

FIGURE 5.6

Ordinary Annuity and Annuity Due.

Type	Notation	Definition	Examples
Ordinary annuity (Annuity immediate) (Annuity in arrears)	*FVA*	A stream of periodic payments for which the payment occurs at the *end* of each payment period	• A series of paychecks a salaried worker receives after the work periods have been completed • A series of bond interest payments in which the first interest payment occurs one period after the bond is issued
Annuity due (Annuity in advance)	*FVAd*	A stream of periodic payments for which the payment occurs at the *beginning* of each payment period	• A series of rent payments • A level series of whole life insurance premiums

Specific problems will require you to decide whether a series of payments is an ordinary annuity or an annuity due. Drawing a time line and marking the valuation date and payment dates make this determination easier. The future value of an ordinary annuity is calculated as of the date of the last periodic payment. The future value of an annuity due is calculated as of the date *one period after* the last periodic payment.

Time Line for an Ordinary Annuity

The following time line represents the future value of an ordinary annuity of $100 per year for three years:

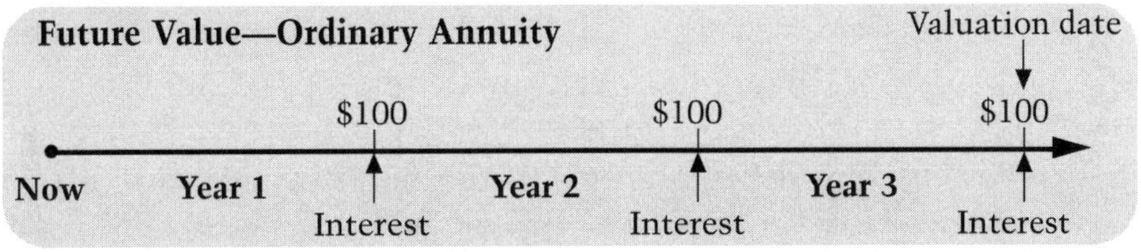

Note that for the ordinary annuity, interest is earned for two years on the first payment. The first payment does not occur until the end of Year 1.

Time Line for an Annuity Due

The following time line represents the future value of an annuity due of $100 per year for three years:

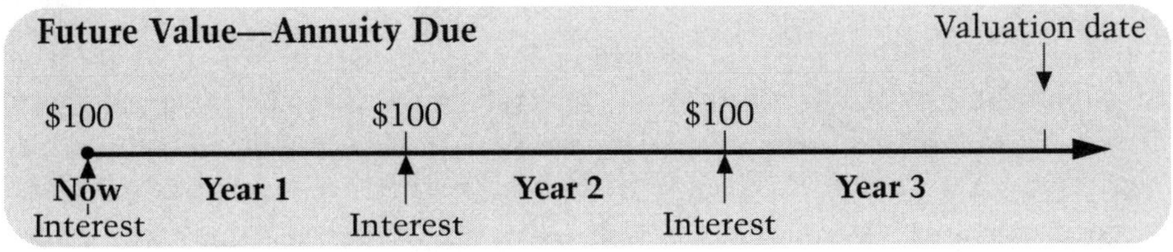

For the annuity due, the first payment occurs at the beginning of Year 1 and interest is earned in each of the three periods.

Future Value Interest Factors for an Annuity

The ***future value of an ordinary annuity*** **(FVA)** is defined as the future value of an annuity in which the payment occurs at the end of each payment period. The *FVA* can be found by adding together the future values of each periodic payment in the series. For a three-year ordinary annuity of $100 earning 5 percent interest compounded annually, the future value can be calculated as shown below. Refer to the following time line and Figure 5-5 for the *FVIF* values used in these calculations.

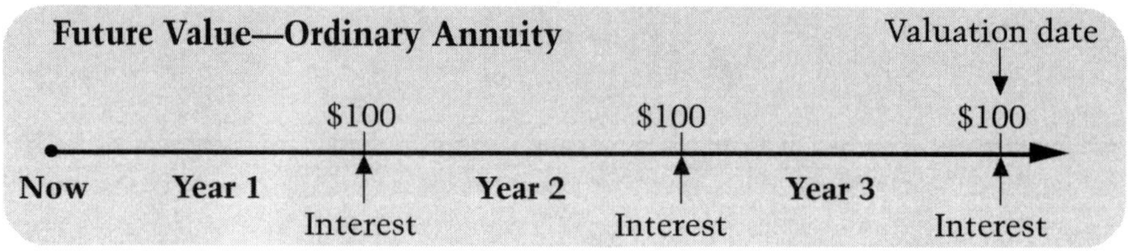

$$
\begin{aligned}
FVA &= [\$100 \times FVIF\,(2, 5\%)] + [\$100 \times FVIF\,(1, 5\%)] + \$100 \\
&= (\$100 \times 1.103) + (\$100 \times 1.050) + \$100 \\
&= \$110.30 + \$105.00 + \$100.00 \\
&= \$315.30
\end{aligned}
$$

For this ordinary annuity, the first $100 payment earns two years of interest and thus is multiplied by *FVIF* (2, 5%). The second $100 payment earns one year's interest, and so it is multiplied by *FVIF* (1, 5%). The third $100 payment is made on the valuation date, and so it earns no interest.

Now, let's look at the calculation for an annuity due of $100 for three years at 5 percent interest. We use the notation *FVAd* to indicate the future value of an annuity due. The ***future value of an annuity due*** **(FVAd)** is defined as the *FV* of an annuity in which the payment occurs at the beginning of each payment period. The *FVAd* is illustrated in the time line below.

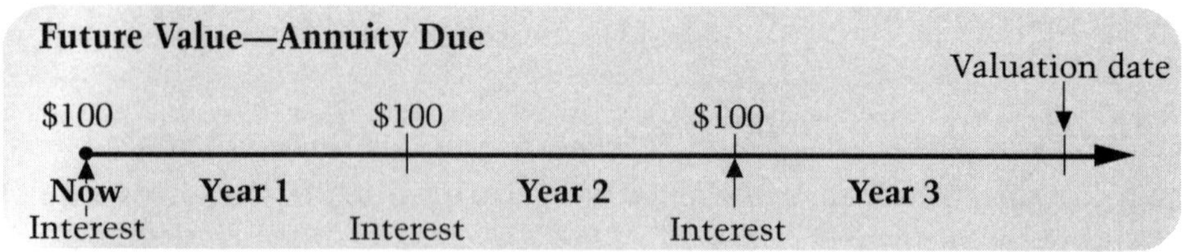

Here, the first $100 payment would earn interest for three full years, the second payment would earn interest for two years, and the final payment would earn interest for one year. As a result, the future value of the annuity due would be greater than the future value of the corresponding ordinary annuity, as demonstrated in the following calculation:

$$
\begin{aligned}
FVAd &= [\$100 \times FVIF\ (3, 5\%)] + [\$100 \times FVIF\ (2, 5\%)] + \\
&\quad [\$100 \times FVIF\ (1, 5\%)] \\
&= [\$100 \times 1.158] + [\$100 \times 1.103] + [\$100 \times 1.050] \\
&= \$115.80 + \$110.30 + \$105.00 \\
&= \$331.10
\end{aligned}
$$

When an annuity has a large number of periods and thus has a large number of payments, calculating the future value of the annuity by adding together the future value of each payment can be time-consuming. The future value of a $1.00 annuity at a given rate of interest and for a stated number of periods is generally referred to as the ***future value interest factor for an annuity (*FVIFA*)*** or the *compound value interest factor for an annuity*. A table that lists values of future value interest factors for an annuity for a variety of interest rates and number of compounding periods is called a ***future value interest factors for an annuity table***. Such tables are similar to the *FVIF* tables. A brief *FVIFA* table appears in Figure 5-7.

FIGURE 5.7

***FVIFA* Table.**

Future value of a $1 annuity per period for *n* periods at *i* interest.

Period (*n*)	Interest Rate (*i*)			
	1%	2%	5%	10%
1	1.000	1.000	1.000	1.000
2	2.010	2.020	2.050	2.100
3	3.030	3.060	3.152	3.310
4	4.060	4.122	4.310	4.641
5	5.101	5.204	5.526	6.105

The general formula for using the *FVIFA* table to solve for the future value of an annuity is

$$
\begin{aligned}
\boldsymbol{FVA} &= \textbf{Periodic payment} \times \boldsymbol{FVIFA\ (n, i)} \\
&= \boldsymbol{PP \times FVIFA\ (n, i)}
\end{aligned}
$$

The general formula for using the *FVIFA* table can be applied without modification to calculate the future value of an ordinary annuity. For example, the future value of the three-year ordinary annuity of $100 earning 5 percent interest can be calculated using the *FVIFA* table as follows:

$$
\begin{aligned}
FVA &= \$100 \times FVIFA\ (3, 5\%) \\
&= \$100 \times 3.152 \\
&= \$315.20
\end{aligned}
$$

By substituting the value from the *FVIFA* table shown in Figure 5-7, we get almost the same result as we did when we summed a series of values derived using the *FVIF* table. The \$0.10 difference reflects rounding.

Using FVIFA Factors for Annuities Due

The factors in *FVIFA* tables are calculated for ordinary annuities. To use the *FVIFA* table to find the future value of an annuity due (*FVAd*), we must modify the *FVA* calculation. The *FVAd* is equal to the future value of a corresponding ordinary annuity of one additional period, minus the amount of one payment. To find the future value of an annuity due of n periods, we first must find the *FVIFA* for the stated interest rate and $n + 1$ periods. Then we subtract 1—remember that the interest factor tables are based on a \$1.00 payment—from this factor and multiply the periodic payment by the result. The method of calculating the future value of an annuity due using the *FVIFA* table can be summarized as

$$\boldsymbol{FVAd = PP \times [FVIFA\ (n + 1, i) - 1]}$$

For example, we can calculate the future value of the annuity due of \$100 for three years at 5 percent interest; this is the same annuity due that we looked at earlier. Here n equals 3, i equals 5 percent, and *PP* equals \$100. Substituting these numbers into the *FVAd* equation yields the following results:

$$\begin{aligned} FVAd &= \$100 \times [FVIFA\ (3 + 1, 5\%) - 1] \\ &= \$100 \times [FVIFA\ (4, 5\%) - 1] \\ &= \$100 \times (4.310 - 1) \\ &= \$100 \times (3.310) \\ &= \$331.00 \end{aligned}$$

Again, substituting the value from the *FVIFA* table shown in Figure 5-7, we get almost the same result as we did using multiple values from the *FVIF* table. The \$0.10 difference reflects rounding.

In this chapter, we have given you a basic introduction to calculations of the future value of money. In Chapter 6, we will do the same for the present value of money.

Key Terms and Concepts

profit margin
time line
valuation date
future value interest factor (*FVIF*)
future value interest factors table
annuity (actuarial definition)

future value of an annuity
ordinary annuity
annuity due
future value of an ordinary annuity (*FVA*)
future value of an annuity due *(FVAd)*
future value interest factor for an annuity (*FVIFA*)
future value interest factors for an annuity table

ENDNOTES

1. The remainder of this chapter was adapted with permission of the publisher from Susan Conant et al., *Managing for Solvency and Profitability in Life and Health Insurance Companies* (Atlanta: LOMA, 1996), chapter 5.

CHAPTER 6

Finding and Using Present Values

After studying this chapter, you should be able to

- Calculate the present value of a single sum
- Calculate the present value of an ordinary annuity and an annuity due
- Use decision rules and the results of profitability analysis to interpret applications of present value techniques
- Identify and apply profitability measures that make use of present value techniques

In many situations, an insurance company estimates the amount of a future sum of money. For example, insurers often estimate the amount and timing of future profits, expenses, investment earnings, payments to customers, and premium income. But because a sum of money in the future does not equal that same sum today, insurers typically need to calculate the present value of such future cash flows. Recall that the present value of a future sum is defined as the amount of money that, if invested at a specified interest rate on a specified valuation date, would grow to equal that future sum. The process of converting a future value to its present value is sometimes referred to as ***discounting***. Discounting can be considered the opposite of compounding.

Present Value of a Single Amount for One Period

Finding present value is similar to finding future value, and the formula used to determine present value can be derived from the formula used to calculate future value.[1] In Chapter 5, we saw the basic formula for calculating the future value of a one-period investment when the present value is known:

$$FV = PV \times (1 + i)$$

When we divide both sides of the future value formula by the expression $1 + i$, where i is the interest rate, the result is a formula for present value. The basic formula for calculating the present value of a one-period investment when the future value is known is

$$PV = FV \div (1 + i)$$

or

$$PV = FV \times \frac{1}{(1 + i)}$$

These formulas can be used to calculate the amount of money we would need to invest today at 5 percent interest, compounded annually, in order to have \$1,050 one year from today. We know that the future value is \$1,050 and that the interest rate is 5 percent; thus, we can use the present value formula, $PV = FV \div (1 + i)$, to find the answer. The calculation appears on the next page.

$$\boldsymbol{PV} = \boldsymbol{FV} \div (\mathbf{1} + \boldsymbol{i})$$

$$\boldsymbol{PV} = \boldsymbol{FV} \times \left[\frac{\mathbf{1}}{(\mathbf{1} + \boldsymbol{i})}\right]$$

$$= \$1{,}050 \times \left[\frac{1}{(1 + 0.05)}\right]$$

$$= \$1{,}050 \times \left[\frac{1}{(1.05)}\right]$$

$$= \$1{,}050 \times 0.9524$$

$$= \$1{,}000.02$$

In our calculation, we discounted \$1,050 to its present value of \$1,000.02. The result of dividing 1 by 1.05 is 0.95238. We rounded this result to 0.9524. If we had used 0.95238, the resulting present value would be exactly \$1,000.

Present Value of a Single Amount for Two Periods

Consider an example of a present value calculation that involves discounting for two periods. Suppose the \$1,050 payment is due two years in the future. We can use the same present value formula, $PV = FV \div (1 + i)$. However, because two discounting periods are involved, we must multiply by $1 \div (1 + i)$ *to the second power* as demonstrated below:

$$FV = PV \times (1+i)^2$$

$$PV = FV \times \frac{1}{(1+i)^2}$$

$$= FV \times \left[\frac{1}{(1+i)\,(1+i)}\right]$$

$$= \$1{,}050 \times \left[\frac{1}{(1.05)(1.05)}\right]$$

$$= \$1{,}050 \times \left[\frac{1}{(1.05)^2}\right]$$

$$= \$1{,}050 \times \left[\frac{1}{1.1025}\right]$$

$$= \$1{,}050 \times [0.9070294]$$

$$= \$952.38$$

The general formula for determining the present value of a future sum when more than one discounting period is involved is derived from

$$\boldsymbol{PV} = \boldsymbol{FV} \times \left[\frac{\mathbf{1}}{(\mathbf{1}+\boldsymbol{i})\,(\mathbf{1}+\boldsymbol{i})}\right]$$

or

$$\boldsymbol{PV} = \boldsymbol{FV} \times \left[\frac{\mathbf{1}}{(\mathbf{1}+\boldsymbol{i})^{n}}\right]$$

PRESENT VALUE INTEREST FACTORS

The ***present value interest factor (*****PVIF*****)*** is the present value of $1.00 discounted at an interest rate of *i* percent for *n* periods. As with future value, tables of factors can simplify the calculation of present value. A ***present value interest factors table*** shows the values of *PVIFs* for many possible interest rates and numbers of periods. The *PVIF* can be substituted for $\frac{1}{(1+i)^n}$ in the present value equation. Thus, the present value of an amount to be paid at a specified later time can be calculated by multiplying that amount by the appropriate *PVIF* as shown in the following equation:

$$PV = FV \times PVIF\,(n, i)$$

Characteristics of All *PVIFs*

A brief *PVIF* table appears in Figure 6-1. *PVIFs* have the following characteristics:

- All of the numbers in the *PVIF* table are less than 1, because the present value of any amount at interest is less than its future value. Thus, the present value of a future value of $1 is less than $1. An investment that earns no interest would have a future value *equal to* its present value.
- A *PVIF* table shows that, at a given interest rate, *i*, the *PVIFs* decrease as the number of discounting periods, *n*, increases. In other words, for a given interest rate, the greater the number of discounting periods, the less a future amount is worth today. Also, the further into the future an amount is, the less the future amount is worth today.
- At a given number of discounting periods, *n*, the *PVIFs* decrease as the interest rate, *i*, increases. In other words, for a specified period of time, the higher the interest rate used in a present value calculation, the less a future amount is worth today.

FIGURE 6.1 ***PVIF* Table.**

Present value of $1 × [1 ÷ (1 + *i*)^n]

Period (*n*)	Interest Rate (*i*)			
	1%	2%	5%	10%
1	0.990	0.980	0.952	0.909
2	0.980	0.961	0.907	0.826
3	0.971	0.942	0.864	0.751
4	0.961	0.924	0.823	0.683
5	0.951	0.906	0.784	0.621

We can use the *PVIF* table to determine the present value of the $1,050 future amount from our earlier example. For a 5 percent interest rate and two periods, the present value can be found as follows:

$$\begin{aligned} PV &= \$1{,}050 \times PVIF\,(2,\ 5\%) \\ &= \$1{,}050 \times 0.907 \\ &= \$952.35 \end{aligned}$$

The present value of $952.35 calculated using the *PVIF* table is very close to the amount of $952.38 calculated earlier, using exponents. The difference of $0.03 results from the rounding of the factors in the *PVIF* table.

PRESENT VALUE OF AN ANNUITY

Insurance companies often need to calculate the present value of a series of equal payments, evenly spaced over a specified time period. In such cases, the value being calculated is the present value of an annuity. (Our discussion of the present value of an annuity applies both to a series of payments *received* and to a series of payments *paid out*.) The ***present value of an annuity*** is the amount that must be invested now in order to provide for a specified, equally spaced series of equal future payments, given a specified interest rate and a specified number of periods. The sum of the present values of the separate periodic payments of an annuity is equal to the present value of that annuity.

We discussed the difference between ordinary annuities and annuities due in Chapter 5. The ***present value of an ordinary annuity (*PVA*)*** is the amount that must be invested now in order to provide for a specified, equally spaced series of equal future payments made at the end of each payment period, given a specified interest rate and a specified number of periods, as follows:

$$PVA \times FVIF\,(n,\ i) = FVA$$

The ***present value of an annuity due*** **(PVAd)** is the amount that must be invested now in order to provide for a specified, equally spaced series of equal future payments made at the beginning of each payment period, given a specified interest rate and a specified number of periods.

Present Value of an Ordinary Annuity

The valuation date for the present value of an ordinary annuity occurs at the beginning of the first period, which is one period before the first payment is made. The time line below represents an ordinary annuity.

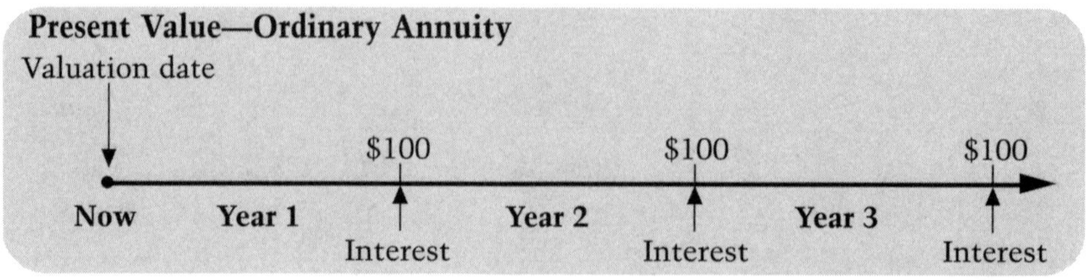

Present Value of an Annuity Due

The present value of an annuity due is represented by the notation *PVAd*. For an annuity due, the valuation date is the beginning of the first period, which is also the date on which the first payment is made. The time line below represents an annuity due.

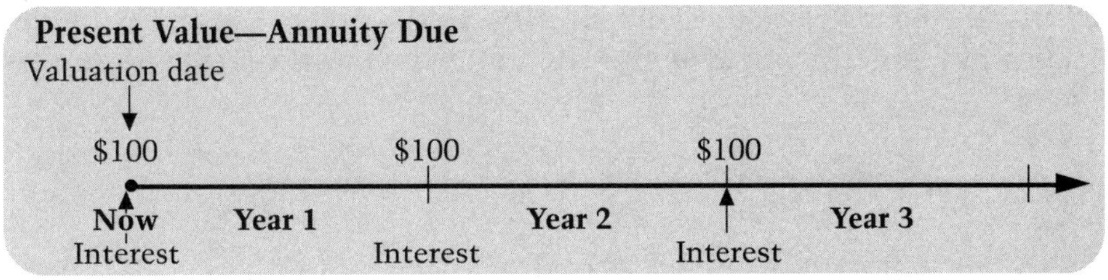

Present Value Interest Factors for an Annuity

The present value of an ordinary annuity (*PVA*) can be found by adding together the present values of each individual payment in the series. This process is similar to finding the future value of an annuity by summing the future values of each payment. As is true for the future value interest factors for an annuity, tables provide factors that simplify these calculations. The present value of a $1.00 annuity at a given rate of interest and for a stated number of periods is generally referred to as the ***present value interest factor for an annuity (*****PVIFA*****)***. A table that lists *PVIFA* values is called a ***present value interest factors for an annuity table***. A sample *PVIFA* table is shown in Figure 6-2. As with the *FVIFA* table discussed earlier, the numbers in the *PVIFA* table apply only to ordinary annuities. Using the *PVIFA*, the formula for calculating the present value of an ordinary annuity is

$$PVA = PP \times PVIFA\ (n, i)$$

By applying this formula, we can determine the present value of an ordinary annuity of $1,000 for three periods at 5 percent interest.

$$\begin{aligned} PVA &= \$1{,}000 \times PVIFA\ (3, 5\%) \\ &= \$1{,}000 \times 2.723 \\ &= \$2{,}723 \end{aligned}$$

FIGURE 6.2 ***PVIFA*** **Table.**

PV **of a $1 annuity per period for *n* periods at interest rate *i*.**

Period (*n*)	Interest Rate (*i*)			
	1%	2%	5%	10%
1	0.990	0.980	0.952	0.909
2	1.970	1.942	1.859	1.736
3	2.941	2.884	2.723	2.487
4	3.902	3.808	3.546	3.170
5	4.853	4.713	4.329	3.791

Calculating the Present Value of an Annuity Due

The *PVAd* is equal to the present value of a corresponding ordinary annuity of one less period plus the amount of one periodic payment. Using the *PVIFA* table to find the present value of an annuity due, we first find the *PVIFA* factor for the interest rate and $(n - 1)$ discounting periods. Then we add 1 to the appropriate present value interest factor and multiply by the amount of the periodic payment. The following equation illustrates this process:

$$PVAd = PP \times [PVIFA\ (n - 1, i) + 1]$$

The *PVIFA* table can be used to find the lump sum to invest today in a 5 percent annuity due in order to receive \$15,000 per year for the next five years. To find the amount of the lump sum payment needed now, we use the *PVIFA* table as follows:

$$\begin{aligned} PVAd &= \$15{,}000 \times [PVIFA\ (5 - 1, 5\%) + 1] \\ &= \$15{,}000 \times [PVIFA\ (4, 5\%) + 1] \\ &= \$15{,}000 \times [3.546 + 1] \\ &= \$15{,}000 \times 4.546 \\ &= \$68{,}190 \end{aligned}$$

The techniques we have described to this point for calculating the *PVA* apply only to annuities (1) for which the payment period equals the length of the discounting period and (2) for which the payments are all equal in amount. If you needed to calculate the present value of a stream of uneven payments, you could not use the *PVIFA* table. See Insight 6-1 for an example of calculating the present value of a stream of unequal payments.

INSIGHT 6.1

PV of a Stream of Unequal Payments.

A proposed investment project with an interest rate of 10 percent is expected to produce the following payments over the next three years:

End of Year 1 .... \$500
End of Year 2 .... \$600
End of Year 3 .... \$200

Normally, this calculation would be made by first calculating the present value of each payment separately, as shown:

\$500 x *PVIF* (1, 10%) = \$500 x 0.909 = \$454.50
\$600 x *PVIF* (2, 10%) = \$600 x 0.826 = \$495.60
\$200 x *PVIF* (3, 10%) = \$200 x 0.751 = \$150.20

The final step in the calculation would be to sum the present values of the separate payments:

\$454.50 + \$495.60 + \$150.20 = \$1,100.30

Using Present Value to Calculate Annuity Cost Factors

Product actuaries use present value techniques to calculate an annuity cost and to construct tables of annuity cost factors. An annuity cost is the present value of future periodic income payments under an annuity. A ***net annuity cost*** is the present value of future periodic income payments, calculated without any specific provision for loading. A ***gross annuity cost*** is the present value of future periodic income payments, calculated with a specific provision for loading. As we saw in Chapter 2, an annuity cost factor is a price for the periodic income payment under an immediate annuity. The annuity cost factor, when applied to a specified dollar amount indicates the amount of periodic income payment the deposit can purchase. If an annuity cost factor is calculated on a net basis without any loading for commissions and other expenses, the cost factor is known as a ***net annuity cost factor***. The cost factors quoted to immediate annuity purchasers are ***gross annuity cost factors***, which are calculated with a specific provision for loading and other expenses. In Chapter 2, we saw that annuity cost factors supplied for use in annuitizing deferred annuity contracts are called annuity conversion factors. In a deferred annuity contract, a ***payout option***, also known as a *settlement option*, is an alternative arrangement for payment of periodic income payments to the contract's payee. (You can review annuity payout options in Chapter 1, where they are outlined in Figure 1-3. Payout options also appear in the sample annuity contracts provided in the CD-ROM that accompanies this book.) Figure 6-3 shows a chart of guaranteed minimum annuity conversion factors for a period certain payout option and shows how these factors are used.

The tabular rates in Figure 6-3 are guaranteed minimum conversion factors. Guaranteed minimum conversion factors typically are less generous than would be actual conversion factors based on marketplace conversion rates. The table in Figure 6-3 does not show different cost factors for different ages because age is immaterial to the calculation.

Annuity payout options can come in many forms, and the cost factors for each different annuity payout option are calculated in a manner suited to that payout option. If the payout option depends upon the annuitant's being alive to collect the periodic income payments, then mortality rates enter into the calculation. (We discuss mortality statistics later, in Chapter 10.) For annuities certain, whether annuitants will survive to the end of the term is immaterial and thus mortality is not an issue. For an annuity certain, the annuity cost factor is properly calculated without any mortality statistics. The net annuity cost for an annuity certain is equal to the present value (PV) of the periodic income payments promised under the contract. The following expressions for finding the net annuity cost are equivalent to each other:

Present value, annuity certain = Present value of future periodic income payments

Present value, ordinary annuity = $PP \times PVIFA\ (n, i)$

$$PVA = PP \times PVIFA\ (n, i)$$

FIGURE 6.3

Annuity Certain Conversion Factors.

Payout Option for an Annuity Certain

Fixed Period Payment Option. Under this option, equal monthly payments will be made for any period selected, up to 30 years. The amount of each monthly payment depends on the total amount applied, the period of years selected, and the monthly payment rates in effect when the first payment is due. The amount of any payment will not be less than the amount produced using the conversion factors shown in the table below.

Minimum monthly payment rates for each $1,000 applied:

Years in Period Certain	Monthly Income Payment
5	$ 18.32
10	$ 10.06
15	$ 7.34
20	$ 6.00
25	$ 5.22
30	$ 4.72

Sample Calculation Using Tabular Rates

Contract owners of deferred annuities can use this table to find the amount of monthly income payment they can purchase with a known accumulation value under a deferred annuity contract. The conversion factor for a five-year period certain is $18.32. With an accumulation value of $100,000, a contract owner could purchase a five-year annuity certain paying monthly income payments of $1,832.00. The amount of the monthly income payments (*PP*) is calculated as

$$PP = (\$100,000 \div \$1,000) \times \$18.32$$
$$PP = 100 \times \$18.32$$
$$PP = \$1,832.00$$

Thus, the contract owner could obtain monthly income payments of $1,832.00 for five years.

Consider an immediate temporary annuity with a period certain of 5 years and guaranteed annual payments of $20,000 per year. To find the present value of this annuity at an assumed investment earnings rate of 10 percent, we apply the formula for the present value of an ordinary annuity. In the formula, we can use 10 percent as the discount rate (i). The number of periods (n) is five. The amount of each periodic payment (PP) is $20,000. We can find the *PVIFA* factor for five periods and 10 percent in Figure 6-2. Thus, to find the *PV* for this five-year annuity certain of $20,000 per year we must solve the following expression:

$$\begin{aligned} PVA &= PP \times PVIFA\ (5, 10\%) \\ &= \$20,000 \times 3.791 \\ &= \$75,820 \end{aligned}$$

Our result means that at an assumed interest rate of 10 percent, an insurance company could provide a periodic income payment of exactly $20,000 per year for exactly five years in return for a single purchase payment of $75,820. The *PVIFA* (5, 10%) factor from the *PVIFA* table is the annuity conversion factor for a payment of $1.

MEASURING PRODUCT PROFITABILITY WITH PRESENT VALUE

Insurance companies use profitability measures when they are deciding how to invest their long-term funds. The numerous profitability measures that companies apply to evaluating investments of long-term funds are known as ***capital budgeting tools***. Examples of types of investments to which insurers apply these tools are investments in (1) the financial markets, (2) computer systems used for product administration, and (3) new financial products. Figure 6-4 shows more examples of situations in which insurers employ capital budgeting tools.

FIGURE 6.4

Applications of Capital Budgeting in Life Insurance Companies.

- Allocating investable general account funds to investments in specific assets or projects
- Allocating product-line capital to investments in specific blocks of business, customer groups, geographic markets, or new products
- Allocating corporate capital to investments in new product lines, existing product lines, or even in purchasing businesses
- Allocating corporate capital to investments in expense reduction strategies such as new information systems, reengineering efforts, and corporate reorganization
- Evaluating the profitability of alternative investment projects
- Evaluating the profitability of proposed new products

Because no single capital budgeting tool covers every issue that an insurer might wish to consider, analysts typically use more than one capital budgeting tool for evaluating a major investment decision. Five profitability measures insurers commonly use in capital budgeting are

1. Internal rate of return (IRR)
2. Net present value (NPV)
3. Profit margin (ratio of the present value of profits to the present value of premiums)
4. Payback period
5. Validation period

In this chapter, we will discuss IRR, NPV, and profit margin. In Chapter 7, we will discuss payback period and validation period. Most insurers employ profitability measures along with a decision rule that indicates whether a proposed investment is acceptable. We mentioned at the outset of Chapter 5 that insurers sometimes use net present value (NPV) techniques for evaluating profitability. For an insurance company using NPV to evaluate a product proposal, the decision rule might be to accept the product if the product's NPV is positive when using a discount rate of 10 percent; otherwise, the company would reject the product.

Cash Flows

Product models for demonstrating potential profitability are based on either the net cash flows or the earnings that a product is expected to generate.

- For an annuity product, the ***net cash flow*** is the product's total cash inflows generated from premiums, investments, and other sources minus the total cash outflows generated for commissions, expenses, benefit payments, etc.
- For an annuity product, ***earnings*** are the monetary amount that the product adds to the insurance company's capital and surplus in a given period.

The definitions of *net cash flows* and *earnings* may seem similar, but there is an important difference. Unlike a measure of net cash flows, a measure of earnings takes into account non-cash items, such as a product's contributions to reserves.

Initial Investment

For a new annuity product, the ***initial investment*** is the amount of capital and surplus that an insurer must invest to establish the new product. New product sales in effect require an insurer to invest capital in its product line. Because first-year costs are high, product sales usually cause a first-year net cash outflow, rather than a net cash inflow. First-year costs for a new annuity product typically include the costs of

- Developing the contract
- Issuing the contract
- Establishing records
- Setting aside reserves
- Compensating producers who sold the contract

Finding the exact amount of an insurer's initial investment in a product is often not a straightforward process. The exact amount designated as the insurer's initial investment in an annuity product depends on the accounting system in use and the insurer's internal practices. For an annuity product, ***surplus strain*** is the loss, or negative earnings, that typically occurs in the annuity product's first year. We discuss surplus strain at greater length in Chapter 11, where we discuss reserves. For many annuity products, insurers consider that the initial investment is equal to the product's surplus strain. However, some annuity products may experience negative net cash flows for longer than one year, whereas others may never experience a negative annual cash flow.

Note that an annuity product need not have repaid its initial investment to produce earnings in a given period. If a product has not yet repaid its initial investment, then its earnings for the given period consist of the amount of the initial investment that was repaid during that period.

Interpreting Internal Rate of Return

For an annuity product, the ***internal rate of return (IRR)*** is defined as the percentage rate at which the product's earnings must be discounted, using present value techniques, in order to exactly repay the insurer's initial investment in the product. IRR, also known as *return on investment (ROI)*, is a popular measure of annuity profitability among insurers. When applied to a new product, the IRR represents the estimated rate of return that the insurer would earn on its investment. An insurer can take into account the level of risk in a product's cash flows by comparing the product's estimated IRR to the product's required IRR. In order for a product's IRR to be acceptable for the level of risk the new product represents, the estimated IRR must exceed the insurer's required IRR for the product.

When calculated by hand, using present value tables, the exact IRR can be arrived at only through a process of trial and error; IRR can be computed much more quickly and exactly with the help of a calculator or computer. We will not demonstrate how IRR is calculated by hand. Figure 6-5 demonstrates the interpretation of IRR results.

FIGURE 6.5

Interpreting IRR Results.

Product A has a predicted IRR of 12 percent. Because the risk associated with the product's expected cash flows is relatively low, the insurer will proceed with developing the product if its expected IRR exceeds 10 percent. In other words, Product A's required return is 10 percent. Because the predicted IRR of 12 percent exceeds the required return of 10 percent, the insurer will proceed with developing the product.

Because Product B is riskier than Product A, the insurer sets a required IRR of 14 percent for Product B. Product B's predicted IRR is also 12 percent. The insurer would not, however, proceed with developing Product B.

Product	Predicted IRR		Required IRR	Decision
A	12%	>	10%	Accept
B	12%	<	14%	Reject

Net Present Value Calculations

One product profitability measure that uses present value techniques is net present value (NPV). The NPV of an investment project is generally calculated by subtracting the project's initial investment from the present value of the project's earnings, as follows:

NPV = *PV* of earnings – Initial investment

An NPV calculation yields a dollar figure representing the present value of the profit that a capital investment project, such as a new product, is expected to earn. Figure 6-6 illustrates the calculation of the net present value of an annuity product. As shown in Figure 6-6, the initial investment in this product is $150. This product has the following characteristics:

- The earnings are $50 per year.
- The earnings are expected to last for five years.
- The earnings occur at the end of each product year.
- The insurer uses a 10 percent discount rate to reflect its evaluation of the time value of money adjusted for the risk associated with the product.

FIGURE 6.6

NPV Calculation at 10 Percent.

Initial investment = $150	Discount rate = 10 percent

Step 1. **Find *PV* of earnings.**

Year	Annual Earnings	×	Present Value Interest Factor	=	Present Value of Annual Earnings
1	$50	×	*PVIF* (1, 10%)	=	$ 45.45
2	$50	×	*PVIF* (2, 10%)	=	$ 41.30
3	$50	×	*PVIF* (3, 10%)	=	$ 37.55
4	$50	×	*PVIF* (4, 10%)	=	$ 34.15
5	$50	×	*PVIF* (5, 10%)	=	$ 31.05
			Total *PV* of earnings	=	**$189.50**

Step 2. **Find difference between *PV* of earnings and initial investment.**

NPV	=	***PV* of earnings**	–	**Initial investment**
	=	$189.50	–	$150
	=	$ 39.50		

When we add together the present value of earnings for each year and then subtract the initial investment, we find that the net present value for this product is $39.50.

When using the NPV approach, the insurer selects the value of the discount rate *i* by considering the time value of money risk associated with the product. If the product has little or no risk, the insurer might use the time value of money only—say 7 percent. Similarly, the insurer can try different interest rates until one calculation produces an NPV of zero. In this example, the interest rate that produces a present value of earnings of $150 is 19.85 percent. Subtracting the initial investment of $150 from the present value of earnings then gives an NPV of zero. This result is interpreted to mean that the earnings represent a return of 19.85 percent on the initial investment. When the funds available to the company cost 2 percent, and when the company believes that a risk-free investment should return at least 12 percent, the insurance company must consider whether this return of 19.85 percent is adequate. The higher the risk associated with the product, the higher the value of *i* the insurer will use to calculate the NPV.

In Figure 6-6, the 10 percent discount rate indicates that the insurer, in compensation for the risk the cash flows represent, is willing to accept the risk so long as the return is at least 10 percent. A higher discount rate—say 15 percent—would indicate that the insurer felt that the product was riskier than a product whose cash flows were discounted at only 10 percent. Generally, the higher the interest rate used for discounting, the lower will be the resulting NPV. As Figure 6-7 shows, a discount rate of 15 percent produces an NPV of $17.65—less than the NPV of $39.50 produced by a 10 percent discount rate in Figure 6-6.

FIGURE 6.7

NPV Calculation at 15 Percent.

Initial investment = $150	Discount rate = 15 percent

***Step 1.* Find *PV* of earnings.**

Year	Annual Earnings	×	Present Value Interest Factor	=	Present Value of Annual Earnings
1	$50	×	*PVIF* (1, 15%)	=	$ 43.50
2	$50	×	*PVIF* (2, 15%)	=	$ 37.80
3	$50	×	*PVIF* (3, 15%)	=	$ 32.90
4	$50	×	*PVIF* (4, 15%)	=	$ 28.60
5	$50	×	*PVIF* (5, 15%)	=	$ 24.85
			Total *PV* of earnings	=	**$ 167.65**

***Step 2.* Find difference between *PV* of earnings and initial investment.**

NPV	**=**	***PV* of earnings**	**–**	**Initial investment**
	=	$167.65	–	$150
	=	$ 17.65		

Profit Margin Calculations

In a general business sense, profit margin is the ratio of profits to sales revenue. Regardless of the situation to which it is applied, the general formula for profit margin is

$$\text{Profit margin} = \frac{\text{Profit}}{\text{Sales revenue}}$$

The precise amount of profit and sales revenue applied in this formula varies depending on the situation, the accounting methods used, and the practices of the company. For annuity products, profit margin must take into account the time value of money. Annuity products usually generate cash flows of premium income, expenses, and profits over many years. In order to compare the cash flows for annuity products, insurers must use present value calculations. As you recall from Chapter 5, the profit margin of an annuity product is calculated by taking the ratio of the present value of profits to the present value of premiums. In other words, the present value of the profits earned on an annuity product is divided by the present value of the premiums collected for the annuity product, as follows:

$$\textbf{Profit margin} = \frac{PV \textbf{ of profits}}{PV \textbf{ of premiums}}$$

For an insurance company evaluating a new product proposal using the profit margin, the decision rule might be to accept the product if the product's profit margin is 10 percent or greater; otherwise, the company would reject the product.

The profit margin ratio is widely used by insurers. Profit margin helps the insurer to understand what share of the product's cash inflows is contributing to the product's profitability. In the profit margin calculation for an annuity product, profit is equal to a product's net cash flows, adjusted for interest income and contributions to reserves. The discount rate *i* used in the calculation is usually set equal to the rate of investment return the insurer earns or expects to earn on the assets that support the product.

For example, Portico Insurance Company is modeling the profitability of a proposed new deferred annuity product for a period of five years into the future. Figure 6-8 shows the assumed future cash flows for Portico's deferred annuity product. For many purposes, we might need to know only the total cash inflows. Here, because we eventually need to find the present value of premiums, we separated the product's cash inflows into two categories: (1) premiums and (2) interest earnings from investments.

FIGURE 6.8

Product Cash Flows.

Year (n)	Premiums	Interest	Cash Outflows	Profit
1	$1,000	-$ 40	$1,400	-$440
2	$ 800	-$ 24	$ 600	$ 176
3	$ 750	-$ 6	$ 550	$ 194
4	$ 700	$ 13	$ 500	$ 213
5	$ 650	$ 34	$ 450	$234

Next, finding profit margin requires us to find both the present value of premiums and the present value of profits. Figures 6-9 and 6-10 show these calculations for the Portico annuity product. Premiums are paid at the beginning of the contract year, and we assume that profits are earned at the end of the year. Recall that the stream of premiums represents an annuity due, whereas the stream of profits represents an ordinary annuity. This difference between premiums and profits requires us to apply different sets of *PVIFs* when calculating the present value of profits and the present value of premiums. Calculating the present value of an annuity *due* requires using the interest factor for $n - 1$ and i, whereas calculating the present value of an *ordinary* annuity involves using the interest factor for n and i.

FIGURE 6.9

Present Value of Premiums.

Year (*n*)	Premiums	×	*PVIF* (*n* – 1, 10%)	=	*PV* of Premiums
1	$1,000	×	1.000	=	$ 1,000.00
2	$ 800	×	0.909	=	$ 727.20
3	$ 750	×	0.826	=	$ 619.50
4	$ 700	×	0.751	=	$ 525.70
5	$ 650	×	0.683	=	$ 443.95
			Total *PV* of premiums	=	**$ 3,316.35**

FIGURE 6.10

Present Value of Profits.

Year (*n*)	Profits	×	*PVIF* (*n*, 10%)	=	*PV* of Profits
1	–$440	×	0.909	=	–$ 399.96
2	$176	×	0.826	=	$ 145.38
3	$194	×	0.751	=	$ 145.69
4	$213	×	0.683	=	$ 145.48
5	$234	×	0.621	=	$ 145.31
			Total *PV* of profits	=	**$ 181.90**

The profit margin for this Portico product is equal to the ratio of the present value of profits to the present value of premiums, as follows:

$$\text{Profit margin} = \frac{PV \text{ of profits}}{PV \text{ of premiums}}$$

$$= \frac{\$181.90}{\$3{,}316.35}$$

$$= 5.48 \text{ percent}$$

KEY TERMS AND CONCEPTS

discounting
present value interest factor (*PVIF*)
present value interest factors table
present value of an annuity
present value of an ordinary annuity (*PVA*)
present value of an annuity due (*PVAd*)
present value interest factor for an annuity (*PVIFA*)
present value interest factors for an annuity table
net annuity cost
gross annuity cost
net annuity cost factor
gross annuity cost factor
payout option
capital budgeting tool
net cash flow
earnings
initial investment
surplus strain
internal rate of return (IRR)

ENDNOTES

1. Much of this chapter was adapted with permission of the publisher from Susan Conant et al., *Managing for Solvency and Profitability in Life and Health Insurance Companies* (Atlanta: LOMA, 1996), chapters 5 and 6.

CHAPTER 7

Product Modeling and Asset-Share Models

After studying this chapter, you should be able to

- Calculate a payback period for a stream of cash flows
- Describe and state the significance of a breakeven point
- Describe the importance of a validation point and a validation period
- Interpret an asset-share analysis and recognize its uses and limitations
- Calculate an asset share and a total fund for a hypothetical product
- Distinguish between user-defined assumptions and fixed assumptions

When insurers design annuity products, they create mathematical models that allow them to consider the long-term financial impact of a product design before the products are actually sold. These models show how the assumptions about various factors—such as interest margin and expenses—will affect expected profit margins and other financial results. This chapter introduces the various ways that a specific type of model, called an asset-share model, is used for demonstrating the potential profitability of annuity products.[1] The input/output screen of a computerized asset-share model appears in Figure 7-1.

The illustration in Figure 7-1 comes from the computer-based asset-share model—*ExecuView: An Asset-Share/Product Profitability Model, Version 2.1*—included on the CD-ROM on the inside back cover of this textbook. The discussion of product models in this chapter makes frequent reference to output from this software. Examples from *ExecuView* appear as illustrations in this chapter and in several other chapters. In this text book, instructions for *ExecuView* users will be marked by the following symbol: EV.

However, you can understand this chapter without using the software. Illustrations within the text demonstrate how the *ExecuView* annuity models behave under the various scenarios discussed here.

ExecuView approximates the type of software that product designers use on the job and provides an opportunity for you to learn by doing. Most personal computers in use today can run the *ExecuView* software. If you have access to a computer that can run *ExecuView*, we encourage you to demonstrate for yourself the *ExecuView* examples presented in this book. *ExecuView* can considerably enhance the effectiveness of your study time. If you intend to use *ExecuView*, you should read the *User's Guide to ExecuView* supplement that appears on the included CD-ROM. This guide includes all of the information you need for using *ExecuView* and for understanding the models included in it.

Overview of Asset-Share Models

To evaluate a new product's potential profitability, insurers typically project the product's

FIGURE 7.1

Input/Output Tables from an Asset-Share Model.

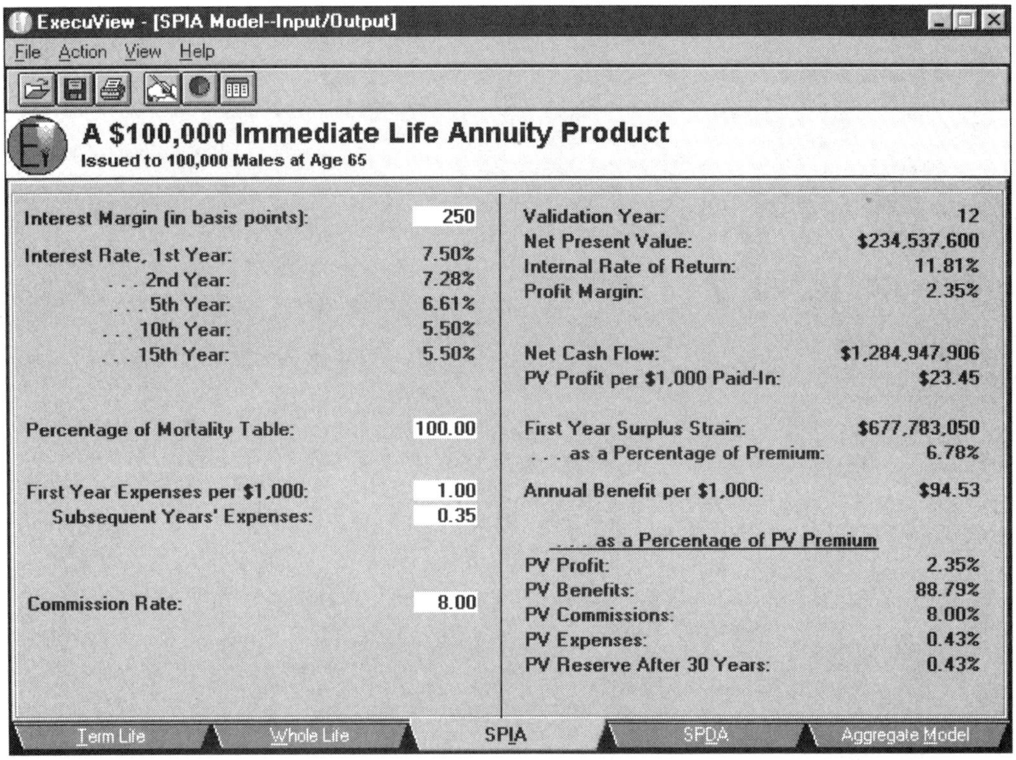

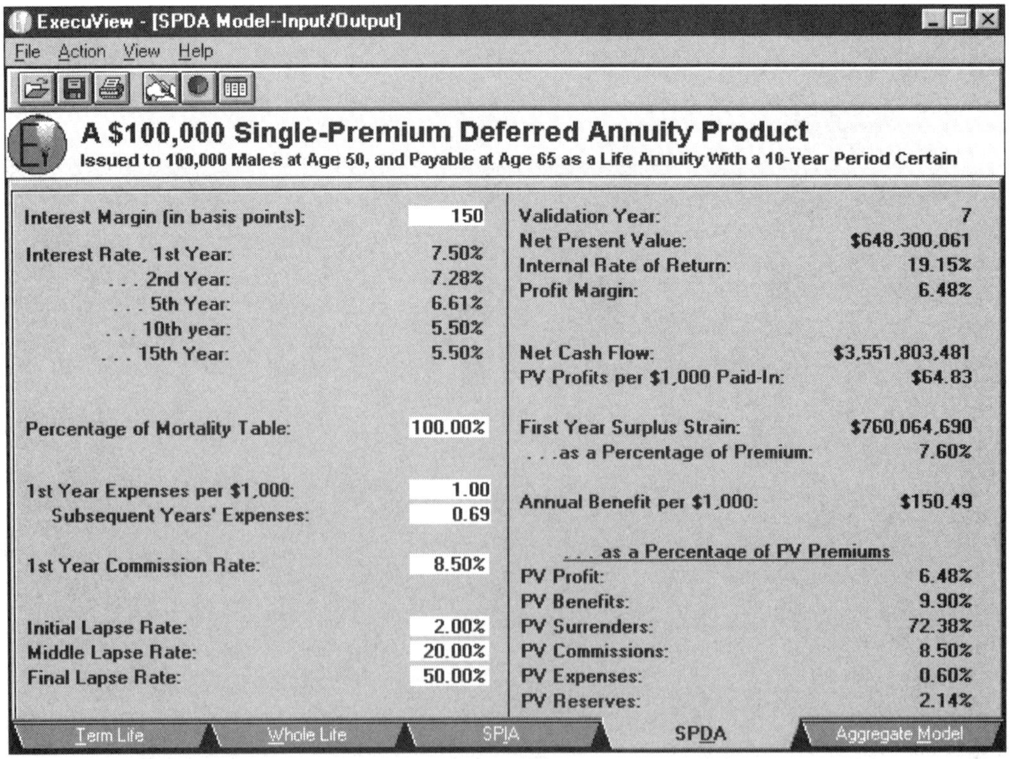

financial results under different sets of assumptions. To test several sets of assumptions, many insurers use asset-share models. For insurance companies, an ***asset-share model*** is a mathematical simulation model used to illustrate how a product's assets, liabilities, and surplus would change from year to year under given sets of conditions. Asset-share models use the concept of an asset share to measure the net cash inflows and outflows created by an annuity product. An ***asset share*** for an annuity product at a given time is the net amount of cash that the product has accumulated per unit of annuity premium—for example, per $1,000 of initial premium.

Asset-share models incorporate assumptions concerning all of the elements—such as expenses, investment earnings, mortality, lapses, and the cost of benefits—that affect a product's financial outcomes. To use an asset-share model, actuaries enter into the model hypothetical values for these elements and then see what values the model produces for profitability. Thus, asset-share models can demonstrate whether a product design can be expected to generate enough revenue to cover the product's costs. However, asset-share models have one notable limitation: the level of product sales is not produced as output by asset-share models, and asset-share models fail to automatically indicate the effect of a product's marketplace appeal on product sales. Asset-share models will produce potentially misleading data showing hypothetical profitability for a product design that would actually have no marketplace appeal and zero sales! For example, a product designed to produce abnormally high profits for the insurer would not be attractive to customers, and sales would be very low—or nonexistent. In such a case, the high profitability results from an asset-share model would not be realized. Accordingly, asset-share models are not used for testing a product design's marketability.

Overview of Assumptions in Asset-Share Models

Asset-share models test the growth of a product's assets based on assumptions about the product and the economic environment. The users of an asset-share model can change some assumptions that make up the product's design and then see the effect of those changes on the product's profitability. A list of some typical assumptions insurers make when developing models of annuity products appears in Figure 7-2.

An asset-share model generates a number of different profitability measures based on a given set of assumed values for the product's cash flows, earnings, and initial investment. Five profitability measures typically analyzed by life insurance companies are

1. Payback period
2. Validation period
3. Profit margin (ratio of the present value of profits to the present value of premiums)

FIGURE 7.2

Typical Assumptions in Product Models.

- The product type and features included
- The gross premium
- The reserve valuation method
- The investment income rate, labeled *interest rate*
- Any mortality table to use in calculating projected benefits
- An expense assumption
- A commission schedule
- A lapse-rate assumption
- A method of calculating accumulated cash values
- A set of profit objectives
- A tax rate

4. Net present value (NPV)
5. Internal rate of return (IRR)

In Chapter 6, we considered profit margin, NPV, and IRR, because they all involve using present value calculations. In the remainder of this chapter, we discuss payback period and validation period. Eventually, our discussion will show that validation period is a crucial profitability measure produced by an asset-share model, and we will discuss asset-share models in greater detail. We discuss the payback period calculation first, because the payback period is the basis for the calculation of the validation period.

Payback Period

Insurers generally want to determine the length of time required to recover their initial investment, and for this purpose they use the measure known as payback period. In general, a payback period is the length of time an investment requires to produce a net contribution to the investor's balance sheet. For an annuity product, the ***payback period*** is defined as the number of years that pass before the insurer's earnings from the product equal the insurer's initial investment in the product. The point in time when a product's cumulative earnings equal its initial investment is known as the ***breakeven point***.

Insurers use payback period calculations in many situations other than deciding whether to invest in the development and marketing of new products. For example, insurers use the payback period as a convenient means of evaluating proposed investments for their investment portfolios. Also, insurers typically calculate a payback period when evaluating a proposed purchase of new operating equipment, such as new computer equipment. For a purchase of new equipment, the payback period would be the length of time before any savings that result from the new equipment would equal the equipment's purchase price. Insight 7-1 illustrates payback period calculations for two financial products.

INSIGHT 7.1

Halcyon's Payback Period Calculations.

	Fixed Annuity Level Payments		Variable Annuity Mixed Payments	
Initial Investment		$22,000		$22,000
	Annual Flows	**Cumulative Totals**	**Annual Flows**	**Cumulative Totals**
Year 1	$5,000	$ 5,000	$ 6,000	$ 6,000
Year 2	$5,000	$10,000	$ 8,000	$14,000
Year 3	$5,000	$15,000	$12,000	$26,000
Year 4	$5,000	$20,000	0	$26,000
Year 5	$5,000	$25,000	0	$26,000

Two products offered by the Halcyon Insurance Company are described in the table above. Note that in the data shown for the fixed annuity and the variable annuity, the cash inflow patterns are different. For the fixed annuity, the annual payments are level. For the variable annuity, the payments are not level from year to year.

Payback Period for Level Periodic Payments

When a product's earnings are uniform from year to year, the payback period can be calculated by dividing the initial investment by the yearly earnings. As an example, consider Halcyon's fixed annuity product. Halcyon's initial investment in the fixed annuity is $22,000. Halcyon's yearly earnings from the fixed annuity are $5,000. The payback period is found by dividing $22,000 by $5,000, for a result of 4.4 years. This result tells us that Halcyon will recover its initial investment in the fixed annuity at the end of 4.4 years.

Payback Period for Mixed Cash Flows

More often, the earnings generated by a product differ from year to year, and the insurer must break down the yearly earnings accordingly. In our example, Halcyon's variable annuity product has an initial investment of $22,000 and then generates earnings of $6,000, $8,000, and $12,000 in its first three years. After two years, the product has generated earnings equal to $14,000, but this cumulative total is still less than Halcyon's initial investment. After three years the variable annuity has generated a cumulative total of earnings equal to $26,000, and this amount exceeds the initial investment. Thus we know that the precise payback period is somewhere between two and three years.

To find the precise payback period, find the share of the third year's earnings that is necessary to complete the payback of the initial investment. In our example, the amount needed in the third year to complete the payback of the initial investment is $8,000. We found the $8,000 by subtracting the $14,000 already earned on the investment from the $22,000 initial investment— $22,000 – $14,000 = $8,000. By dividing the $8,000 yet to be paid off by the $12,000 earned in Year 3, we find that the remainder of the investment is paid off in $^2/_3$ of a year. Thus, the payback period is $2^2/_3$ years.

The main appeal of the payback period calculation is that it provides a relatively straightforward way to estimate how long a product will tie up the insurer's capital before the product begins to make a net contribution to capital and surplus. However, the payback period calculation has a number of limitations.

- The payback period calculation usually takes into account only the amounts of cash flows.
- The payback period calculation does not automatically take into account the likelihood that projected earnings will actually materialize.
- The payback period calculation ignores any timing differences between cash flows because it does not distinguish between cash flows earned in different years. By ignoring timing differences, payback period also ignores the time value of money.
- The payback period calculation also ignores the total length of time cash flows are expected to continue.

VALIDATION PERIOD AND ASSET-SHARE MODELS

The key comparison in an asset-share model of annuity products is that of reserves to asset shares. When an annuity product is first issued, the product's reserve exceeds its asset share, and the product is a drain on the insurer's capital and surplus. In asset-share models of annuity products, the first year in which the asset share grows to equal the reserve and the product breaks even is the ***validation point***. The ***validation period*** of an annuity product is the time period beginning when a product is issued and ending when the product's asset share grows to equal its reserve—that is, when the product reaches its validation point. During the new annuity product's validation period, the insurance company covers the gap between assets and reserves by allocating existing surplus—generated by other products—to the new product's reserve account. When an annuity product's asset share equals its reserve, the validation period ends, and the product has paid off the company's initial investment in it. You might observe that the breakeven point and the validation period are similar to the payback point and the payback period. The validation point found by using an asset share model can be thought of as being a special application of a breakeven point, and the validation period is a special application of a payback period. Figure 7-3 depicts the charts and graphs that ExecuView uses for illustrating the validation point.

PROCEDURE FOR FINDING A PRODUCT'S ASSET SHARE

For the purpose of introducing an asset-share model, we have developed an abbreviated asset-share model of a new fixed-rate SPDA product, as shown

FIGURE 7.3

***ExecuView* Display of Growth in Reserves and Assets.**

By looking at *ExecuView's* Chart screen for each of the annuity product models, you can easily see where the trend line for total fund assets crosses and rises above the trend line for reserves.

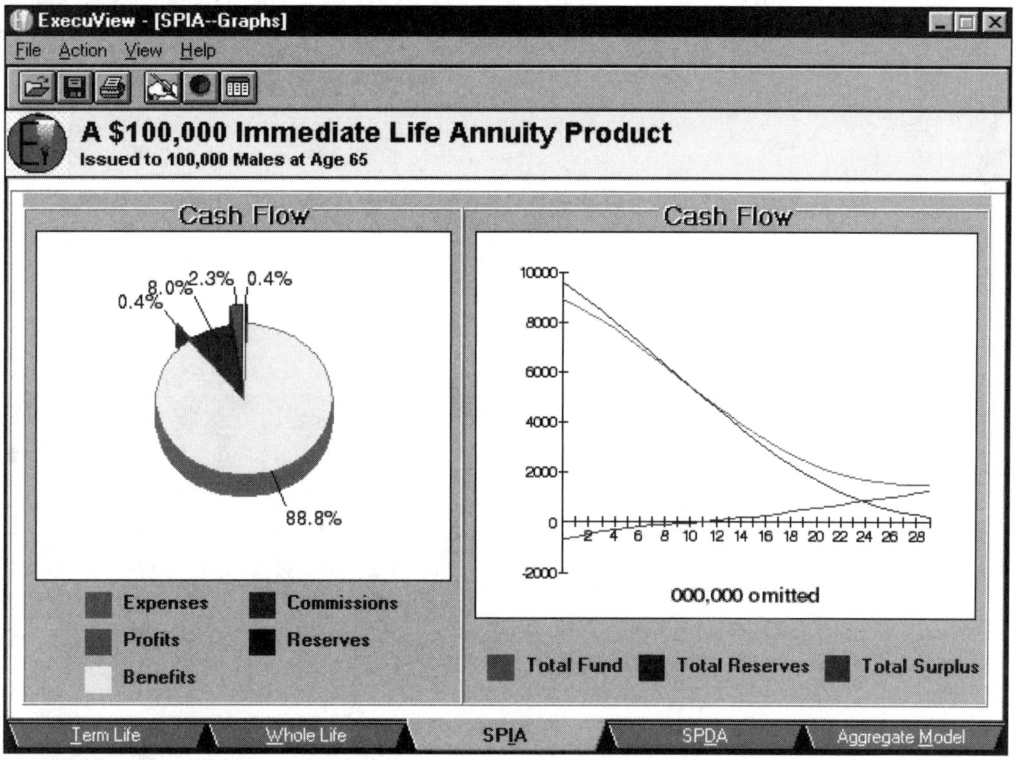

in Figure 7-4. (More extensive asset-share calculations appear in the worksheets for the *ExecuView* product models.)

For the sake of this example, we have combined all of the product's premium and interest income into Column 3, labeled *Total Cash Inflows.* Also, we have combined all of the product's expenses, benefit payments, and commissions into Column 4, labeled *Total Cash Outflows*. The difference between the inflows and the outflows determines the total fund for each year, which is shown in Column 5.

Find the Total Fund for Year 1

At the end of the product's Year 1, the value of the total fund is found by taking the cash inflows generated by the product during Year 1 and subtracting the cash outflows for Year 1.

  Year 1 cash inflows
– Year 1 cash outflows
= Total fund, end of Year 1

FIGURE 7.4

Simplified Asset-Share Model.

Worksheet: Asset Shares, SPDA Product, EV Life Insurance Company
1,000 Contracts, each with $1,000 Single Premium

(1) Year	(2) Contracts (units of $1,000 initial premium), end of year	(3) Total cash inflows	(4) Total cash outflows	(5) Total fund, end of year [Previous (5) + [(3) – (4)]]	(6) Asset share per $1,000 of initial premium [(5) ÷ (2)]	(7) Reserve per $1,000 of initial premium	(8) Surplus per $1,000 of initial premium [(6) – (7)]
1	976	$1,068,379	$ 110,278	$ 958,101	$ 982	$1,060	$ –78
2	952	$ 69,494	$ 26,388	$1,001,207	$1,052	$ 1,121	$ –69
3	927	$ 70,395	$ 27,820	$1,043,782	$ 1,126	$ 1,184	$ –58
4	903	$ 71,068	$ 29,252	$1,085,598	$1,202	$ 1,247	$ –45
5	880	$ 71,503	$ 30,677	$ 1,126,424	$1,280	$ 1,310	$ –30
6	857	$ 71,690	$ 32,084	$1,166,030	$ 1,361	$ 1,374	$ –13
7	834	$ 71,621	$ 33,465	$1,204,186	$1,445	$1,439	$ 6
8	661	$ 71,292	$258,469	$ 1,017,009	$1,538	$1,503	$ 35
9	590	$ 57,954	$ 111,483	$ 963,480	$ 1,631	$1,566	$ 65
10	526	$ 52,766	$103,936	$ 912,310	$1,732	$1,629	$ 103

Find the Total Fund for Years After Year 1

For each year after Year 1, the year-end total fund for Year n is equal to the fund at the end of the previous year (Year $n - 1$) plus the cash inflows during Year n minus the cash outflows during Year n.

	Total fund, end of Year $n - 1$
+	Year n cash inflows
–	Year n cash outflows
=	Total fund, end of Year n

In Year 3, for example, EV Life's new annuity product has cash inflows of $70,395 and cash outflows of $27,820. The total fund at the end of Year 2 was $1,001,207. The total fund for Year 3 is calculated as follows:

	Total fund, end of Year 2	→	$1,001,207
+	Year 3 cash inflows	→	+ $ 70,395
–	Year 3 cash outflows	→	– $ 27,820
=	Total fund, end of Year 3	→	= $1,043,782

Find the Asset Share

The total fund value is used to calculate asset shares. To find the asset share per unit for a given year, divide the total fund by units of product in force, as follows:

$$\frac{\text{Total fund, year end}}{\text{Number of units in force, year end}} = \text{Asset share}$$

In our example, we are calculating the asset share per $1,000 of initial premium. Recall that each contract has an initial premium of $1,000. Thus, for our example, one contract is equal to a unit of coverage represented by $1,000 of initial premium. Column 2 of Figure 7-4 shows that 927 contracts are in force at the end of Year 3. The asset share for Year 3, shown in Column 6, is calculated as follows:

$$\frac{\text{Fund, year end}}{\text{Number of contracts, year end}} = \text{Asset share, year end}$$

$$\frac{\text{Fund, Year 3}}{\text{Number of contracts, Year 3}} = \text{Asset share, Year 3}$$

$$\frac{\$1{,}043{,}782}{927} = \$1{,}126$$

For Year 3, the asset share indicates that each unit of coverage has accumulated assets of $1,126.

Next, we compare the product's asset share at the end of each year to the reserve, shown in Column 7. The asset share represents the amount of assets that each remaining unit of product has generated for the insurer. Along with surplus, asset share and reserve can be plugged into the insurance accounting equation, in which assets equal liabilities plus capital and surplus. As you recall, the general accounting equation is

Assets = Liabilities + Owners' equity
or
Assets – Liabilities = Owners' equity

For an annuity product, we can validly substitute *asset share* for assets, and *reserve* for liabilities. The insurance company's owners' equity in a single annuity contract is that contract's total surplus or the amount of the insurer's capital and surplus that is attributable to that contract or other unit of premium. Figure 7-4 illustrates this amount in Column 8. Thus, for an annuity contract we can express the accounting equation as

Reserve		Asset share
+ Surplus	**or**	– Reserve
= Asset share		= Surplus

We can see an illustration of these relationships for a product by looking at data from our simple asset-share model in Figure 7-4. At Year 10, the values for the model's asset share, reserves, and surplus are as follows:

Year	Asset share	–	Reserve	=	Surplus
10	$1,732	–	$1,629	=	$ 103

Find the Validation Point and the Validation Period

The validation point for EV Life's new product can be identified from Figure 7-4 as the first year that the asset share in Column 6 exceeds the contract reserve in Column 7. The validation point can also be identified as the first year that the product maintains a positive surplus. You can find surplus in Column 8. The worksheet in Figure 7-4 shows that the validation point for EV Life's product is Year 7, and the product's validation period is seven years. The information for Years 6 and 7 is reproduced below:

Worksheet: Asset Shares, New SPDA, EV Life Insurance Company

(1) Year	(2) Contracts, end of year	(3) Total cash inflows	(4) Total cash outflows	(5) Total fund, end of year	(6) Asset share per $1,000 of initial premium	(7) Reserve per $1,000 of initial premium	(8) Surplus per $1,000 of initial premium
6	857	$71,690	$32,084	$1,166,030	$1,361	$1,374	–$13
7	834	$71,621	$33,465	$1,204,186	$1,445	$1,439	$6

This information tells us that the product takes seven years to return EV Life's initial investment in it.

Unlike the payback period calculation, the validation period calculation explicitly takes into account the time value of money by (1) including investment income among the cash inflows entered into the model and (2) comparing the asset share and the contract reserve for the same year. However, like the payback period calculation, the validation period calculation does not automatically take into account the expected life of cash flows and does not explicitly account for the risk associated with the cash flows—the possibility that the projected earnings will not actually occur.

OTHER PROFIT MEASURES

Different insurance companies use different profit measures to evaluate their products. Some insurers use measures we do not cover in this text. In fact, we could not possibly cover every profitability measurement in use today. However, validation period, net present value, internal rate of return, and profit margin are the measures most commonly used. *ExecuView* illustrates several other profit measures, which are described in Figure 7-5.

FIGURE 7.5

Additional Profit Measures Shown in ExecuView.

- **Total profit on product**. The cumulative monetary total of profits that a product has generated by the end of a given period, with no reference to the time value of money.
- **Net annual premium**. For *ExecuView's* life insurance products, net annual premium shows the exact amount of premium that is needed from each contract to pay for the surrender expenses and any mortality expenses.
- **Surplus strain**. The monetary net loss in Year 1.
- **Surplus strain as a percentage of first-year premium**. Surplus strain is divided by the premium for Year 1, and the result is shown in percentage form.
- **Present value of profits per $1,000 of premium**. PV Profits at the end of a test period is divided by the number of $1,000 units of premium collected in Year 1. This measure shows the amount that each unit sold contributed to the product's profitability by the end of a profit test period.
- **Ratio of a chosen cash outflow to the present value of premiums**. Insurers can calculate the ratio of the present value (PV) of each cash outflow to present value of premiums. Profit margin, discussed in Chapter 6, is the most common of these measures. (Recall that profit margin is PV profits divided by PV premiums.) Sometimes, though, insurers look at a ratio with PV expenses, PV commissions, PV surrenders, or another outflow. These ratios show the share of premiums devoted to each type of cash outflow.

When insurers develop new products, they set profit objectives for their products to achieve both during product testing and after product implementation. Using typical insurance industry standards, we have created profit objectives for each of the *ExecuView* product models. As you try various *ExecuView* scenarios, refer to these objectives. The profit objectives for the *ExecuView* annuity products appear in Figure 7-6.

ASSUMPTIONS USED IN ASSET-SHARE MODELS

Asset-share models and other computer-based product models generally have two types of assumptions for values and formulas used in the model: user-defined assumptions and fixed assumptions.

- ***User-defined assumptions*** in a mathematical model are the assumptions for values and formulas that the end user of the model

FIGURE 7.6

***ExecuView* Profit Objectives.**

	Acceptable Values
Profit Test	**SPDA and SPIA Products**
Validation Year	Year 2 to Year 15
IRR	10.0% to 25.0%
Profit Margin	1.5% to 10.0%

can easily change. Models are designed to allow the user to change the values of user-defined assumptions. Thus, users are able to test a wide variety of scenarios. Product models generally give a model's user the opportunity to change the values for either (1) product design elements that represent competitive product features or (2) environmental features that are volatile, such as market interest rates. The intended purpose of a financial product model is to demonstrate the financial outcomes from a set of user-defined assumptions and thus to evaluate the profitability of a product.

- ***Fixed assumptions*** in an asset-share model are those for which the user cannot readily change the assumed values. It is possible to adjust the fixed assumptions in an asset-share model, but this is a more complicated process than changing the user-defined assumptions. Fixed assumptions reflect how the model's designer expects an annuity product to behave in the real world. The model's fixed assumptions are mainly reflected in the mathematical formulas that calculate the model's output. The asset-share model's fixed assumptions determine how the model applies the user-defined assumptions to calculate the model's output. The fixed assumptions in a product model come from a variety of sources:
    - Forecasting techniques
    - An insurer's previous experience with similar products in similar markets
    - An expert's educated guess

The accuracy of an outcome from a product model necessarily depends on the accuracy of the modeling assumptions. In practice, insurers base their values for most of these assumptions on forecasts of one type or another. An entire set of assumptions will never be entirely correct, because at least some of the forecasts are certain to be incorrect. Thus, a model will never be 100 percent accurate in its projections. However, if properly constructed with reasonable assumptions, a model can approximate what is likely to happen to an annuity product under various scenarios. The information that financial models generate can be a great help to insurers when they are making product design decisions.

Because insurance companies use asset-share models that are specific to their needs, most asset-share models differ from one another. The same can be said for other product testing models. Depending on the product an insurer is modeling and the kinds of scenarios it wants to test, a model can include different sets of assumptions. A fixed assumption in one model may be a user-defined assumption in another. Despite these obvious variations, some assumptions are commonly used. Therefore, we are going to look at lists of common user-defined assumptions and common fixed assumptions for asset-share models.

User-Defined Assumptions for Annuity Products

A model's user-defined assumptions for annuity products typically include

- Market interest rates
- Interest margin
- Expenses
- Commission rates
- Lapse rates
- Mortality rates

Market Interest Rates

In a product model, an assumption for the investment earnings rate reflects the net investment returns the insurer projects will be earned on product-related investments. The insurer's investment returns are subject to fluctuations in the investment markets at large. In *ExecuView*, the product models allow the user to alter the interest-rate assumption. The insurer may anticipate that market interest rates will be level, rising, or falling, or will rise and fall over time. By testing a number of scenarios for market interest rates, an insurer can test the soundness of its product design. Insurers in the United States and Canada are sometimes required to test products using a variety of specified interest-rate scenarios.

Interest Margin

As we discussed in Chapter 2, a crediting rate is the interest rate applied to the fixed annuity customer's account value. The interest margin represents the amount of investment earnings that the insurer retains. When insurers calculate a fixed annuity contract's account value, they generally credit the contract holder with a crediting rate that is slightly lower than the rate of return the insurer is actually earning on its asset portfolio. The insurer's interest margin is the difference between the rate of investment return the insurer is actually earning and the crediting rate. The interest margin is typically expressed in terms of a number of ***basis points***, or one-hundredths of a percent (0.01 percent). If an insurer's investment portfolio is earning 8 percent interest and the desired interest margin on an annuity product is 150 basis points—that is, 1.5 percent—then the crediting rate to customers is 6.5 percent, as summarized in the simplified example below:

Interest rate realized	→	8.0%
– Interest margin retained	→	– 1.5%
= Declared crediting rate	→	= 6.5%

The actual method an insurer uses to set a crediting rate can be quite complicated. Note that, in any event, the declared crediting rate must at least equal the contract's guaranteed minimum crediting rate. In the *ExecuView* annuity models, the guaranteed minimum crediting rate is 4 percent. For many real-world annuity products, the guaranteed minimum crediting rate may be 3 percent or 3.5 percent.

For a given level of realized investment earnings, in general, the higher a fixed annuity product's interest margin, the lower the fixed annuity product's crediting rate. For some fixed annuity products, the interest margin can be the insurer's primary source of profits on the product. Testing a number of interest margins can help an insurer to select the optimal annuity product design.

Expenses

Introducing a new product generates a variety of administrative and other expenses, such as selling expenses and issuing expenses. Insurers must decide how expenses will be allocated to each contract. Generally, a product model uses an annual expense charge in the form of both a fixed expense per contract and a percentage of premium expense per contract. (Recall from Chapter 2 that, in this context, expenses do not include the cost of benefits.)

Commission Rates

Commission rates represent the percentage of premiums the insurer pays to compensate sales producers. Product models include an assumption for commission rates. Annuity products marketed through traditional distribution systems incur commission expenses. For these products, commission rates are an important product design consideration, and rates can vary considerably. First-year annuity commission rates in the United States are usually lower than 8 percent. With an 8 percent commission rate, a $100,000 single-premium annuity would pay a commission of $8,000. Such large commissions would be difficult for insurers to support. A more typical commission rate for a single-premium annuity would be around 4 percent, which would amount to a total commission of $4,000 on a $100,000 premium.

Lapse Rates

Lapse rates describe the percentage of business in force that is terminated each year. For most products, a high lapse rate can tremendously diminish profitability. Testing a number of lapse-rate scenarios can help insurers predict the effects of different lapse rates on profitability.

Fixed Assumptions for Annuity Products

Product models often incorporate the following specific types of fixed assumptions:

- Gross premium
- A product's basic features

- A reserve valuation method
- A cash value accumulation method

Gross Premium

The gross premium is the amount contract owners pay to the insurance company. For the *ExecuView* annuity products, the amount of gross premiums is a fixed assumption; however, the amount of the gross premium is a user-defined assumption for the *ExecuView* life products.

Basic Product Features

A product model's fixed assumptions typically incorporate a product's basic features. Does the product call for fixed premiums, flexible premiums, or a single premium? Is it an individual or a group product? Is the product fixed or variable?

Reserve Valuation Method

A product's reserve greatly affects the product's projected profitability for the test period. Different reserve valuation methods produce different reserve amounts for each year. Within any applicable regulatory limits, the insurer selects the method of reserve valuation to use in a product model. Additionally, for benefits that require the use of mortality rates, the insurer selects a mortality table.

Cash Value Accumulation Method

The insurer must specify a method for the model to use in calculating cash value accumulations. For most annuity products, the cash value accumulation method is quite similar to the reserve valuation method. We will discuss cash value accumulations again in Chapter 11.

How Insurers Select Assumption Values

We saw earlier in this chapter that insurers use various forecasts as the basis for the values assigned to various assumptions in product modeling. We should emphasize that an insurance company is not limited to creating and using only one forecast as an assumed value. After all, if an insurer based its business plans and decisions on a single forecast, and the forecast turned out to be wrong, then the insurer could encounter serious financial trouble. Instead, insurers typically create an entire set of predicted values. They then evaluate the likelihood that each different predicted value will accurately reflect future conditions.

Point Estimates and Range Estimates

When forecasters assign a single value to an assumed value, the forecasters are creating a point estimate. For example, a predicted first-year lapse rate of 15 percent is a point estimate. Many analysts believe that using a point estimate encourages forecasters to be highly cautious and conservative, because they are afraid to be wrong.

Alternatively, forecasters can create a range estimate of possible values for an assumed value by specifying a range of values for the expected outcome. For example, a predicted first-year lapse rate of 10 to 20 percent is a range estimate. If an insurer forecasts a range of values, then the insurer can take steps to protect itself against potential unfavorable situations and to position itself to take advantage of potential favorable situations.

When forecasters create range estimates, they can also assign probabilities to various individual outcomes within each range; each probability would represent the likelihood that a particular outcome will occur. For example, suppose Rachel Robins works for an insurance company and is asked to forecast what the prime interest rate will be at the end of the next quarter. She might forecast that the prime rate will fall somewhere between 7.25 percent and 7.75 percent. In addition, she might attach the following probabilities to various interest-rate forecasts within that range:

Prime Interest Rate	Probability
7.25%	15%
7.50%	60%
7.75%	25%

A second approach forecasters sometimes use when creating range estimates employs a statistical tool called a confidence limit. A ***confidence limit*** is an expression of the probability that a specific outcome will fall within a stated range. For example, suppose that Richard Clifford, like Rachel Robins in the example above, also needs to forecast what the prime rate will be at the end of the next quarter. Mr. Clifford decides to apply confidence limits to this forecasting problem. Thus, his forecast might look like this:

Prime Interest Rate	Confidence Limit
Between 7.25% and 7.75%	68.0%
Between 7.00% and 8.00%	95.0%
Between 6.75% and 8.25%	99.7%

As this example demonstrates, the wider the range of outcomes, the more confident the forecaster can be that the actual outcome will fall within that range.

Even when the insurer has predicted a range of possible outcomes, the insurer may want to analyze each predicted situation. Or, the insurer may want to analyze conditions that fall outside the predicted range. In this way, insurers can test how variations in assumptions might affect the company's economic condition.

Scenario Analysis

Scenario analysis is a quantitative modeling process that involves changing data entered into a model and then determining how the changed data affected the model's output (results). Insurers generally apply scenario analysis to the product design process. Although insurers everywhere use scenario analysis, insurers in Canada must use scenario analysis in developing contractual reserves for nonparticipating products. In scenario analysis for reserve valuation, an analyst develops numerous reserve calculations, or scenarios, for each product. Each scenario reflects a different set of actuarial assumptions for interest rates, mortality rates, and persistency rates. Guidelines provided by the Canadian Institute of Actuaries help insurers select the actuarial assumptions used in scenario analysis for reserve valuations.

Scenario analysis helps insurers identify a likely range of values for a product's future experience. Insurers can then use this information in calculating a range of values for the reserves they need to maintain in order to safeguard their contractual obligations. Given a range of possible values for their reserves, insurers are expected to use conservative reserving practices, and so are expected to select a reserve value near the high end of the range.

KEY TERMS AND CONCEPTS

asset-share model
asset share
payback period
breakeven point
validation point
validation period
user-defined assumption
fixed assumption
basis point
confidence limit
scenario analysis

ENDNOTES

1. Much of this chapter was adapted with permission of the publisher from Susan Conant et al., *Managing for Solvency and Profitability in Life and Health Insurance Companies* (Atlanta: LOMA, 1996), chapter 6.

CHAPTER 8

Testing Product Designs

After studying this chapter, you should be able to

- Identify reasons that insurance companies use interest-sensitive cash-flow testing
- Describe the steps in a cash-flow testing (CFT) process
- Differentiate between cash-flow testing (CFT) and dynamic solvency testing (DST)
- Compare results from product modeling to related profitability objectives

We have seen that asset-share models and profitability measures are based on assumptions an insurer makes about a product, mortality rates, and the economic environment. In this chapter, we explore how changes in those assumptions relate to product profitability. All of the real-world interactions among interest rates, lapse rates, profit margins, and profitability are too complex for us to explore fully. Nevertheless, some general rules and general relationships among these factors hold true in many cases.

In Chapter 6, we examined profitability measures using present value techniques. In Chapter 7, we covered product modeling and the basic assumptions that product models use. In this chapter, we proceed to the actual product testing process that uses product models. Here, we will use the *ExecuView* software to demonstrate concepts with examples.

Testing Assumptions About Cash Flows

Because the values of assumptions used in financial models are crucial to the results of financial modeling, insurers use quantitative models to test the effects of different values for these assumptions. Recall from Chapter 7 that insurers sometimes enter both a range of predicted values and the confidence limits associated with those values into a computer model, and the model then runs simulations based on those different inputs. The insurer can then analyze the results to see if any of the simulations has an output that represents financial distress.

Simulation modeling is the use of mathematical models to represent a complex system in order to study how the system behaves under various circumstances. The objective of simulation modeling is to explore a number of "what if" situations—not to produce a single forecast based on a known or even an expected set of conditions. Insurers use financial simulations in a number of ways. For example, insurers typically like to explore best-case, worst-case, and most-likely case scenarios. A simulation model can be used as a testing ground for trying out different possibilities.

Sensitivity analysis is a technique for using mathematical models for the purpose of measuring the responsiveness of the outcome produced by changing the value of one of a model's input variables—or, in more familiar terms, one of its user-defined assumptions. In quantitative modeling, a ***dependent variable*** is a modeling outcome, and its value can change in response to changes in inputs to the model; an ***independent variable*** is a modeling input that a model's user can change in order to observe any effect on the model's outcomes. In other words, the user-defined assumptions in *ExecuView* models are independent variables. Specifically, sensitivity analysis can provide insight into the effect that changing a model's independent variables has on the model's dependent variables. For example, by testing the sensitivity of a dependent variable Y to changes in an independent variable A, an analyst would learn how changing the value of A would affect the value of Y. So, sensitivity analysis shows how responsive or sensitive the model's outcomes are to changes in the model's input variables.

Scenario analysis, which we introduced in Chapter 7, is commonly applied to simulation models. In scenario analysis, an insurer has the opportunity to learn how several changes in the values of a model's variables will affect results. Scenario analysis is an important part of an insurance company's financial planning process. If scenario analysis identifies a specified set of circumstances that would produce a financial disaster for the company, management can then take steps to manage the particular risks associated with that scenario.

In Chapter 4, we saw that life insurance companies have a particular interest in tracking their exposure to risks from changes in market interest rates. In this section, we discuss the use of two specific forms of cash-flow testing to examine how changes in assumed interest rates will alter a product model's cash-flow forecasts.

Interest-Sensitive Cash-Flow Testing

Interest-sensitive cash-flow testing is a way of analyzing the effects of various interest-rate scenarios on cash flows by incorporating many types of internal and external forecasts. Interest-sensitive cash-flow testing is a regulatory requirement for many insurance companies in the United States and for all insurance companies in Canada. Product design strategies and investment strategies strongly influence an insurer's cash flows. If interest-sensitive cash-flow testing suggests that a selected scenario produces undesirable financial results, then the insurer would try to avoid ever facing the conditions reflected in that scenario.

An insurer might perform interest-sensitive cash-flow testing on a number of levels—for example, on a single annuity product, on a block of annuity products, or on an entire annuity product line. Furthermore, interest-sensitive cash-flow testing can be performed for a number of reasons. Life insurance companies use interest-sensitive cash-flow testing for purposes of

- Testing to support an actuarial opinion and memorandum required by regulators
- Voluntary testing for use in constructing investment portfolios
- Voluntary testing for use in technical product design

Two important types of interest-sensitive cash-flow testing are known as cash-flow testing and dynamic solvency testing. ***Cash-flow testing (CFT)*** is the use of simulation modeling to project into a future period the cash flows associated with an insurance company's existing business, as of a given valuation date, and to compare the timing and amounts of asset and liability cash flows after the valuation date. ***Dynamic solvency testing (DST)*** is the use of simulation modeling to project into a future period an insurance company's existing and future business, as of a given valuation date, and to compare the amounts of assets, liabilities, and owners' equity at various times after the valuation date. (Some practitioners prefer to refer to DST as *dynamic analysis of financial condition*, or *dynamic capital adequacy testing*.) We discuss both CFT and DST in the next several sections.

The Cash-Flow Testing Process

The process of cash-flow testing (CFT), as summarized in Figure 8-1, can be divided into four steps:

1. *Match the liabilities (products) to be tested with the assets (investments) corresponding to those liabilities.* If CFT is being performed on an entire company, then this step is not necessary, because all the insurer's assets and products are tested. However, if an entire company is not being tested, then the insurer must identify which assets are backing the products being tested.
2. *Select the scenarios to be tested.* Typically, cash flows are tested under a variety of interest-rate scenarios.
3. *Project the cash flows associated with each selected scenario.* The insurer would project cash flows by testing the different scenarios in the quantitative model that it uses for CFT. The model would account for the ways that changes in one variable cause changes in other variables.
4. *Analyze the results.* The insurer would compare the CFT modeling results to the insurer's desired results. For example, the insurer's desired results might be that total cash inflows exceed total cash outflows under all scenarios that could potentially materialize.

Required Cash-Flow Testing

Insurers in the United States are required to use cash-flow testing for the purpose of evaluating the adequacy of the assets backing their reserves.

FIGURE 8.1

Steps in Cash-Flow Testing.

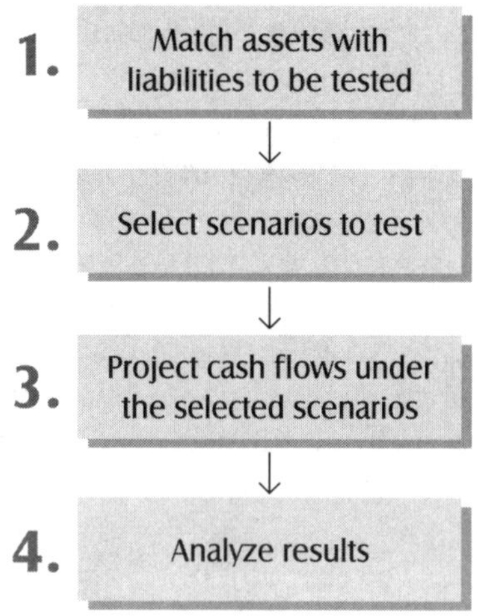

Required cash-flow testing is intended to ensure that a company's policy reserves are adequate to cover anticipated cash outflows, given the assets backing the reserves. The NAIC's Revised Standard Valuation Law, adopted by most states, requires insurers to test cash flows under seven specified interest-rate scenarios. The scenarios are sometimes called the *New York Seven* because they were first described in New York's Regulation 126. Although Regulation 126 required insurers to test only cash flows related to specified types of annuities, the Revised Standard Valuation Law requires insurers to test the cash flows related to all products. Figure 8-2 shows the seven required interest-rate scenarios. As you can see, the required scenarios give equal consideration to scenarios of rising and falling interest rates.

FIGURE 8.2

Interest-Rate Scenarios for Required Cash-Flow Testing.

1. Interest rates remain level.
2. Interest rates increase 0.5% per year for 10 years and then remain level.
3. Interest rates increase 1% per year for 5 years; decrease 1% per year for 5 years; then remain level.
4. Interest rates increase 3% immediately and then remain level.
5. Interest rates decrease 0.5% per year for 10 years and then remain level.
6. Interest rates decrease 1% per year for 5 years; increase 1% per year for 5 years; then remain level.
7. Interest rates decrease 3% immediately and then remain level.

After this mandatory CFT is completed, the insurer's appointed actuary is required to sign an actuarial opinion and memorandum. The ***actuarial opinion and memorandum (AOM)*** is a formal written statement attesting that the actuary has analyzed the insurer's projected cash flows under the required scenarios, and that, in the actuary's opinion, the insurer's reserves make adequate provision for the insurer to meet future obligations to customers, given the assets backing the reserves.

Dynamic Solvency Testing[1]

The use of dynamic solvency testing (DST) is voluntary for U.S. insurers, but it is a regulatory requirement for Canadian insurers. DST involves modeling the company's future financial condition under a number of business-growth scenarios and a number of interest-rate scenarios. One function of DST is to identify scenarios that would threaten a company's solvency. Standards of professional practice established by the Canadian Institute of Actuaries (CIA) require each insurer in Canada to perform DST annually. In addition, Canada's 1992 Insurance Companies Act requires each insurer to file a statement about the insurer's financial prospects based on the results of DST. The DST required in Canada is more far-reaching than the CFT required in the United States. In practice, many U.S. insurers perform DST voluntarily for their own management purposes.

DST involves all of the steps applied in CFT, but DST is more comprehensive. The Canadian Institute of Actuaries' DST standards require actuaries first to test the insurer's financial condition based on a best estimate of actual future conditions and then to test ten additional required scenarios. Each of the ten prescribed scenarios requires an actuary to change a single element of the best-estimate scenario, such as mortality, withdrawal rate, interest rate, or expenses. Additionally, the actuary should use the results of the ten required scenarios to select a wide variety of other scenarios to test. The actuary is also expected to test the effects of changes in the insurer's operating strategies. For example, the actuary might project the effects of new product introductions, stockholder dividends, changes in investment or marketing strategy, or changes in underwriting standards. Generally, the actuary's objective is to determine that the insurer will be able to maintain the level of surplus required by law.

Comparison of CFT and DST

Dynamic solvency testing (DST) is similar in many ways to the cash-flow testing (CFT) required for the United States. Like CFT, DST involves projecting an insurer's cash inflows and outflows and their effect on the insurer's financial situation under a variety of scenarios. However, as summarized in Figure 8-3, points of contrast between CFT and DST include the following:

- U.S. mandatory CFT primarily tests the adequacy of an insurer's reserves, whereas Canadian mandatory DST also tests the adequacy of the insurer's capital and surplus.

- U.S. mandatory CFT involves testing the insurer's in-force business only, whereas Canadian mandatory DST requires the insurer to project both its inforce and new business and the effects of future developments on that new business.
- U.S. mandatory CFT requires insurers to test seven specified scenarios based only on different interest rates, whereas Canadian mandatory DST requires insurers to test ten specified scenarios based on changes in interest rates and other variables.
- U.S. mandatory CFT operates as a pass/fail test, whereas Canadian mandatory DST does not require insurers to pass any test. Instead DST is used to identify potential threats to an insurer's solvency; the insurer can then take steps designed to reduce its exposure to any identified threats.

FIGURE 8.3

Cash-Flow Testing and Dynamic Solvency Testing.

	CFT	DST
Tests adequacy of...	Reserves only	Reserves and surplus
Business considered...	In-force business only	In-force and future business
Scenarios tested...	Interest-rate scenarios only	Various types of scenarios
Purpose of testing...	Pass/Fail	Diagnostic

STRUCTURE OF THE *EXECUVIEW* MODELS[2]

Insurers need to explore how changes in some unknown variables, such as interest rate or lapse rate, as well as changes in determinable variables, such as product price or commission, affect product profitability. Insurers test combinations of these variables using asset-share models.

To illustrate the kinds of assumptions insurers make when creating asset-share models, this section presents the assumptions used in the *ExecuView* software that accompanies this text. In addition to providing examples of the assumptions insurers use in asset-share models, this section serves as a reference for information about *ExecuView*.

ExecuView consists of five models—four product models and an aggregate model combining results of the product models. *ExecuView*'s product models depict two fixed annuity products and two life insurance products. Our discussions in this book focus on *ExecuView's* two fixed annuity product models—the single premium deferred annuity (SPDA) model and the single premium immediate annuity (SPIA) model. Figure 8-4 describes *ExecuView's* annuity products. Figure 8-5 describes the structure and assumptions of the Aggregate Model.

FIGURE 8.4

Annuity Products in *ExecuView*.

	SPIA Model	SPDA Model
Product summary	• An immediate straight life annuity issued to a male at age 65	• A single premium deferred annuity paid in by a male at age 50 with an accumulation period of 15 years, after which the annuity is payable for life with a 10-year period certain
Number of contracts	• 100,000	• 100,000
Premium	• $100,000	• $100,000
Crediting rate	• The interest applied when calculating the benefit is the current interest rate minus the *Interest Margin*.	• The interest applied to cash value is the current interest rate minus the *Interest Margin*.
Minimum crediting rate	• None	• 4%
Profit test period	• 30 years	• 30 years
Mortality basis	• The *1983 Basic Table* for annuities	• The *1983 Basic Table* for annuities
Lapse rates	• Lapses not permitted	• The *Initial* rate applies for the first seven years. The *Middle* rate applies in the eighth year, the first year with no surrender charges. Half of the *Middle* rate applies in Years 9 through 14. In Year 15, the last year lapses are allowed, the *Final* rate applies.
Surrender charges	• Surrenders are not available, so surrender charges do not apply.	• A 7% surrender charge is levied in the first year. This rate drops one percentage point a year for 7 years. From Year 8, no surrender charges apply.
Commission rates	• The percentage in *Commission Rate* is applied to the initial premium only.	• The percentage in *Commission Rate* is applied to the initial premium only.
Expenses	• *First Year* for the first policy year, *Subsequent Years* for every year thereafter	• *First Year* for the first policy year, *Subsequent Years* for every year thereafter
Cash value	• Surrenders are not available, and thus cash values do not apply.	• **Accumulation period**. Initial premium accumulated at the crediting rate • **Payout period**. No cash value
Reserve basis	• Calculated using mortality rates from the *1983 Basic Table* and 7.75% interest	• **Accumulation period:** Equal to cash surrender value • **Payout period**. Calculated using mortality rates from the *1983 Basic Table* and 7.25% interest
Miscellaneous assumptions	• Deaths occur in the middle of the year.	• Death claims result in surrenders without penalties. • Lapses and deaths occur in the middle of the year.

FIGURE 8.5

***ExecuView's* Aggregate Model.**

The Aggregate Model combines the output of the four product models based on a product mix set by a user. (Italics in the paragraphs below indicate user-defined assumptions in the *ExecuView* software.)

- Total number of contracts sold across all product models is 400,000.
- *Percentage of Policies (Contracts) Sold.* The user applies a percentage value for each product type and thus sets the product mix. This percentage is applied to the total of 400,000 contracts sold.
- The assets, reserves, and surplus generated by the four product models are first multiplied by the percentages users set under *Percentage of Policies (Contracts) Sold;* then multiplied by four; and finally added together to produce the aggregate assets, reserves, and surplus.
- Interest rates used in the aggregate model and in the product models are a user-defined assumption in the aggregate model. For Year 1, interest rates are equal to the *First-Year Interest Rate.* In subsequent years, the interest rate for a given year equals the interest rate for the previous year plus the *% Change* applicable to that year.

Within the *ExecuView* product models, some of the fixed assumptions are the same for all product models. Each *ExecuView* product model includes the following assumptions:

- 100,000 contracts are issued at the beginning of the first contract year.
- The average annuity contract has an initial premium of $100,000.
- Deaths occur in the middle of a contract year.
- Premiums, expenses, and commissions are paid at the beginning of a contract year.
- Interest credited is compounded annually.

ExecuView's Single Premium Deferred Annuity

ExecuView's SPDA Model depicts an annuity product with a single $100,000 premium paid by each member of a group of 100,000 males at age 50. The annuity accumulates for a period of 15 years and then becomes payable as a life annuity with a 10-year period certain. A life annuity continues to provide periodic income payments for at least the life of the annuitant. As we also saw in Chapter 1, a period certain is a period over which the insurer guarantees to make benefit payments whether the annuitant is living or dead. Most contract owners withdraw from deferred annuity products before the payout period begins. Accordingly, many insurers would model only the accumulation period of a deferred annuity product such as this one. The SPDA Model uses the assumptions that we describe in the following sections.

Mortality Rates

For the payout period of the SPDA Model, *ExecuView* uses mortality rates from the *1983 Basic Table* for annuities, currently the most widely used mortality table for annuities. For *ExecuView*'s SPDA Model, deaths during the accumulation period result in contract surrenders. Figure 8-6 shows these mortality rates.

FIGURE 8.6

Excerpt from the *1983 Basic Table*.

Age	Mortality rate per 1,000	Age	Mortality rate per 1,000	Age	Mortality rate per 1,000
50	4.52	66	15.76	82	76.55
51	4.94	67	17.47	83	84.23
52	5.37	68	19.37	84	92.50
53	5.81	69	21.49	85	101.26
54	6.26	70	23.81	86	110.42
55	6.72	71	26.35	87	119.89
56	7.18	72	29.12	88	129.61
57	7.66	73	32.12	89	139.64
58	8.15	74	35.40	90	150.10
59	8.67	75	38.99	91	161.28
60	9.27	76	42.93	92	172.70
61	9.96	77	47.27	93	185.05
62	10.79	78	52.05	94	198.22
63	11.77	79	57.33		
64	12.92	80	63.12		
65	14.25	81	69.52		

Source: Reprinted with permission from "Report of the Committee to Recommend a New Mortality Basis for Individual Annuity Valuation (Derivation of the 1983 Table a)," *Transactions of the Society of Actuaries* XXXIII (1981): 695. Copyright 1982 by the Society of Actuaries.

Cash Values

Many deferred annuities allow contract owners to withdraw their account values during the accumulation period, but many do not allow withdrawals during the payout period; *ExecuView*'s SPDA Model reflects this restriction. Moreover, many deferred annuities apply a surrender charge to all withdrawals that occur during the early years of the accumulation period, and the SPDA Model includes such a charge.

During the accumulation period, the SPDA Model builds cash value at a crediting rate equal to the model's Interest Rate minus the number entered in the Interest Margin cell, but with a minimum guaranteed crediting rate of 4 percent. You can see the input table to the SPDA Model in Figure 7-1 on page 112. Thus, if the interest rate is 6 percent and the interest margin is 150 basis points, the crediting rate will be 4.5 percent. However, if the current interest rate is 5 percent and the interest margin is 150 basis points, the crediting rate will be the minimum guaranteed rate of 4 percent, leaving the company with a margin of only 1 percent. A surrender penalty of 7 percent applies to withdrawals in the first accumulation year.

This surrender penalty decreases 1 percent each year for seven years. Starting in Year 8, surrender charges no longer apply. No penalties apply to a surrender resulting from the death of an annuitant.

Reserves

Reserves during the accumulation period equal cash values. Reserves during the payout period are calculated using mortality rates from the *1983 Basic Table* (shown in Figure 8.6) and an interest rate of 7.75 percent.

Annual Income Payments

At the beginning of the first year of the payout period—Year 16—*ExecuView* calculates the cost of a $1 life annuity with a 10-year period certain, based on the mortality rates in the model and the interest crediting rate from Year 15. *ExecuView* then calculates the amount of annual income payments that each surviving contract owner's account value can purchase. In this way, the model calculates the annual income payments that are payable throughout the payout period.

Lapse Rates

Annuity products with surrender charges, such as the one illustrated in *ExecuView*'s SPDA Model, tend to experience very low lapse rates so long as surrender charges apply. After surrender charges no longer apply, lapse rates increase markedly. [3] At the end of the accumulation period, during the last year lapses are allowed, many real-world deferred annuities experience even greater lapse activity.

ExecuView reflects real-world trends in deferred annuity lapse rates by allowing users to set three lapse rates, as follows:

- The model applies the *initial lapse rate* during Years 1 through 7.
- The model applies the *middle lapse rate* in Year 8—the first year no surrender charges apply. From Years 9 through 14, the model applies one half of the middle lapse rate.
- The model applies the *final lapse rate* only in Year 15, the last year the product allows surrenders.

Expenses

The SPDA Model applies user-defined first year expenses to the first year and user-defined expenses to every year thereafter. The SPDA Model applies no assumption as to an expense based on a percentage of premium.

Commissions

The commission rate assumption applies to the initial $100,000 premium only.

ExecuView's Single Premium Immediate Annuity

As we saw in Chapter 1, an immediate annuity begins paying periodic income payments exactly one period after the initial premium is paid. *ExecuView*'s Single Premium Immediate Annuity (SPIA) Model depicts a single premium life annuity—one with no period certain—purchased at age 65. The assumptions in *ExecuView's* SPIA Model are the same as those in the SPDA Model except for the following differences:

- There is no accumulation period; therefore, the SPIA Model does not need to show the impact of deaths during the accumulation period.
- The SPIA Model's cost of benefits is calculated at the beginning of Year 1.
- The SPIA Model has no period certain.
- The SPIA Model's initial $100,000 premium is used to purchase the periodic income payments before the premium accumulates any interest.
- The SPIA product prohibits withdrawals, so cash value accumulations and surrender charges are unnecessary.
- The crediting rate is implicit in the calculation of the annual income payment and thus remains constant for the life of the contract.
- The insurer pays annual income payments at the end of the year. The first annual income payment is paid at the end of Year 1, and each subsequent annual income payment is paid at the end of the year.

ExecuView's Aggregate Model

ExecuView's Aggregate Model functions differently from the four product models. This model's purpose is to provide a companywide picture of profitability from product operations, using the profitability results of the four *ExecuView* product models. Because this book is about annuities, we assume that you are interested in seeing results for only annuities. Company-wide effects of product mix, for example, are beyond the scope of this text. If you would like to see aggregate model results that include only the annuity products, then for the life insurance models you should set the values for *% of contracts sold* to zero, as shown in Figure 8-7.

The Aggregate Model assumes that a total of 400,000 contracts are sold at the beginning of the profit test period. The user can select the portion of these 400,000 contracts attributable to each product by entering a *% of contracts sold* for each product. For example, if you would like for the model to assume that 50,000 immediate annuity contracts are sold out of the 400,000 total contracts, you would enter 12.5 percent for *% of contracts*

FIGURE 8.7

Settings in *ExecuView's* Aggregate Model.

ExecuView **screen with default values.**

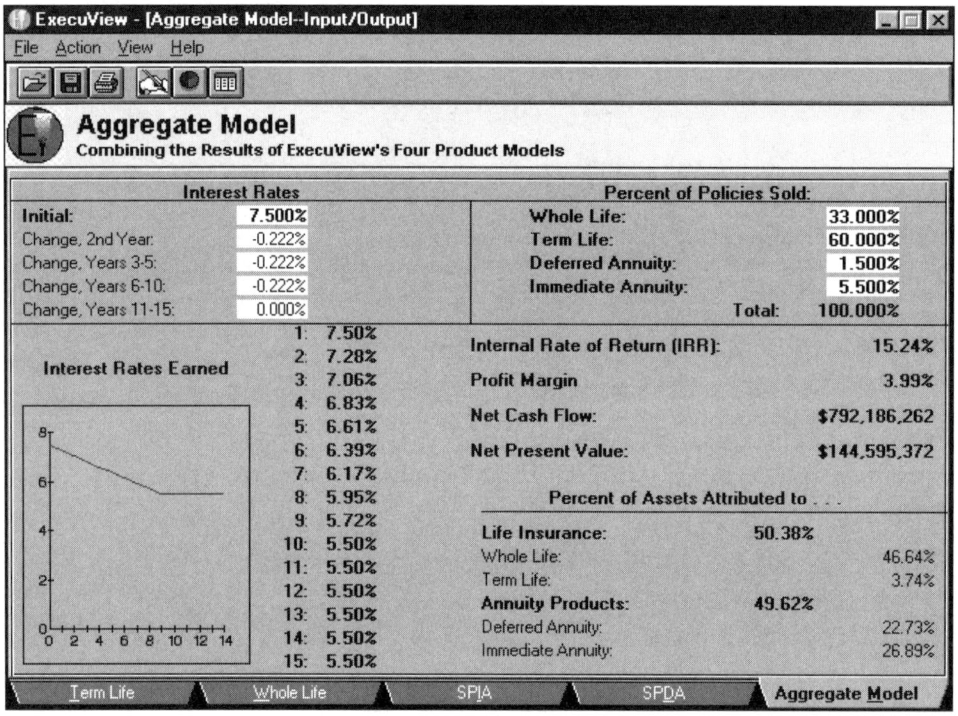

ExecuView **screen with no life insurance products sold.**

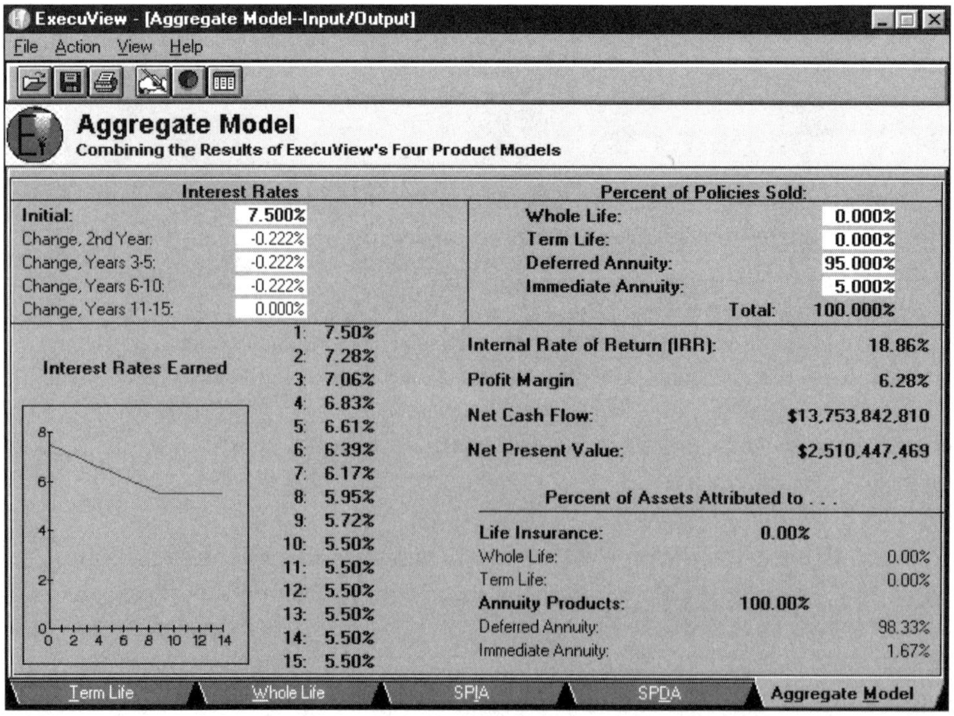

sold, immediate annuity. You would then proceed to allocate the remaining 350,000 contracts among the three remaining *ExecuView* products. If you wanted all remaining products to be SPDA contracts, you would set both life products to zero percent and the SPDA product to 87.5 percent. *ExecuView*'s Aggregate Model calculates the total net cash flows, IRR, and NPV for all four products, in proportions reflecting the percentages entered by the user. The Aggregate Model also displays the percentage of aggregate assets attributable to each of the four products.

CHANGING USER-DEFINED ASSUMPTIONS IN *EXECUVIEW*[4]

As mathematical approximations of real-world processes, models must simplify the processes they simulate. The real-world processes that determine the profitability of an annuity product are extremely complex and almost impossible to predict accurately. Sometimes, a change in one factor causes changes in several others. For example, in the real world, a large increase in an annuity product's interest margin would likely trigger reduced sales and higher lapse rates. Generally, asset-share models do not automatically account for such interrelationships. Typically, an asset-share model would show an increase in profitability as a result of the increase in interest margin, but would not show the offsetting loss of income that an insurer might experience in the competitive marketplace. Asset-share models almost never exactly reflect the real-world behavior of a product. When coupled with other techniques that compensate for the limitations of asset-share models, however, these models can be used to illustrate the mathematical results of a given set of hypothetical circumstances.

In this section we look at how changing the user-defined assumptions in the *ExecuView* models affects the profitability shown in these models. This section discusses each assumption in isolation, though in the real world the factors being simulated could affect one another. Each of the examples we discuss—for example, a result showing that a decrease in interest margin results in decreased profitability—shows part of the complex real-world picture. By isolating the effect of changes in each assumption, insurers can better predict the likely profitability results when many interrelated changes are combined.

Our discussion refers to *ExecuView* for examples. The exact effects of the changes in assumptions discussed in this section apply only to the *ExecuView* models in which these effects are demonstrated. In order to evaluate a set of outcomes from the *ExecuView* models, you should compare the profitability results to the acceptable profitability ranges shown below.

	Acceptable Values
Profit Test	**SPDA and SPIA Products**
Validation Year	Year 2 to Year 15
IRR	10.0% to 25.0%
Profit Margin	1.5% to 10.0%

If a given test produces profitability values outside of the ranges shown, you should consider the results unacceptable.

If you use ExecuView *to test the scenarios presented here, be sure to reset the models before each scenario by selecting "Reset, All Models" from the Action menu on the* ExecuView *toolbar.*

Changes in Interest Margin

Increases in the interest margin in an asset-share model cause increases in the model's profit measures, and decreases in the interest margin cause decreases in profitability. In an effort to increase profitability, however, insurers must not set interest margins too high, because a product with too high an interest margin will have trouble attracting new customers. The effect that a change in interest margin has on an asset-share model is greatly affected by any guarantees in the crediting rate that are built into the model. For example, *ExecuView*'s SPDA Model contains a guaranteed minimum crediting rate of 4 percent. The guaranteed minimum crediting rate is a fixed assumption of the product model. No matter how high the interest margin assumption is set, the crediting rate will never be lower than 4 percent. For *ExecuView*'s SPDA Model with the default values for the interest rate, Figure 8-8 shows how different interest margins affect profitability.

In Figure 8-8, we can see the effect of this product's minimum guaranteed crediting rate of 4 percent. In Scenario 3, when the interest margin is 350

FIGURE 8.8 **Changes in Interest Margin, *ExecuView*'s SPDA Model.**

	Scenarios				
	Scenario 1	Scenario 2	Scenario 3	Scenario 4	
	User-Defined Assumptions				
Interest Margin	150 bp	80 bp	350 bp	400 bp	**Acceptable values**
	Results of Modeling				
Validation Year	7	None	3	3	2–15
Net Present Value	$648,300,061	-$22,064,454	$1,360,468,031	$1,360,468,031	Positive value
Internal Rate of Return	19.15%	5.94%	52.81%	52.81%	10%–25%
Profit Margin	6.48%	-0.22%	13.60%	13.60%	1.5%–10%
Acceptable Values?	Yes	No	No	No	

basis points (bp), the results are the same as in Scenario 4, when the interest margin is 400 bp. An example can explain this occurrence. The interest margin of 350 bp can be converted to 3.5 percent. Then, the interest margin of 3.5 percent can be subtracted from 7.5 percent for a result of 4 percent. Thus, an interest margin of 350 bp creates a crediting rate of 4 percent, the minimum crediting rate guaranteed by the product. Any interest margin greater than 350 bp would still require the minimum crediting rate of 4 percent, and thus the model would show the same overall profitability results as the 350 bp interest margin. An interest margin of 350 bp results in crediting rates that are probably too low to attract many customers.

Changes in Interest Rates

In *ExecuView*, the interest-rate assumption reflects the assumed investment earnings rate on the investment portfolio supporting the product. Products that are strongly affected by changes in market interest rates, or investment earnings rates, are sometimes referred to as *interest-sensitive products*. Within *ExecuView*, the effect of changes in interest rates on product profitability varies greatly from one product type to another. As a rule, profits for products that maintain more assets for longer periods of time will be more sensitive to fluctuations in interest rates. Another general rule for behavior of the asset-share model is that higher interest rates will show increased product profitability, and lower interest rates will show decreased product profitability. In the real world, however, higher interest rates can actually decrease profitability because customers sometimes remove money from a financial institution in order to earn a higher investment return elsewhere. When interest rates are high, fixed annuity products sometimes provide lower investment returns than do competing financial products. Most asset-share models do not automatically account for the effect that changes in market interest rates might have on the value of an insurer's existing assets. Figure 8-9 shows the effect of various interest-rate scenarios on the profitability of *ExecuView*'s annuity product models.

ExecuView's SPIA Model shows strong sensitivity to changes in interest rates, with a 2.35 percent profit margin under falling rates, 9.39 percent under level rates, and 15.10 percent under rising rates. Notice that this profit margin of 15.10 percent under Scenario 3 for the SPIA exceeds the acceptable range of 1.5 percent to 10 percent for profit margin.

The SPDA Model's profit margin actually decreases when interest rates rise. This effect results from the way the model applies the interest margin to produce a crediting rate. During the SPDA's accumulation period, the interest credited to contract owners varies with the model's interest rate. When the SPDA Model's interest rates are higher, a number of interrelated effects occur:

- Contract owners earn more interest and accumulate larger annuity account values.

- With the larger annuity account values, contract owners can purchase a greater amount of annual income payments for the annuity payout period.
- As a result of the greater amount of annual income payments, the insurer pays out a greater percentage of its assets in annual income payments and surrenders.

Although the dollar amount of profit the insurer earns on the SPDA product increases as interest rates rise, the SPDA's profit margin decreases. A lower profit margin will not necessarily result from rising market interest rates in all deferred annuities.

FIGURE 8.9

Interest Rates and Profitability in *ExecuView*.

Here we look at a scenario of falling interest rates, a scenario of level interest rates, and a scenario of rising interest rates. In the *ExecuView* input tables for assumptions, interest-rate assumptions are set to change at Year 1, Year 2, Year 5, Year 10, and Year 15. In the annuity models' default scenarios, which is Scenario 1 in this example, Year 1 interest rates start at 7.5%, and fall 0.222% at Years 2, 5, and 10. Thus, the actual interest rates represented in our scenarios are as follows:

	Scenario 1 Falling	Scenario 2 Level	Scenario 3 Rising
Year 1 only	7.50	7.50	7.50
Year 2–Year 4	7.28	7.50	7.72
Year 5–Year 9	6.61	7.50	8.39
Year 10–Year 14	5.50	7.50	9.50
Year 15 and beyond	5.50	7.50	9.50

These interest-rate scenarios produce the following profitability results in the *ExecuView* models.

	Product Model	Validation Year	Profit Margin	IRR
Scenario 1: Falling Interest Rates (Default values)	SPIA	Year 12	2.35%	11.81%
	SPDA	Year 7	6.48%	19.15%
Scenario 2: Level Interest Rates (7.5% throughout)	SPIA	Year 6	9.39%	25.57%
	SPDA	Year 7	6.39%	20.02%
Scenario 3: Rising Interest Rates	SPIA	Year 5	15.10%	35.15%
	SPDA	Year 7	6.24%	20.88%

Changes in Mortality Rates

As mortality rates increase and more annuitants die, the amount of periodic income payments an insurer makes each year decreases. As a result, the annuity product's profitability increases. For *ExecuView*'s SPIA Model, Figure 8-10 shows the effect of a 10 percent increase in mortality rates.

FIGURE 8.10

Changing the Mortality Assumption in *ExecuView's* SPIA.

Immediate Annuity Model		
% of Mortality Table	**100%**	**110%**
Validation Year	Year 12	Year 8
Net Present Value	$234,537,600	$481,218,000
Internal Rate of Return	11.81%	16.81%
Profit Margin	2.35%	4.81%

Changes in Expense Assumptions

Insurers sometimes try to improve the profitability of annuity products by reducing expenses. Asset-share models can demonstrate how even a slight adjustment in an expense rate assumption can have a powerful effect on profitability. As expenses come down, profitability can improve dramatically, and as expenses increase, profitability can suffer. Figure 8-11 shows the profitability of *ExecuView*'s SPDA Model under several expense scenarios. Notice that all of these expense scenarios produce acceptable results for the chosen profitability measures.

FIGURE 8.11

Expense Assumptions for *ExecuView's* SPDA.

	Scenarios			
	Scenario 1	**Scenario 2**	**Scenario 3**	**Scenario 4**
	Expenses			
Year 1 expenses	$1.00	$0.75	$1.00	$3.50
Subsequent years	$0.69	$0.50	$3.00	$3.00
	Results of Modeling			
Validation year	Year 7	Year 7	Year 8	Year 9
Net present value	$648,300,061	$664,678,325	$479,569,585	$454,569,583
Internal rate of return	19.15%	19.50%	15.89%	15.13%
Profit margin	6.48%	6.65%	4.80%	4.55%

Changes in Commission Rates

Asset-share models show greater product profitability as commission rates are lowered and poorer product profitability as commission rates are increased. In the real world, the relationship between commission rates and product profitability is more complex, so that a higher commission rate might generate more product sales than a lower commission rate. However, this positive effect is limited, because the number of potential customers is limited. After a certain point, increased commissions will actually have no positive effect on product sales. An insurer must find the right balance between the level of commissions that must be paid to generate the desired level of sales and the level of sales that can actually be generated. For *ExecuView*'s SPIA Model, Figure 8-12 shows the effect of different commission schedules.

FIGURE 8.12

Commission Assumptions in *ExecuView*'s SPIA Model.

	Scenarios			
	Scenario 1	Scenario 2	Scenario 3	Scenario 4
	Commissions			
Year 1 Commission	5.00%	6.50%	8.00%	9.50%
	Results of Modeling			
Validation Year	Year 4	Year 6	Year 12	Year 20
Net Present Value	$534,537,700	$384,537,700	$234,537,600	$84,537,690
Internal Rate of Return	32.4%	18.55%	11.81%	7.86%
Profit Margin	5.35%	3.85%	2.35%	0.85%

Changes in Lapse Rates

We noted in earlier discussions that a lapse rate is a percentage of contracts lapsing. A set of product design assumptions might include a different lapse rate for each year of a product modeling period. For any given year, the lapse rate shows the percentage of contracts in force that will terminate during that year.

The relationship between product lapse rates and product profitability is complex. In general, higher lapse rates—in product models and in product experience—reduce profitability, though not in every case. The effect on profitability in an asset-share model from a given change in lapse rate assumptions is mostly determined by whether this change is in an early contract year or a later contract year. Annuity contracts that lapse before the validation point will never pay off the insurer's initial investment in them. Annuity contracts that lapse after the validation point have made a net contribution to the insurer's capital and surplus. Thus, high lapse rates occurring during the validation period have a stronger negative effect on profitability than do the same lapse rates occurring after the validation point. For *ExecuView*'s SPDA Model, Figure 8-13 shows the effects of different lapse rates.

FIGURE 8.13

Changes in Lapse Rates* in *ExecuView*'s SPDA Model.

	Scenarios			
	Scenario 1	Scenario 2	Scenario 3	Scenario 4
	Lapse Rates			
Default values, SPDA Model				
Initial lapse rate	2.00%	50.00%	10.00%	45.00%
Middle lapse rate	20.00%	20.00%	10.00%	40.00%
Final lapse rate	50.00%	2.00%	10.00%	20.00%
	Results of Modeling			
Validation year	7	NA	7	N/A
Net present value	$648,300,061	-$5,334,763	$546,351,648	-$532,627
Internal rate of return	19.15%	6.21%	18.37%	6.96%
Profit margin	6.48%	-0.05%	5.46%	-0.01%

*Note that lapse rates are applied to the number of contracts in force at the time the lapse rate is applied.

Scenario 1 shows the default values for the SPDA Model. In Scenario 3, the product's profit measures demonstrate acceptable profitability because the lapse rates are relatively low throughout the profit test period. In Scenarios 2 and 4, the product shows losses; in these scenarios, the highest lapse rates are early in the profit test period.

Changes in Multiple Assumptions

While asset-share models can be used to test the effects of changes in a single assumption, insurers more commonly use asset-share models to test whole sets of assumptions. By testing changes in multiple assumptions and incorporating forecasts about the way assumptions are likely to affect one another, insurers can more accurately picture the way an annuity product is likely to behave after the business is in force.

Insight 8-1 illustrates how multiple assumptions can be tested together for *ExecuView*'s SPDA Model. Although *ExecuView* simplifies the process of product testing, the *ExecuView* models and the following example provide a useful overview of how insurance companies use asset-share models when designing annuity products. If you have access to a computer that can run *ExecuView*, we suggest that you follow this example on your computer. However, you may follow the example by reading along and examining the reproductions of the *ExecuView* screens that show the results of the changes in assumptions.

INSIGHT 8.1 Testing a Deferred Annuity.

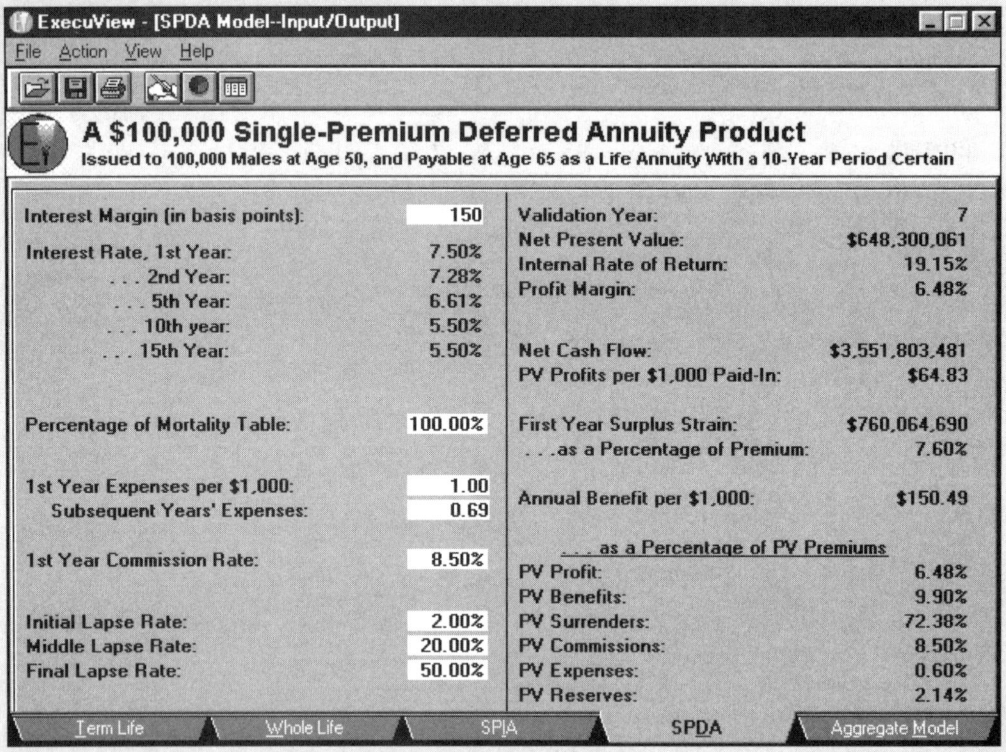

The EV Life Insurance Company is developing a fixed-rate SPDA product that it plans to market to males in their early fifties. This product will have a 15-year accumulation period and will become payable as a life annuity with a 10-year period certain. The minimum crediting rate EV Life plans to offer on this product is 4 percent. The profit objectives for this product are

- A validation period of between 2 and 15 years
- An internal rate of return (IRR) between 10 and 25 percent
- A profit margin between 1.5 and 10 percent

Insight 8.1 Testing a Deferred Annuity. *(continued)*

Experimenting with Interest Margin

EV Life is setting the crediting rate it will offer on this product. Originally, the product was expected to offer a crediting rate 150 basis points (bp) below the rate EV Life actually earns on its investments. The marketing department now would like to make this product more competitive by decreasing the interest margin, thereby increasing the interest rate credited to EV Life's SPDA customers. As an experiment, EV Life decreases the interest margin assumption in its asset-share model to 95 bp—thus increasing the interest crediting rate by 55 bp.

Set the SPDA Model's *Interest Margin* to 95 bp.

When the interest margin is thus reduced, EV Life's asset-share model shows a validation period of 14 years, an IRR of 8.87 percent, and a profit margin of 1.26 percent. Thus, the product no longer meets the company's profit objectives. If EV Life introduced the SPDA product to the market using this pricing strategy, it would be in danger of suffering a loss if conditions were even slightly different from EV Life's test scenario. Making a few adjustments, therefore, EV Life's actuaries suggest an interest margin of 115 bp, which allows the product to meet its profit objectives.

Set the SPDA Model's *Interest Margin* to 115 bp.

The profitability results of this interest margin, as demonstrated by EV Life's asset-share model, are shown in the following *ExecuView* screen.

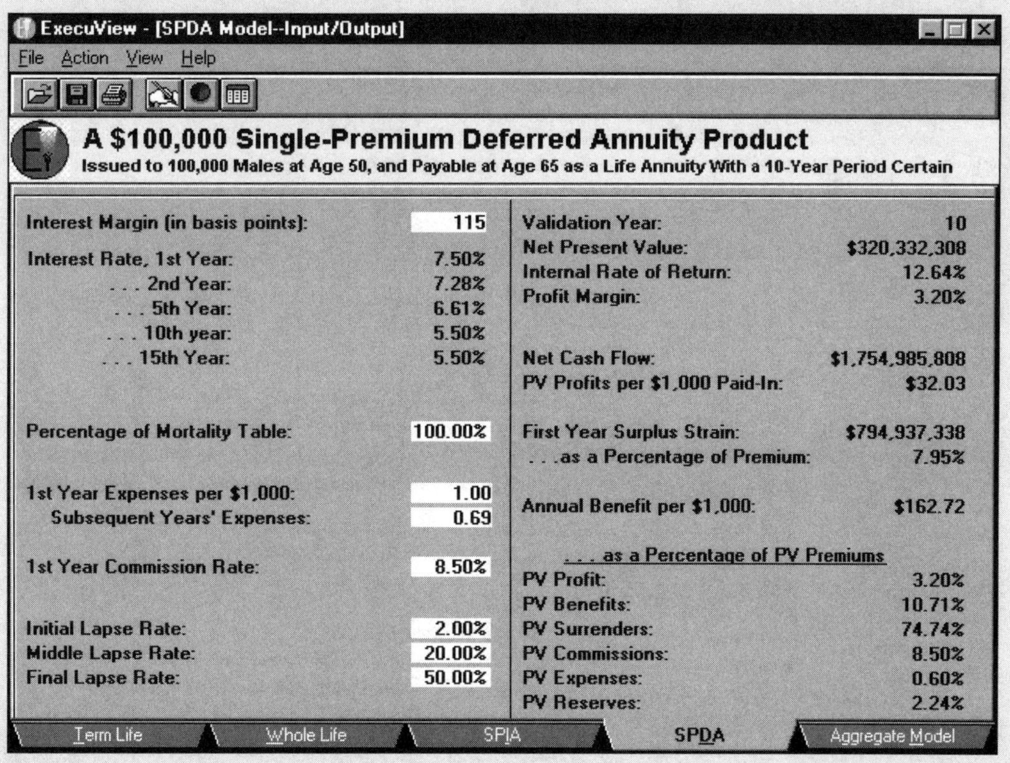

Insight 8.1 Testing a Deferred Annuity. *(continued)*

Experimenting with Mortality and Lapse Rates

After an interest margin is settled upon, new information becomes available about the mortality experience of EV Life's annuitants, who are living longer than expected. To compensate, EV Life needs to decrease the mortality rate in its asset-share model by at least 15 percent. Also, EV Life's latest persistency studies suggest that the asset-share model's middle lapse rate assumption is too low by at least 20 percentage points. The same studies indicate that currently initial lapse rates are around 4 percent and final lapse rates are close to 55 percent.

Set the SPDA Model's *Percentage of Mortality Table* to 85 percent. Change the *Initial Lapse Rate* assumption to 4 percent, the *Middle Lapse Rate* to 35 percent, and the *Final Lapse Rate* to 55 percent.

Readjusting to Meet Profit Objectives

As a result of these changed assumptions, the annuity product no longer meets its profit objectives. The validation point at Year 10 is acceptable. IRR and profit margin, however, are below profit objectives. EV Life again increases the interest margin until the profit measures fall within an acceptable range. This time, EV Life's actuaries decide to try an interest margin of 130 bp.

Set the SPDA Model's *Interest Margin* assumption to 130 bp.

The profitability outcome projected by EV Life's asset-share model is shown in the following *ExecuView* screen:

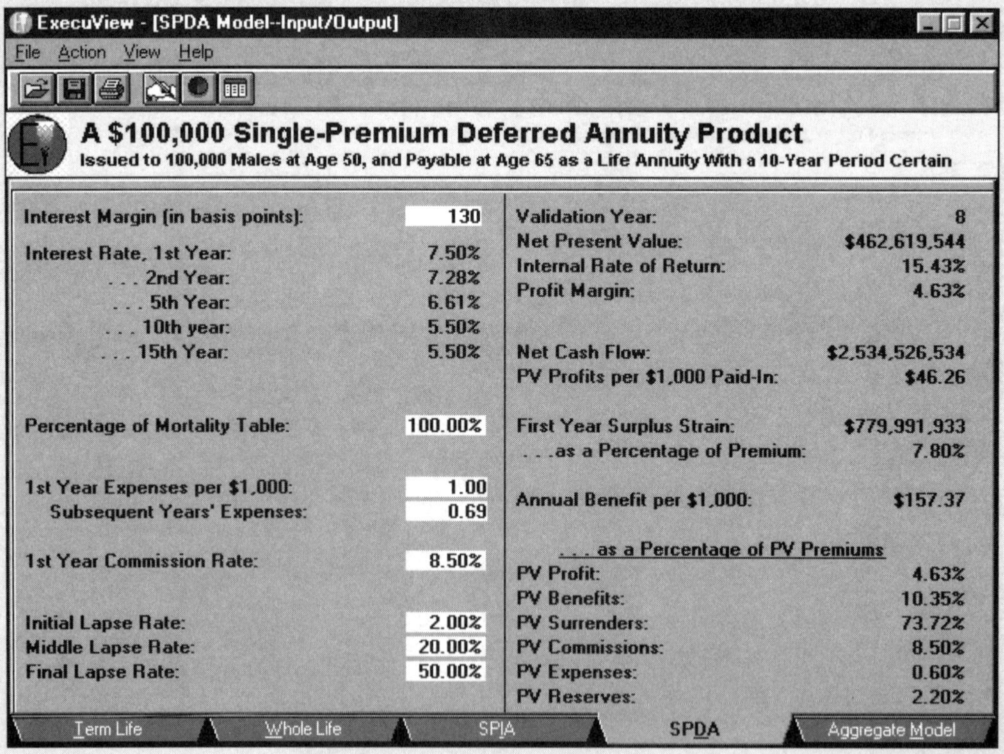

KEY TERMS AND CONCEPTS

simulation modeling
sensitivity analysis
dependent variable
independent variable
interest-sensitive cash-flow testing
cash-flow testing (CFT)
dynamic solvency testing (DST)
actuarial opinion and memorandum (AOM)

ENDNOTES

1. Allan Brender, "The Evolution of Solvency Standards for Life Insurance Companies in Canada." *Research Report 91-10,* Institute of Insurance and Pension Research, University of Waterloo, Ontario.
2. Adapted with permission of the publisher from Susan Conant et al., *Managing for Solvency and Profitability in Life and Health Insurance Companies* (Atlanta: LOMA, 1996), 179–89.
3. Samuel H. Cox et al., "Single-Premium Deferred Annuity Persistency Study," *Transactions of the Society of Actuaries,* 1991–92 Reports, 290.
4. Adapted with permission of the publisher from Susan Conant et al., *Managing for Solvency and Profitability in Life and Health Insurance Companies* (Atlanta: LOMA, 1996), 189–202.

CHAPTER 9

Expenses and Annuity Product Design

After studying this chapter, you should be able to

- Identify examples of acquisition expenses, maintenance expenses, and overhead expenses for annuity products
- Distinguish between direct expenses and indirect expenses, as well as give examples of each
- Describe unit costs and standard costs
- Distinguish between full costing and marginal costing and be able to calculate expenses for a product using full costing and marginal costing
- Recognize the characteristics of product loading in annuity product designs for the accumulation period and the payout period

Insurers must design annuity products that will at least recover the operating expenses for supporting the product. In a broad accounting sense, expenses are the amount a company spends to obtain a specified benefit or service. Expenses are a major account classification on an income statement. The component in an annuity product design that is intended to cover the insurer's administrative expenses—and, in some instances, a profit margin—is the loading. As we have discussed, the loading is one of three basic components of an annuity product design. The other two are (1) expenses for contractual benefits and (2) any anticipated investment earnings. Thus, as preparation for annuity product design, insurance companies must project their expenses for annuity products. To do so, insurers accumulate, track, and analyze their known costs through their accounting systems.

As you will recall from Chapters 7 and 8, expenses are explicitly included in product models. In the context of product design, expenses include the costs of doing business, but do not include the amounts of the contractual benefits that an insurer pays out. In this chapter, we discuss how insurance companies analyze and classify costs from their accounting records, and then assign the identified costs to specific annuity products. Our discussion of expenses describes the difference between product models that consider only direct expenses and those that consider both direct and indirect expenses. Finally, we examine how insurers incorporate these costs into their annuity product designs for the accumulation period and the payout period.

Overview of Insurance Company Expenses

Insurance companies undertake financial accounting activities so that they can compile formal financial reports, whereas managerial accounting activities are designed to obtain information for effective managerial decisions. Our interest in this section is in the management accounting activities that focus on studying costs to derive information needed for use in product models and technical product design. Because each insurance company's management accounting system is designed to meet the company's internal needs, terminology used in reference to management accounting systems varies widely.

The portion of a management accounting system that provides needed cost information for use in product models is the cost accounting system. A ***cost accounting system*** is an accounting subsystem that accumulates expense data for the dual purposes of effective cost control and accurate product design activities. ***Cost accumulation*** is the process of capturing all of a company's costs and categorizing them in meaningful ways.[1] Cost accumulation is a crucial first step toward assigning costs to products and lines of business, as appropriate.

Classification of expenses helps insurers to assign costs to various annuity products. Insurance company expenses are properly divided into two main categories of (1) investment expenses and (2) general and administrative expenses.

Investment Expenses

For life insurance companies, ***investment expenses*** are the costs associated with investing the company's general account and separate account assets. Examples of investment expenses include the costs of investment analysis, purchasing assets, selling assets, and servicing assets. Even for general accounting purposes, investment expenses are generally viewed as an offset to investment income. Thus, fixed annuity product designs typically recognize investment expenses by reducing the crediting rate on investments—that is, by crediting a "net" interest rate.

General and Administrative Expenses

The insurance company's non-investment expenses are classified as ***general and administrative expenses***, which can be defined as the expenses that occur as a result of undertaking normal business activities to generate sales of insurance and annuity products and to support annuity and insurance products. Insurance operating expenses can be subdivided into

- Expenses for contractual benefits
- Operating expenses

Expenses for Contractual Benefits

Important types of expenses for benefits associated with annuity contracts include paying

- Cash surrender values
- Partial withdrawals of the account balance prior to the scheduled maturity date
- Survivor benefits upon the death of the annuitant
- Periodic annuity income payments

Operating Expenses

Three important types of operating expenses can be identified from an insurance company's accounting records: acquisition expenses, maintenance expenses, and overhead expenses.

- ***Acquisition expenses*** for annuity products are the insurer's expenses related to obtaining and issuing new annuity business. Many companies consider all first-year expenses to be acquisition expenses, whereas other companies consider that acquisition expenses encompass only expenses incurred before contract issue. Examples of acquisition expenses are advertising expenses, agents' first-year commissions, some agency management expenses, and the costs of preparing new contracts and new customer records.
- ***Maintenance expenses***, also known as *renewal expenses*, are the product-related expenses that arise once a contract is in force. Examples of maintenance expenses include renewal commissions; premium taxes; costs of disbursing periodic income benefit payments under immediate annuities; costs of disbursing cash surrender values, partial withdrawals, and survivor benefits; costs for customer service activities such as changes in data, including address, beneficiary, and name changes; and, again, certain agency management expenses.[2]
- ***Overhead expenses*** are costs incurred during normal business operations and not directly associated with a specific product or service. Examples of overhead costs for annuity operations include the costs of furniture and fixtures, telephone service, electricity, actuarial analysis, research, general legal services, accounting services, taxes, costs of licenses, and other business fees.

Figure 9-1 illustrates the relationships among the types of insurance company expenses we have discussed.

FIGURE 9.1

Relationships Among Insurance Company Expenses.

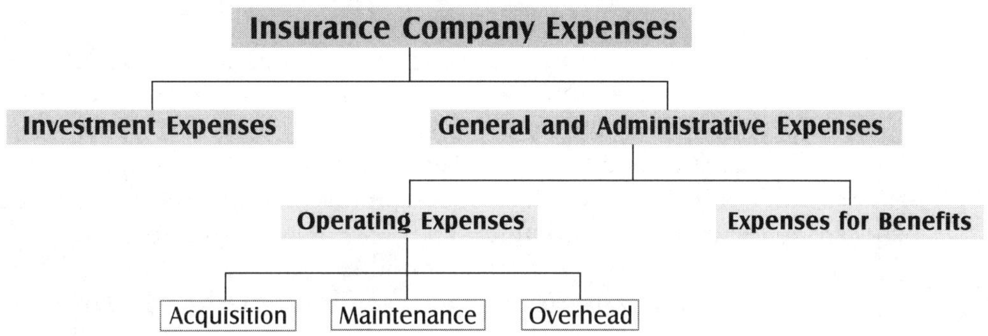

Figure 9-2 shows examples of acquisition expenses, maintenance expenses, and overhead expenses.

FIGURE 9.2

Acquisition, Maintenance, and Overhead Expenses.

Overhead Expenses	• Actuarial analysis	• Accounting services	• Information systems
Maintenance Expenses	• Premium taxes	• Customer service operations	• Some agency expenses
Acquisition Expenses	• First-year commissions	• Contract issue expenses	• Some agency expenses

Expense Analysis

Now that we have defined and described the primary types of expenses insurers incur, we can discuss how insurers analyze these expenses. An important goal of expense analysis is to design product models with expense patterns that match likely future expense patterns. Although an insurance company's accounting records provide valuable information about historical patterns of expenses, these exact historical expense amounts are not used directly in product loading, because historical events are not completely accurate as forecasts of future developments. Product models must reflect expectations of future developments, and thus insurers generally build relevant expected economic and societal trends into expense loadings.

Direct and Indirect Expenses

Expenses can also be classified as direct or indirect expenses. For our purposes, ***direct expenses*** of an annuity product, also known as *traceable costs*, are expenses incurred for or physically traceable to that specific product. Assigning direct expenses to a particular product is fairly straightforward. For example, a sales commission expense is a direct expense. When a sales producer sells a single premium deferred annuity (SPDA) contract, the insurer's commission expense arises directly from that SPDA contract. ***Indirect expenses***, also called *common costs*, of an annuity product are expenses that cannot be traced to or are not incurred for one specific product. Indirect expenses result from activities that relate to several or all of an insurer's products. An insurer incurs the same level of indirect expenses whether or not it offers a specific product. For example, each insurance company typically uses the same information system to provide customer service for several lines of business, such as individual annuity products, pension products, individual life insurance products, and group life insurance products. The costs of such an information system are not directly attributable to the individual annuity product line. If an insurer stopped maintaining its individual annuity product line by transferring that product line to another insurer, the costs associated with maintaining and operating the company's information system would remain essentially the same. The costs of this information system are an indirect expense from the point of view of the individual annuity product line.[3] Figure 9-3 shows examples of direct and indirect expenses.

FIGURE 9.3

Direct and Indirect Expenses for Annuity Products.

Direct Expenses

- Agents' commissions
- Issue expenses
- Transaction processing expenses

Indirect Expenses

- Information systems expenses
- Accounting expenses
- Expenses for chief executive officer's compensation

Cost Allocation

Cost allocation, also known as *expense allocation*, is the accounting process of assigning or distributing an indirect cost to a cost object according to a method or formula. A ***cost allocation method*** is the procedure or formula used for assigning an indirect cost to a unit of product.

Insurance companies use cost allocation in many ways, some unrelated to product design. Thus, insurance companies may choose to allocate indirect costs to a designated cost object such as a profit center, cost center, function, or unit of product. For product design needs, insurance companies identify direct expenses and also assign indirect expenses to a unit of product such as a business unit, product line, product, contract, dollar amount of contract value, or customer.

Units of Product and Unit Costs

Insurers can choose to designate different units of annuity product, depending on the information needed. A ***unit cost*** is the incurred expense that can be attributed to a single measured amount of product. Thus, a unit cost may include both indirect and direct expenses. A unit cost is found by dividing the relevant cost by the number of designated units of product. In the context of product loading, ***relevant costs*** are the costs that are important to include as expenses in the product design. An example of a unit cost calculation for contract issue expenses appears in Figure 9-4.

One important structure for a unit cost is a flat dollar amount of expense per contract. Some expenses are assumed to be the same for all contracts of

FIGURE 9.4

Unit Cost Calculation, Contract Issue Expenses.

		Annual Data
1. Number of contracts issued	→	20,000
2. Employee-related expenses	→	$1,500,000
3. Other contract expenses	→	$5,500,000
4. Total expenses (2 + 3)	→	$7,000,000
5. Unit cost (1 ÷ 4)	→	$350

Source: Elizabeth A. Mulligan and Gene Stone, *Accounting and Financial Reporting in Life and Health Insurance Companies* (Atlanta: LOMA, 1997), 491. Adapted with permission of the publisher.

a specific type, no matter how large the contract, and for these expenses, insurers apply a flat amount per contract. For example, an insurer's costs for preparing and mailing annual account statements to customers are the same for all contracts of the same type, independent of the size of a customer's account. Other expenses vary with some variable embedded in a contract, and for these expenses, insurers state the amount of an expense as a percentage of the associated contract variable, such as the

- Customer's initial premium
- Customer's account value
- Amount of account activity

When an insurer loads expense charges into an annuity product model, the insurer sometimes converts the expenses per contract to a dollar amount per $1,000 of initial premium, usually associated with the average contract size. On this basis, insurers might classify an annuity product's expenses as some expense per $1,000 of initial premium, and another expense per contract.

For example, suppose Tri-Star Life's single premium immediate annuity (SPIA) product needs to be loaded for expenses of $50 per contract, and Tri-Star Life's average contract size for this product is $100,000 of initial premium. To convert this per-contract expense to a per $1,000 of initial premium basis, Tri-Star would divide $50 by 100, resulting in a loading of $0.50 per $1,000 of initial premium.

Figure 9-5 shows a simplified expense analysis for first-year unit costs of a single premium deferred annuity product.

Standard Costs

Insurers sometimes find performing a thorough cost analysis for every one of their products to be impractical. Instead, insurers sometimes estimate

FIGURE 9.5

First-Year Unit Costs, SPDA Product.

The worksheet below shows a simplified expense analysis for first-year unit costs of a single premium deferred annuity product.

Expense Categories	Flat Amount per Contract	Percentage of Value
Acquisition expenses (Year 1)		
Commissions		X
Issue expense	X	
Premium taxes		X
Business licensing and fees	X	
Overhead	X	X
Maintenance expenses (after Year 1)		
Commissions and trails		X
Premium taxes		X
Overhead	X	X

some costs. ***Standard costs*** are cost estimates representing the average amount of a given type of expenditure for normal business operations. Most insurers have calculated standard costs for the entire administration of a given type of annuity product. For a new product design, an insurer may use standard costs, particularly if the new product is similar to one of the insurer's existing products. Although standard costs provide insurers a quick, efficient method of estimating expenses for use in product design, standard costs must be tested and revised periodically to ensure that they accurately reflect actual conditions.[4]

MARGINAL AND FULL COSTING[5]

The process used during technical product design to set a product's expense assumptions is called ***costing***. Two methods are commonly used in the life insurance industry for costing annuity products: (1) marginal costing and (2) full costing. These methods differ in the way they treat indirect costs.

- ***Marginal costing***, also known as *variable costing* or *direct costing*, is a method for estimating product-related expenses so that only direct expenses are treated as product-related expenses. Under marginal costing, indirect expenses are not allocated to products.
- ***Full costing***, also known as *absorption costing*, is a method for estimating product-related expenses in which both direct and indirect expenses are treated as product-related expenses. Because indirect expenses are not directly attributable to any given product, full costing requires the insurer to allocate indirect expenses to each product line and potentially to each product.

Traditionally, the insurance industry has used full costing. However, insurers are increasingly using marginal costing.

Note that the size and function of a product's expense margin differ depending on whether the company uses full or marginal costing. Under full costing, both direct and indirect costs are treated as relevant costs. In contrast, under marginal costing only direct costs are treated as relevant costs. Under full costing, a product's expense margin contributes to profit, but not to indirect costs. Under marginal costing, however, the expense margin contributes to both indirect costs and profit. These differences are illustrated in Figure 9-6.

FIGURE 9.6

Direct/Indirect Costs and Expense Margins Under Full Versus Marginal Costing.

	Full Costing	Marginal Costing
Direct and Indirect Costs	Both direct and indirect costs are relevant product costs.	Only direct costs are relevant product costs.
Expense Margin	The expense margin contributes to profit.	The expense margin contributes to both indirect costs and profit.

Insight 9-1 uses an example to illustrate how the same product's expenses are treated under full costing and marginal costing, resulting in very different total expense margins.

ESTABLISHING LOADING

We have seen in this chapter that the loading in a product is designed to reimburse the insurer for its general operating expenses, not including benefit costs or investment expenses. Our discussion to this point has covered operating expenses that have a strong historical basis in the company's accounting system. Loading additionally covers some items that the company cannot collect from its accounting system, including contingencies, margins, and provision for lapses.

Provision for Contingencies

Contingencies are exposures to risk. Contingencies consist of exposures to events such as severe swings in market interest rates, unfavorable regulatory decisions, or unfavorable tax legislation. Contingencies are important in product design because they can cause adverse deviations from actuarial assumptions. Even the uncertainty associated with the forecasting process can produce small adverse deviations. When unexpected events cause investment earnings, mortality rates, persistency rates, or expenses to vary significantly from assumptions, adverse deviations result.

INSIGHT 9.1

Full or Marginal Costing Example.

The numbers and the assumptions used in this example are simplified. The example assumes that all of the product's expenses are incurred and all premiums paid at the same time—something that probably never occurs with annuity products.

The Avalon Insurance Company sells a product line with the expense profile shown below:

Expense Profile of an Annuity Product	
Expense charge	$100
Direct expenses	$50
Allocated indirect expenses	$30

The *expense charge* is the portion of the product line's price that is intended to account for the product's expenses.

Expense Margin Under Full Costing

First, Avalon Insurance calculates the product's expense margin using full costing. The expense margin under full costing can be calculated by summing a product's direct and indirect expenses and subtracting this sum from the expense charge, as shown in the following equation:

Expense margin, full costing = Expense charge – (Direct expenses + Indirect expenses)

Assume that Avalon will allocate $30 of indirect expenses to the product line we are examining. Under full costing, the expense margin for this product line can be calculated as follows:

Expense margin = $100 – ($50 Direct expenses + $30 Indirect expenses)
= $100 – $80
= $20

Marginal Costing Example

Under marginal costing, the only expenses that are treated as product expenses are direct expenses; indirect expenses are not considered. The following formula can be used to calculate the expense margin under marginal costing:

Expense margin, marginal costing = Expense charge – Direct expenses

When Avalon uses marginal costing to calculate the expense margin of the same product line we have described, the expense margin is calculated as follows:

Expense margin = $100 Expense charge – $50 Direct expenses
= $50

Source: Susan Conant et al., *Managing for Solvency and Profitability in Life and Health Insurance Companies* (Atlanta: LOMA, 1996), 230–32. Adapted with permission of the publisher.

Insurers usually add an amount to a product's loading to protect themselves and their customers from the potentially damaging financial results of adverse deviations. In group insurance, this amount is called the risk charge. This additional loading helps ensure that an insurer will be able to fulfill its contractual obligations even under difficult circumstances.[6]

Margins[7]

Actuaries generally design an annuity product so that its expected cash inflows exceed its projected cash outflows, so as to provide the insurer with an appropriate margin. A product's margin is intended to contribute to the insurer's profit and to provide a further cushion to provide for contingencies. Most insurers rely upon tools such as asset-share models to analyze the potential profitability of products.

We can distinguish between assumed values, expected values, and actual values. Accordingly, we can distinguish among an assumed margin, an expected margin, and an actual margin. During product design, any margin built into a product is an *assumed margin*. When actuaries establish a product's technical design, they assume different values from the expected values so that the product design will have an adequate margin.

Expected values are the values that the insurer's actuaries believe are most likely to occur. So, an *expected margin* is one that the insurer expects to be achieved.

The *actual margin* is the margin that emerges after the product has been in force and is the difference between the assumed values for benefit costs, expenses, or investment income, and the actual values for these factors. The actual margin may be higher or lower than the assumed or the expected margin.

Product margins are described as being either thin or wide. As these terms imply, a thin product margin is a small margin, and a wide product margin is a large margin. Deferred annuity products tend to have relatively thin margins, whereas other product types tend to have wider margins. Insight 9-2 discusses important influences that affect the size of a product's expected margin.

INSIGHT 9.2

Influences on a Product's Margin.

Competition. A competitive market environment often acts to force prices down. Thus, if a product is competing with other products for customer dollars, then the product's expected margin is likely to be thin. Accumulation products, such as annuities, have thin margins partly because the financial marketplace includes numerous products offered by banks and mutual fund companies.

The risk assumed by the insurer. The greater the level of risk an insurer assumes with a product, the greater must be the potential reward of assuming that risk. Thus, the greater the level of risk a product represents for an insurer, the wider the product's expected margin. The wider margin provides a safety net, in case the insurer's experience is worse than expected.

The length of interest crediting guarantees. The insurer's opportunity to revise a product's crediting rate reduces the insurer's risk of supporting the product. The more frequently an insurer can revise a product's crediting rate while the product is in force, generally, the thinner the product's expected margin.

With a fixed deferred annuity, for example, the insurer can adjust the insurance charge and the crediting rate on a frequent basis. The insurer does not need to build in such a wide margin to protect itself against adverse experience on this type of product. If experience is unfavorable, the insurer can adjust the product's charges or its crediting rate.

Customer emphasis on return. When customers purchase accumulation products, they are generally drawn to products that offer the highest return available within their personal risk tolerance. Shifting risk to customers allows insurers to offer thin expected margins. Customers with a low tolerance for risk seek products that offer more investment guarantees but lower potential returns. Products with investment guarantees require insurers to build wide expected margins into their pricing.

Deterrents to surrenders and withdrawals. Some deferred annuity product designs contain charges or penalties that deter customers from making surrenders and partial withdrawals.

Source: Susan Conant et al., *Managing for Solvency and Profitability in Life and Health Insurance Companies* (Atlanta: LOMA, 1996), 221–22. Adapted with permission of the publisher.

Provision for Lapses

Product expenses can be high during a product's early years, when the insurer pays commissions and other acquisition expenses. The insurer generally recovers first-year expenses over the course of several years. The more contracts the insurer expects to lapse in the early years, the higher the loading charge the insurer must establish in order to recover its expenses. Insurers have analyzed product features and product markets for their influence on different persistency rates. Any factor that influences persistency should influence loading. Higher persistency generally calls for lower loading, and lower persistency generally calls for higher loading. Figure 9-7 shows a sample calculation of a loading charge for expected lapses.

FIGURE 9.7

Lapse Expense of the Primo Life Insurance Company.

The Primo Life Insurance Company plans to sell 15,000 contracts in a new product's first year and to recover $1 million of the first-year expenses in the product's second year. The table below shows the amount Primo will have to charge per customer in order to recover these expenses if the persistency rate is expected to be 80 percent and 70 percent, respectively.

First-Year Persistency	80 Percent Persistency	70 Percent Persistency
Number of first-year customers	15,000	15,000
Number of customers lapsing after first year	3,000	4,500
Number of customers remaining, second year	12,000	10,500
Expense per customer = ($1 million ÷ customers)	$83.33	$95.24

As the table shows, if the expected first-year persistency rate for this product is 80 percent, the Primo Company would need to charge each remaining customer $83.33 in the second year to cover first-year expenses. If the expected persistency rate drops to 70 percent, then the charge would need to be $95.24 per customer.

Source: Susan Conant et al., *Managing for Solvency and Profitability in Life and Health Insurance Companies* (Atlanta: LOMA, 1996), 238–39. Adapted with permission of the publisher.

UNBUNDLED AND BUNDLED PRODUCT DESIGNS

Insurers use different approaches to incorporating the expense charge into a product's structure, depending on whether the product has an unbundled or a bundled product structure.

- An ***unbundled product structure*** is one in which the insurer explicitly discloses various expense charges to customers and also specifies the rate of investment return being credited to customers.
- A ***bundled product structure*** is one in which the insurer presents a product to customers as a package of benefits provided in exchange for a given sum of premium.

Most annuity products in the accumulation period have an unbundled product structure. An example of an unbundled product structure is a fixed

SPDA contract in which the customer pays an annual administration charge, the contract is subject to surrender charges, and the insurance company discloses the rate of interest being credited to the customer's account. However, most annuity products have a bundled product structure for the payout period. An example of a bundled structure is the annuity cost factor for an immediate annuity. The insurer does not necessarily specify what portion of the premium goes to cover expenses, what portion goes to provide benefits, or how much interest the insurer is crediting to the customer.

Expense Charges in Fixed SPIAs

The most prominent examples of bundled annuity products are fixed annuity contracts in the payout period. For bundled annuity products, the insurer specifies to the customer neither the interest the insurer is crediting on the product nor any charges to cover administrative expenses, commissions, or mortality expenses.

When a customer purchases an SPIA contract, one form for expressing the price of the product is the annuity purchase cost for $1, which is the insurer's charge to the customer for a life annuity of $1 per period. For a fixed annuity, whenever the amount of the single premium is known, the annuity purchase cost is used to determine the amount of periodic income payments available during the payout period. Annuity purchase costs for SPIAs incorporate the elements of mortality, interest, and loading. Annuity purchase costs for SPIAs that are sold through a sales producer include a load to cover the expense of commissions. For use in annuitization of deferred annuity contracts, insurers develop prices known as annuity conversion costs. These annuity conversion costs are very similar to annuity purchase costs, except that annuity conversion costs typically do not provide for loading, because no sales producer is involved in the annuitization of a deferred annuity.

Expense Charges in Deferred Annuity Products

Expense charges are the portion of a product's structure designed to reimburse the insurer for its operating expenses—specifically, commissions, premium taxes, and general operating expenses. Note that these operating expenses do not include benefit costs or investment expenses.

Expense charges are used most often in connection with deferred annuities. Most fixed deferred annuities are unbundled products, but they are not required to be unbundled. However, all variable annuity products in the United States must have unbundled expense charges. For the unbundled annuity products, the insurer designs expense charges to offset specific expenses. In addition, the insurer often charges more than one type of expense fee within the structure of a given product.

Fees in Fixed Deferred Annuities[8]

Four types of explicit fees are commonly used to incorporate loading into the design of fixed deferred annuities. Such an annuity product might feature one of these fees, a combination of two or three of these fees, or all of these fees. As we discussed in Chapters 7 and 8, a fixed deferred annuity product might also provide for loading through an interest margin. Types of fees that may be applied to fixed deferred annuities include

- Front-end loads
- Surrender charges
- Periodic fees
- Service fees

In an annuity product, a ***front-end load***, also known as a *front load*, is a charge deducted from a premium at the time the customer pays a premium. Front-end loads are usually expressed as a percentage of the customer's payment to the company. Contracts that have front-end loads typically do not have surrender charges. The front-end load is intended to compensate the insurer for any sales commission it pays to a sales producer for selling a product.

To illustrate, assume that the Easton Insurance Company's fixed deferred annuity has a 2.5 percent front-end load. If Gary Nielsen purchases a fixed deferred annuity from Easton for $50,000, Easton will deduct 2.5 percent of the $50,000 and invest the remainder on behalf of Mr. Nielsen's accumulation account. In this situation, the amount of the front-end load would be calculated as 2.5 percent multiplied by $50,000, equaling $1,250. Thus, Mr. Nielsen's annuity accumulation value in the beginning of Year 1 would be calculated as $50,000 minus $1,250, equaling $48,750.

As you recall from Chapter 2, a surrender charge, also known as a back-end load, back load, or withdrawal charge, is an amount charged when a customer withdraws money from an annuity. Surrender charges are intended to discourage customers from withdrawing their money and to compensate the insurer for the costs it incurs in issuing a new contract. Thus, surrender charges can support annuity persistency. Also, surrender charges offer the insurer an opportunity to recover sales commissions and issue costs. The amount of a surrender charge is typically set to decrease over time.

Another type of expense charge is the periodic fee. We saw in Chapter 2 that some annuity products include a flat annual administrative charge of $30 to $50 annually. Another similar charge is the mortality and expense charge, also discussed in Chapter 2. A ***periodic fee*** is an amount that must be paid at predetermined intervals, for example, every year or every month. A periodic fee is generally intended to compensate the insurer for its administrative expenses. A periodic fee can be either a flat amount or a percentage of the customer's account value. Typically, these fees are found in flexible premium deferred annuity contracts (FPDAs).

Finally, some insurers charge customers one-time fees for specific services. For example, an insurer might charge a fee of $10 to transfer money from one variable annuity subaccount to another. Fees such as these may be called *service fees* or *transaction fees.* Fees for specific services are generally deducted from the amount of the transaction being handled.

Figure 9-8 summarizes the expense charges that are commonly used for fixed deferred annuity products.

FIGURE 9.8

Expense Charges for Fixed Deferred Annuity Products.

	Formula	Insurer Deducts from	Purpose
Front-End Load	• Specified percentage	Premium	• Covers commission expenses • Covers issue expenses
Surrender Charge	• Specified percentage	Withdrawal amount	• Covers commission expenses • Covers issue expenses • Discourages withdrawals • Can provide some protection of market value of investments
Periodic Fee	• Stated flat amount per period • Stated percentage of account value per period	Account balance	Offsets general administrative expenses
Service Fee	• Stated flat amount per transaction	Transaction amount	Offsets specific administrative expenses

Fees for Variable Deferred Annuities

Under SEC and NASD rules, all charges in variable annuities must be shown separately, and thus, all variable annuities are unbundled. Under U.S. rules that apply to securities, variable annuities cannot impose a penalty charge for early withdrawals, such as a surrender charge. In place of a surrender charge, variable annuities commonly have a charge termed a contingent deferred sales load (CDSL). The most common of the types of charges used in variable annuities are the

- ◆ Mortality and expense (M&E) charge, a charge generally expressed as a percentage of variable annuity assets, and designed to cover the company's mortality risk and expense contingencies
- ◆ Administration expense charge, an expense charge generally expressed as a percentage of variable annuity assets, and designed

to cover expenses such as the costs of preparing and mailing account statements

- Account fee, an annual charge generally expressed as the lesser of $30 per year or 2 percent of account value
- ***Contingent deferred sales load (CDSL)***, an expense charge deducted from withdrawals and applied for recovery of sales expenses

Insight 9-3 shows a common structure for variable annuity expense charges to customers.

INSIGHT 9.3

Hypothetical Variable Annuity Expenses.

Judy, Warren, and Jeff have invested in variable annuities. All have chosen variable investment subaccounts. The table below illustrates the expense charges for each of their accounts, based on the average amounts of annual expense charges and their investment amounts.

Company Charges	Expenses	Judy	Warren	Jeff
Initial investment		$10,000	$ 15,000	$25,000
Sales charge*	0	0	0	0
Average administrative charge	0.21%	$ 21	$ 32	$ 53
Average management fee	0.61%	$ 61	$ 92	$ 153
Average mortality and expense risk charges	1.11%	$ 111	$ 167	$ 278
Average annual contract maintenance charge**	$27	$ 27	$ 27	$ 27
Total		$ 220	$ 318	$ 511

* Please note that most annuities have no sales charges.

** Many companies waive this fee if there is a minimum contract value.

Source: Data from Lipper Inc., 1999.

KEY TERMS AND CONCEPTS

cost accounting system
cost accumulation
investment expense
general and administrative expense
acquisition expense
maintenance expense
overhead expense
direct expense
indirect expense
cost allocation
cost allocation method
unit cost

relevant cost
standard cost
costing
marginal costing
full costing
contingencies
unbundled product structure
bundled product structure
front-end load
periodic fee
contingent deferred sales load (CDSL)

ENDNOTES

1. Elizabeth A. Mulligan and Gene Stone, *Accounting and Financial Reporting in Life and Health Insurance Companies* (Atlanta: LOMA, 1997), 493.
2. Adapted with permission of the publisher from Susan Conant et al., *Managing for Solvency and Profitability in Life and Health Insurance Companies* (Atlanta: LOMA, 1996), 227.
3. Ibid., 229.
4. Ibid., 228.
5. Ibid., 230–32.
6. Ibid., 228.
7. Ibid., 217–21
8. Ibid., 236–38.

CHAPTER 10

Annuity Products and Mortality

After studying this chapter, you should be able to

- Read data from a mortality table
- Use data for the number living and the number dying to calculate a mortality rate for a given age
- Use data for the number living and the associated mortality rate to calculate the number of deaths for a given age group
- Identify the purposes and characteristics of different types of mortality data and mortality tables
- Recognize the function and behavior of the mortality margin in technical product design for life annuities

As noted in Chapter 1, an insurer must be able to estimate accurately the amount and timing of future benefit payments in order to learn how much money will be needed to pay those future benefits. For immediate annuities with life contingencies, mortality rates are an important factor (1) in determining an insurance company's cost to provide periodic income payments, (2) in setting the annuity purchase rates that insurers use to determine the periodic income payment for a given single premium amount, and (3) in calculating annuity reserves. However, mortality rates do not affect the accumulation of value in deferred annuities. Deferred annuities make no distinction as to sex or mortality.

For immediate annuity products with life contingencies, an insurer must be able to predict the approximate number of deaths that will occur each year among a given group of annuitants. Estimating the cost of periodic income benefits requires first selecting an appropriate mortality table. Mortality information is organized into tables showing the expected mortality rates for each age. As we mentioned in Chapter 2, a mortality table is a chart that shows the expected death rates among a particular group of people at given ages—that is, how many of the people in each age group may be expected to die in a particular year. A mortality rate is the percentage rate at which death occurs among a defined group of people of a specified age and sometimes of a specified gender. Keep in mind that insurance companies are interested in the rate at which people in a given group are expected to die, not in trying to predict an individual's death. ***Expected mortality***, or *tabular mortality*, refers to the number or rate of deaths that have been predicted to occur in a group of people at a given age according to the mortality table. The mortality rates shown in mortality tables are called ***tabular mortality rates***. ***Mortality experience*** refers to the number or rate of deaths that *actually* occur in a given group of people.

Mortality tables are differentiated by the group of people included in the mortality data. A mortality table showing rates of death for the general population, based on data from a population census, is known as a ***population mortality table***. However, for life insurance business, insurance companies consult mortality tables that cover a population of life insureds only. Similarly, insurers consult special annuity mortality tables for life annuities. ***Annuity mortality tables*** show the projected mortality rates and survival rates for a population of annuitants only. Because annuity benefits are payable while the annuitant continues to live, a life annuity protects the annuitant against the personal risk of outliving her financial resources. The ability to pay life annuities has been made possible by the life insurance industry's studies of mortality rates and its development of mortality tables. Insurers can use this information to predict the amount of annuity benefits they will be liable to pay in a given year. Establishing accurate estimates of mortality rates allows the insurer to establish adequate mortality charges in its product expense structures. In the rest of this chapter, we will explain how to read data from mortality tables and discuss several types of mortality tables and the situations in which they are used.

READING A MORTALITY TABLE

Figure 10-1 shows a mortality table excerpt based on the rates in the 1996 *Annuity 2000* basic mortality table for men. (A separate mortality table is available showing statistics for women.) To illustrate how mortality tables are designed, we'll read and interpret a section of the table in Figure 10-1.

FIGURE 10.1

Basic Annuity Mortality Table—Men.

(1) Age	(2) Mortality rate per 1,000	(3) Number living	(4) Number dying
65	11	100,000	1,100
66	12	98,900	1,187

Source: Reprinted with permission from "Annuity 2000 Mortality Tables," *TSA 1995–96 Reports of Mortality, Morbidity, and Other Experience*, p. 265. Copyright 1998 by the Society of Actuaries.

The table in Figure 10-1 is divided into four columns:

- *Column 1* shows the ages of men included in the mortality table.
- *Column 2* shows, for each age, the number of men per thousand dying during the year, which is the mortality rate.
- *Column 3* shows, for each age, the total number of men living at the beginning of the year.
- *Column 4* shows, for each age, the total number of men expected to die at that age.

In this table, the group of men aged 65 begins the year with 100,000 members. From statistics insurers have gathered about expected mortality, actuaries have been able to estimate that 1,100 of the original 100,000 men aged 65 are expected to die before they reach age 66.

Calculating the Mortality Rate

Mortality rates are often expressed in terms of deaths per thousand lives. We can convert this mortality information to a mortality rate by dividing the number dying at age 65 (column 4) into the number living at age 65 at the beginning of the year (column 3). Thus, to find the mortality rate for our mortality data, we could divide 1,100 by 100,000, for a result of 0.011. According to our table, 11 out of every 1,000 men will die after attaining age 65 but before attaining age 66.

Calculating the Survival Rate

Mortality tables also permit us to find survival rates for each age. Referring back to the mortality table, if you go down to the row of numbers for age 66, you will see that 98,900 men from the group depicted in the mortality table are expected to survive to age 66. We can find this number of survivors by subtracting the 1,100 deaths from the original 100,000 lives, as follows:

$$100{,}000 - 1{,}100 = 98{,}900$$

To find the number of men dying at age 66, we must find the tabular mortality rate for age 66, which is equal to 12 per thousand. When we multiply the mortality rate of 12 per thousand by 98,900—the number living at age 66—the result is 1,187 men. Thus, the mortality rate of 12 per thousand indicates that 1,187 of the 98,900 men living at age 66 are expected to die before reaching age 67.

To find the number of men surviving to age 67, we can begin with the number of men reaching age 66 and subtract the number of men dying at age 66, as follows:

Number living, age 66		Number dying, age 66		Number living, age 67
↓		↓		↓
98,900	–	1,187	=	97,713

Although here we show only an excerpt from this table, the full table shows mortality rates through age 115. By age 115, the last men in the original group of 100,000 can be expected to die. Thus, you can follow the progression of the mortality table from age 65 to age 115. Although this mortality table concludes at age 115, other mortality tables may conclude at a lower or higher age. Although some people actually live beyond the age of 115, the number of people living beyond that age is statistically insignificant.

An insurer uses several types of mortality tables, and it chooses which mortality table to use depending upon

- The product type being developed
- The purpose of the calculation it is undertaking calculating

- The characteristics of the population being studied
- The availability of appropriate statistics based on the insurance company's own experience

PRODUCT-DIFFERENTIATED MORTALITY TABLES

Insurers must predict the cost of benefits using the most appropriate data available for a product type. Accordingly, insurers use morbidity data showing incidences of sicknesses for health insurance calculations; for disability products, insurers use morbidity data from continuance tables; and for life insurance and annuity product calculations, insurers use mortality data. However, insurers do not use the same sets of mortality data for life insurance as they use for annuities.

Purchasers of life insurance and annuity products exhibit different mortality patterns. Because annuitants tend to live longer than life insureds, insurers use lower mortality rates for annuity product design than for life insurance rate making. Although medical underwriting is seldom used for annuity products, the purchase of an immediate annuity indicates the annuitant's confidence in his longevity.

Life expectancy, which is the number of years of life remaining for a group, is an important factor in calculating the cost of life annuities, and thus is a critical factor in technical annuity design. Demographers recognize a long-term trend of increased life expectancy for the population as a whole. This trend represents a decrease in risk for issuers of life insurance, but an increase in risk for issuers of annuities. Because of increasing longevity, issuers of life annuities must expect to provide increasing periods of annuity payments under life annuities.

Finally, an insurer might use different sets of mortality data for different annuity products. For example, insurers often use lower mortality rates for individual annuities than they use for group annuities, because annuitants of individual annuities tend to live longer than annuitants of group annuities.

BASIC AND VALUATION MORTALITY TABLES

Two of the most important uses insurers have for annuity mortality tables are (1) forecasting the cost of a product's benefit payments and (2) calculating the amount of the statutory reserves. In the United States, insurers use different mortality tables for calculating statutory reserves than they use for technical product design and for setting purchase rates for immediate annuity products with life contingencies.

Mortality Tables for Technical Product Design

The mortality tables that are used for technical design of annuity products are known as ***basic mortality tables,*** which are mortality tables with no safety margin built into the rates. Basic mortality tables are inherently less conservative than statutory reserve valuation tables. Basic mortality tables are designed to provide realistic mortality rates so that an insurer can design annuity products to reflect the mortality costs most likely to occur.

As mentioned in Chapter 7, the basic mortality table most widely used for annuities is the SOA's *1983 Basic Table.* The SOA has developed a newer table for annuities, but to date it has not come into widespread use.

Mortality Tables for Reserves

Statutory policy reserves are reserves calculated to satisfy the requirements of state insurance regulators. The mortality tables used to calculate statutory policy reserves are called ***valuation mortality tables***, and these tables are considered to be conservative because they have a safety margin built into their rates. This safety margin, which for life annuities consists of a lower-than-expected mortality rate, is intended to ensure that, even under adverse conditions, insurers will be able to pay benefits as they become due.

SEX-DISTINCT AND UNISEX MORTALITY TABLES

Mortality tables can be constructed on a sex-distinct or unisex basis. Actual mortality rates and life expectancies differ by gender: on the average, women live longer than men. Thus, insurers generally must pay life annuity benefits to females as a group for a longer period than to males as a group.

The mortality rate of females at any given age—up to the end of a mortality table—is lower than that for males. Mortality rates of both males and females start high at birth and then decrease dramatically at age 1. Mortality rates for both genders steadily decrease until about age 10. Mortality rates of females then increase steadily until old age. However, mortality rates for males begin to climb sharply during the teenage years, then drop again in the mid-twenties, and begin to rise again in the early thirties. Finally, in old age, the mortality rates of both males and females accelerate sharply with each passing year. Figure 10-2 shows the different mortality curves for men and women.

Sex-Distinct Mortality Tables

Sex-distinct mortality tables, also known as *gender-based mortality tables,* are mortality tables that show different mortality rates for males and females. Annuity premium rates based on sex-distinct mortality rates are

FIGURE 10.2

Mortality Curves for Men and Women.

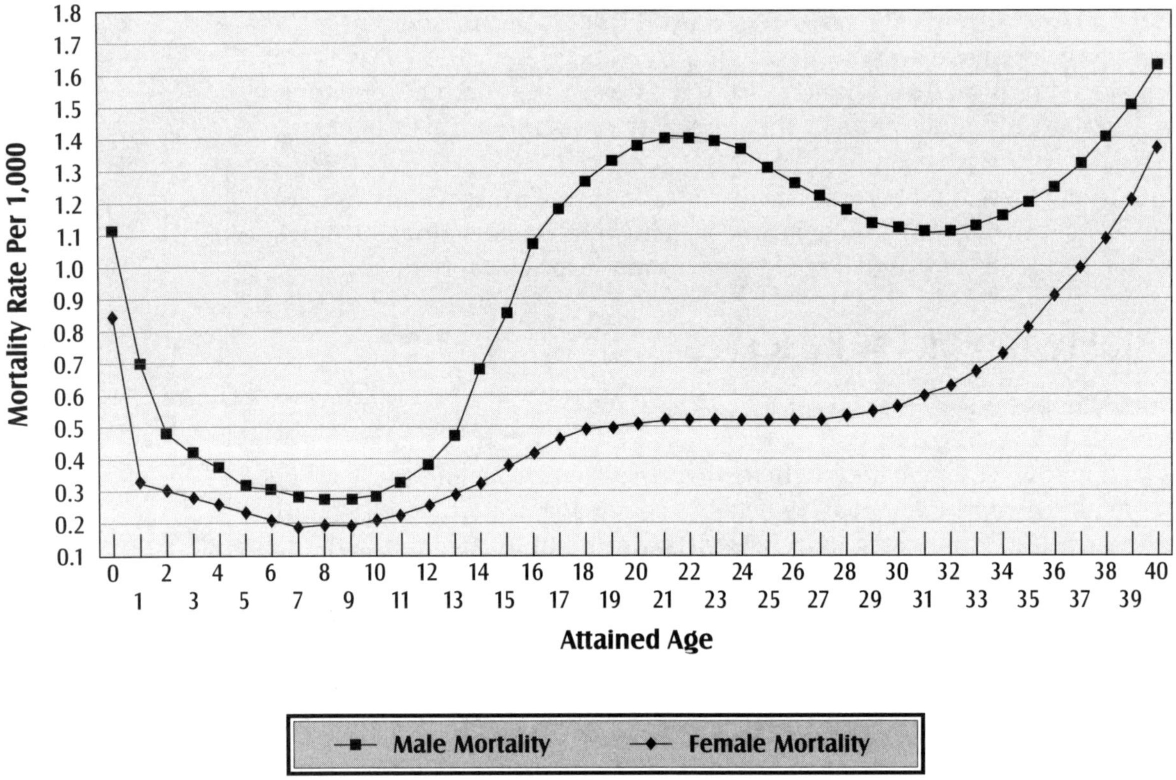

generally higher for females than for males having otherwise similar characteristics. Insurers sometimes compensate for female annuitants' lower mortality rates—and longer life expectancy—by charging female annuitants higher premium rates than they charge male annuitants having otherwise similar characteristics.

Unisex Mortality Tables

Unisex mortality tables are mortality tables that show a single set of mortality rates to be used for both males and females. When an insurer uses unisex mortality tables, men and women of the same age are charged the same rates for the same types of coverage.

For several reasons, most retirement products are based on unisex mortality rates. First, law in the United States prohibits the use of sex-distinct mortality rates in connection with employer-sponsored benefits. Second, in recent years, insurers have received public pressure to charge the same rates for both females and males. Third, the legislatures and courts are examining whether the use of sex-distinct rates is a form of unlawful discrimination on the basis of sex. Finally, some jurisdictions have enacted

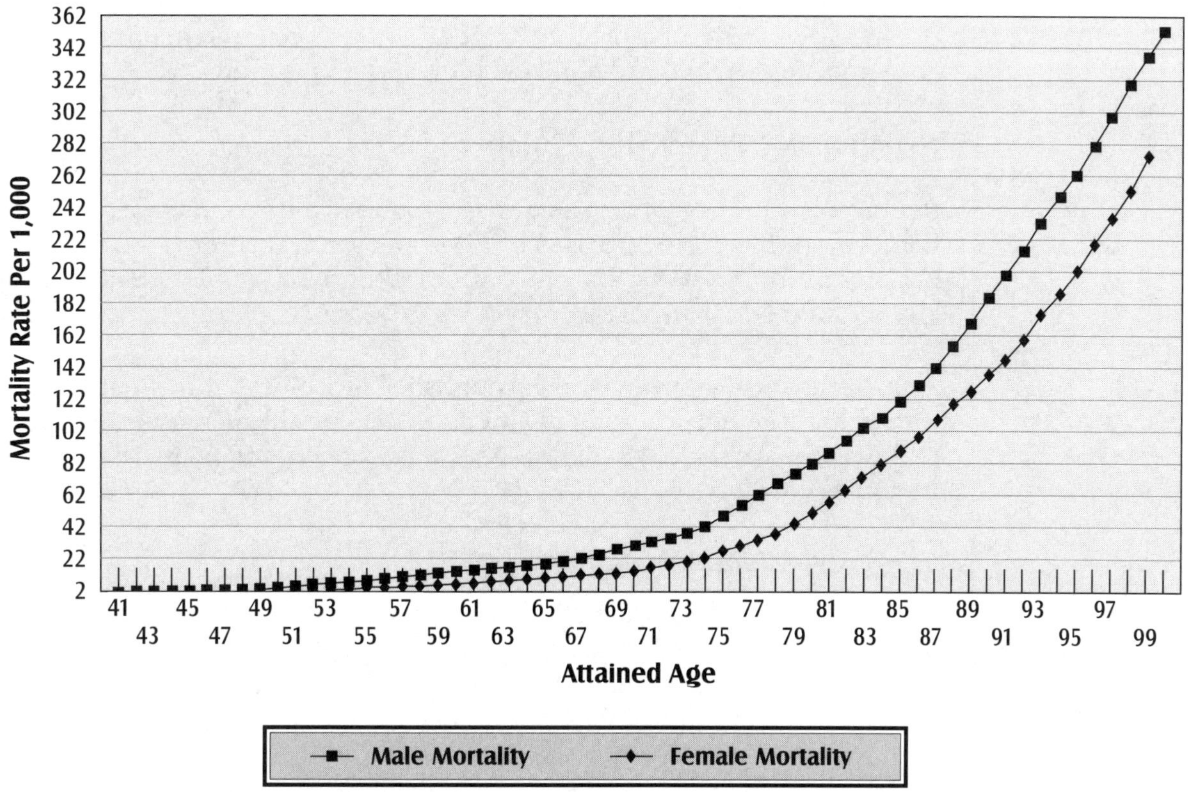

laws requiring that insurers charge the same rates for both men and women for some product types.

Proprietary and Published Mortality Tables

Insurers use both proprietary and published mortality tables. The mortality tables a single insurance company develops, based largely on its experience with its own customers, are known as ***proprietary mortality tables***. Through the coordination of the National Association of Insurance Commissioners (NAIC), the insurance industry's overall mortality experience can be published. ***Published mortality tables***, also called *public mortality tables*, are mortality tables that are made available to the general public through printed documents and electronic sources.

Proprietary Mortality Tables

In general, larger insurers are more likely to develop proprietary tables than are smaller insurers. Smaller insurers may not have sufficient experience with their own insureds and typically may not possess adequate resources to perform the necessary mortality studies to produce reliable mortality data. Larger insurers, on the other hand, generally prefer to construct proprietary mortality tables for use in rate making. Typically, insurers that use proprietary basic mortality tables use them for rate making. Proprietary mortality tables are not used for reserve valuations.

Published Mortality Tables

Published mortality tables can be basic tables or valuation tables, and published mortality tables are used by large and small insurers for calculating net premiums, reserves, and cash values. Proprietary tables are not generally used for such purposes.

Among the most commonly used published mortality tables are the statutory valuation tables compiled and published by the Society of Actuaries at the request of the NAIC. The SOA's statutory annuity valuation mortality tables currently in use are the

1. *1983 Table a*
2. *1983 Group Annuity Mortality (GAM)*

The SOA has developed new *Annuity 2000* mortality tables showing longer life expectancies. These tables are gradually coming into use in a few states.

As we mentioned earlier in this chapter, some published mortality tables are basic tables. Excerpts of the SOA's *1983 Basic Table* appear in Figure 10-3.

Figure 10-4 summarizes the characteristics of various mortality tables we have discussed.

MODIFYING TABULAR MORTALITY RATES

Most mortality tables are based on past data, which has not always kept pace with recent dramatic increases in human life spans, and which failed to caution insurers of the AIDS epidemic that reduced life spans for some portions of the population. Thus, mortality tables based on experience alone generally provide inaccurate predictions of future mortality. Insurers often modify tabular mortality rates using either a projection method or a setback method.

Projection Method

Using the projection method, the analyst multiplies the mortality rates found in a mortality table by a chosen percentage. For example, the insurer could multiply the rate found in the table by 95 percent or 110 percent. If the insurer expects people in the specified group to live longer than the

FIGURE 10.3

1983 Basic Table.

Deaths per thousand.

Age	Males	Females	Age	Males	Females	Age	Males	Females
65	14.248	8.241	**85**	101.261	72.368	**105**	440.707	378.434
66	15.761	9.114	**86**	110.424	81.137	**106**	477.634	412.352
67	17.467	10.012	**87**	119.894	90.907	**107**	518.120	451.160
68	19.373	10.931	**88**	129.609	101.721	**108**	562.412	495.376
69	21.486	11.916	**89**	139.643	113.454	**109**	610.761	545.521
70	23.810	13.027	**90**	150.099	125.936	**110**	663.417	602.115
71	26.353	14.326	**91**	161.082	138.997	**111**	720.626	665.676
72	29.120	15.872	**92**	172.699	152.469	**112**	782.640	736.725
73	32.123	17.717	**93**	185.049	166.187	**113**	849.708	815.782
74	35.398	19.883	**94**	198.219	180.008	**114**	922.077	903.367
75	38.986	22.383	**95**	212.291	193.111	**115**	1000.00	1000.00
76	42.930	25.228	**96**	227.346	207.411			
77	47.272	28.433	**97**	243.467	220.718			
78	52.054	32.017	**98**	260.903	234.236			
79	57.325	36.029	**99**	279.903	248.485			
80	63.132	40.525	**100**	300.716	263.985			
81	69.523	45.561	**101**	323.592	281.255			
82	76.547	51.194	**102**	348.780	300.815			
83	84.229	57.483	**103**	376.529	323.185			
84	92.498	64.512	**104**	407.088	348.885			

Source: Reprinted with permission from "Report of the Committee to Recommend a New Mortality Basis for Individual Annuity Valuation (Derivation of the 1983 Table a)," *Transactions of the Society of Actuaries* XXXIII (1981): 695. Copyright 1982 by the Society of Actuaries.

tabular rates indicate, the proper adjustment to tabular mortality rates would be to multiply the tabular rates by a factor smaller than 100 percent. However, if the insurer expects people in the specified group to die sooner than the tabular rates indicate, the proper adjustment to tabular mortality rates would be to multiply the rates by a factor greater than 100 percent. The mortality rates used for annuities must be adjusted to show a projection for any future improvements in mortality. Tables that have been adjusted using the projection method are called ***mortality tables with projection***, in contrast with ***static mortality tables***—mortality tables that have not been adjusted in this manner.

Setback Method

Under the setback method of modifying tabular mortality rates, insurers can show future improvements in mortality for annuitants of a given age by using the tabular mortality rate for a younger age. For example, if an insurer chooses to use a two-year setback to tabular mortality for age 35, the insurer would use the tabular mortality rate for age 33. A setback from age 35 to age 33 is a two-year setback, because it uses an age two years earlier than the attained age. When using an age setback, insurers typically use values of one to five years to allow for future improvements in the mortality of annuitants. Generally, insurers avoid using a large setback, because a large setback could create distortions of the mortality curve.

FIGURE 10.4

Types of Mortality Tables.

Type	Purpose, Characteristics
Population mortality tables	Show mortality data for the population as a whole or for a cross-section of the general population
Annuity mortality tables	Show mortality data for a population consisting of annuitants only; show lower mortality rates than do life insurance mortality tables
Life insurance mortality tables	Show mortality data for a population consisting of life insureds only
Basic mortality tables	Show realistic mortality rates; can be used for rate making
Valuation mortality tables	Show conservative mortality rates; are used to calculate reserves
Unisex mortality tables	Show mortality data for groups consisting of males and females, whereas sex-distinct mortality tables show separate mortality rates for males and females
Published mortality tables	Are available to the public and are based on the mortality of the public at large or the general insured population
Proprietary mortality tables	Are insurers' private tables; based on the mortality of each insurer's own insureds
Mortality tables with projection	Tables that have been adjusted by the projection method to show future mortality improvements
Static mortality tables	Show mortality rates that have not been adjusted to provide for future mortality improvements

MORTALITY RATES AND ANNUITY CONVERSION COSTS

As discussed in Chapter 2, when a deferred annuity reaches maturity, the contract owner can convert the annuity's accumulation value to an immediate life annuity. For converting a deferred annuity contract's accumulation value to an immediate life annuity, the factor that the insurer uses for establishing the amount of the periodic income payments available in exchange for the contract's accumulation value is the annuity conversion cost. We can look at annuity conversion costs to demonstrate how mortality rates affect the costs for annuitants of different ages.

In general, the higher the mortality rate is for a group of annuitants of the same age and gender, the lower the annuity conversion cost will be for annuity coverage issued to that group. Conversely, the lower the mortality rate is for a group of annuitants of the same age and gender, the higher the annuity conversion cost will be for annuity coverage issued to that group. Figure 10-5 shows mortality rates and annuity conversion cost factors for men aged 65 to 69.

FIGURE 10.5

Mortality Rates and Annuity Conversion Costs.

Mortality Rate per 1,000 Lives	Men	Annuity Conversion Cost *
	Age	
17.405	65	$10.53
18.767	66	$10.28
20.290	67	$10.03
21.992	68	$9.77
23.890	69	$9.50

**Annuity conversion cost* represents the actuarial present value of periodic income payments of $1 per period.

In Figure 10-5, we can see that the insurer charges a higher annuity conversion cost to provide an annuity benefit of $1 to men with a lower mortality rate than to men with a higher mortality rate. Men aged 65 have a lower mortality rate—and correspondingly higher expected longevity—than do men aged 69. Men aged 65, with a mortality rate of 17.405 per 1,000, pay a higher annuity conversion cost than do men aged 69, with a mortality rate of 23.890 per 1,000.

THE MORTALITY MARGIN

An annuity product's ***mortality margin*** is the excess of the insurer's actual mortality experience over the assumed mortality used in rate making for the product—for example, in calculating annuity conversion costs. A positive mortality margin can be viewed as a source of company profits. Thus, for life annuities, mortality profits increase as the actual mortality rates increase; correspondingly, mortality profits decrease as the actual mortality rates decrease. Insurers can build an expected mortality margin into a life annuity product design by setting an assumed mortality rate that is lower than the actual mortality rate. Building an expected mortality margin into a product's technical design creates a safety margin that may help the insurer meet its benefit obligations if actual mortality rates turn out to be lower than assumed.

Although an insurer can build an assumed mortality margin into a product's technical design, the actual mortality margin may be considerably different from the assumed margin. Insurers can attempt to build a mortality margin into an annuity's technical design in a number of ways:

- **Using a conservative mortality table**. A conservative annuity mortality table understates expected mortality, and thereby overstates the corresponding life expectancy. To create a mortality margin, an insurer can use a lower-than-expected mortality rate assumption in an annuity product's technical design.

- **Using a multiple of the expected mortality rate**. In designing an annuity contract, an insurer might create a mortality margin by using 90 percent of the expected tabular mortality rate. This method is consistent with the projection method of modifying tabular mortality rates.
- **Adding a flat amount to the product's mortality charge**. If a product's annuity conversion cost based on expected mortality is $12.50, then the insurer might create a mortality margin by adding a charge of $0.25 and using an annuity conversion cost of $12.75.

KEY TERMS AND CONCEPTS

expected mortality
tabular mortality rate
mortality experience
population mortality table
annuity mortality table
life expectancy
basic mortality table
valuation mortality table
sex-distinct mortality table
unisex mortality table
proprietary mortality table
published mortality table
mortality table with projection
static mortality table
mortality margin

CHAPTER 11

Annuity Reserves and Cash Surrender Values

After studying this chapter, you should be able to

- Distinguish among contractual reserves, noncontractual reserves, modified reserves, net reserves, gross reserves, and several other types of reserves
- Recognize the types of actuarial assumptions that create conservative values for reserves
- Identify the benefits and drawbacks of conservative reserving practices
- Recognize the importance of the Standard Valuation Law and the Commissioners' Annuity Reserve Valuation Method (CARVM)
- Recognize features of the policy premium method (PPM) used for setting reserve amounts in Canada
- Recognize how annuity cash surrender values are calculated

In this chapter, we discuss reserves for annuities. Generally, reserve values are closely related to an annuity contract's accumulation value. In addition, a deferred annuity contract's accumulation value, with a few adjustments, is used to determine the annuity contract's cash surrender value. Because these values are closely related to the values of annuity reserves, we also discuss annuity cash surrender values in this chapter.

Reserves make up most of an insurer's liabilities. For some annuity contracts, determining the amount of the reserve liabilities that an insurer needs to set aside to meet future business obligations is a relatively straightforward process. However, the amount of other future business obligations—for example, obligations for annuity benefits subject to life contingencies—is not known precisely in advance. Where the exact amount of the future obligation is not known in advance, the insurer's actuaries must set reasonable reserve amounts by identifying and consistently applying the proper (1) values for actuarial assumptions, (2) reserve valuation methods, and (3) procedures for ensuring reasonable values for reserves.

Reserve valuations are formal calculations of reserve values. Reserve values are critical to the usefulness of the information a life insurer generates about its financial strength and performance. Within a life insurer's financial reporting system, reserve values are important for the following reasons:

1. Reserve values are developed using a degree of estimation.
2. Reserve values represent the vast majority of an insurance company's liabilities.
3. Reserve values strongly influence the values of published measures of an insurance company's overall solvency and profitability.

In Chapter 7, we saw that an annuity product's asset-share calculation employs a balance-sheet format as a useful model for the operation of the product. Surplus for an insurance company is also found by subtracting liabilities from assets, as shown:

Assets – Liabilities = Surplus

In regard to assets, liabilities, and surplus, we can view an annuity product's assets at a given time as being more or less equal to the product's collected premiums plus accumulated interest earnings. The annuity product's liability is the annuity reserve. Thus, the product's surplus is the difference between the product's assets and its reserves.

CONTRACTUAL AND NONCONTRACTUAL RESERVES

Insurers have several types of contractual and noncontractual reserves. ***Contractual reserves*** are liabilities that identify the amount that, together with future premiums and interest earnings, represents the expected amount of future benefits payable on an insurer's in-force business. Thus, contractual reserves represent the insurer's obligations to customers. Contractual reserves for annuities are the largest segment of contractual reserves for U.S. life insurers. In this chapter, we describe contractual reserves for annuities in terms of their purpose and methods of calculation.

Reserve valuation can be applied to a block of business, a specific product, a contract, or a unit of coverage. For most purposes, reserves are calculated for a block of contracts. The reserves for a block of contracts, a line of business, or an entire company are sometimes called aggregate reserves.

We can refer to all types of reserves that are not contractual as ***noncontractual reserves***. Although contractual reserves make up the largest share of all reserves, several types of noncontractual reserves represent insurers' business obligations that are not directly attributable to paying benefits for a specified product. Three types of noncontractual reserves are defined as follows:

- ***Contingency reserves*** are voluntary, noncontractual reserves that supply added reserve protection against various special categories of risk, usually related to the C-1 through C-4 risks that we discussed in Chapter 4. On an insurer's balance sheet, contingency reserves differ from other reserves in that they represent surplus, not liabilities.
- ***Asset fluctuation reserves*** are noncontractual reserves that are designed to absorb short-term fluctuations in the gains and losses affecting an insurer's invested assets. These reserves allow the effects of short-term investment gains and losses to be reflected only gradually in capital and surplus.
- ***Supplemental reserves*** are usually noncontractual reserves established, often voluntarily, for the purpose of strengthening required reserves. Insurers might establish supplemental reserves after adverse experience shows that the original assumptions used in a product's design were overly optimistic.

TYPES OF ACCOUNTING RECORDS

In addition to maintaining various contractual and noncontractual reserves, insurers operating in the United States must calculate each reserve for several different purposes. Insurers operating in the United States must keep different sets of accounting records for different purposes. These various sets of accounting records typically include statutory accounting records, generally accepted accounting principles (GAAP) accounting records, internal (modified GAAP) accounting records, and tax accounting records. These sets of accounting records give rise to reserves that are respectively labeled (1) statutory (required) reserves, (2) GAAP reserves, (3) internal (modified GAAP) reserves, and (4) tax reserves. Each set of accounting records meets a distinct need for financial reporting, as follows:

- ***Statutory accounting records*** in the United States are designed for financial reporting to state insurance regulators, whose primary interest is in evaluating insurance companies' long-term financial stability. For calculating U.S. statutory reserves, each state sets guidelines based on the NAIC's model laws. As we will discuss later in the chapter, statutory annuity reserves are governed by the NAIC's Standard Valuation Law and the method of calculating reserves that these laws prescribe—the Commissioners' Annuity Reserve Valuation Method (CARVM). In Canada, one set of GAAP accounting practices applies to all required accounting records, and statutory accounting records do not exist.
- ***GAAP accounting records*** are designed for financial reporting to investors and the public at large, and these records focus on showing the company's financial stability along with its profitability. GAAP accounting in the United States differs considerably from GAAP accounting in Canada. To distinguish the two from each other, we refer to U.S. GAAP and Canadian GAAP. An organization known as the Financial Accounting Standards Board (FASB) sets guidelines for U.S. GAAP, with significant participation from the Securities and Exchange Commission (SEC). The guidelines for determining U.S. GAAP reserves for most fixed-rate and variable annuity products are specified in Financial Accounting Standard (FAS) 97. For Canada, GAAP accounting records are used for reporting to insurance regulators.
- ***Internal accounting records***, also known as *modified GAAP accounting records*, are designed for financial reporting to company management, whose main interest is in having appropriate data for making sound decisions. For internal accounting purposes, each insurer freely makes its own desired modifications to standard U.S. GAAP. Most insurers believe that their internal accounting system produces the most realistic picture of their financial situation.
- ***Tax accounting records*** are designed for financial reporting to federal and state or provincial taxing authorities. Tax issues, including tax reserves, are outside of the scope of our discussion.

For much of our discussion, differences among the accounting systems will be irrelevant. However, when appropriate, we will discuss specific requirements affecting specific sets of reserves. We will not cover internal reserves or tax reserves but instead will limit our coverage to U.S. GAAP, U.S. statutory, and Canadian statutory reserves. Figure 11-1 summarizes our discussion of United States accounting records and annuity reserves.

FIGURE 11.1

U.S. Accounting Records and Their Audiences.

	Primary Audience	Reserve Type Used
U.S. Statutory Accounting	Insurance regulators	U.S. statutory reserves
U.S. GAAP Accounting	Potential investors	U.S. GAAP reserves
Internal Accounting	Company managers	Internal reserves
Tax Basis Accounting	Taxing authorities	Tax reserves

Annuity reserve valuation varies depending upon the following factors:

- Whether an annuity product is in its accumulation period or its payout period
- Whether an annuity reserve valuation is designed for statutory or GAAP accounting records
- How much conservatism is reflected in the annuity reserve valuation
- How an annuity reserve takes into consideration the problem of surplus strain in the product's early years

CONSERVATISM IN ANNUITY RESERVES

Conservatism in annuity reserves results in maintaining larger reserves. The larger and more conservative an insurer's reserves, the more protection the reserves provide against adverse deviations in experience and the possibility that the insurer could become insolvent. Conservative reserve valuations are derived by using actuarial assumptions that are generally less favorable to the insurance company than the expected (realistic) values. However, one drawback of conservative reserves is that they can limit an insurer's prospects for profitability and growth.

Conservative reserving typically improves an insurer's quality rating from the insurance rating agencies. An ***insurance rating agency*** is an independently owned, private organization that evaluates the financial condition of insurers and provides information to potential customers of and investors in insurance companies. A ***quality rating*** is an alphabetical grade or rating assigned to an insurance company by an insurance rating agency to indicate the level of the insurance company's financial strength, its ability to pay its obligations to customers, or its ability to pay its obligations to creditors. A strong quality rating can improve the insurer's competitive position, because customers generally prefer doing business with a highly rated insurer.

On the other hand, conservative reserving can damage an insurer's competitive position by forcing up charges for the insurer's products. An insurer may need to set relatively high contract charges in order to cover the amount of reserves it chooses to maintain. In addition, conservative reserving can hurt an insurer's competitive position by increasing the insurer's surplus strain from new business.

Insurers have considerable latitude in setting their reserve amounts. Consider the following examples:

- U.S. GAAP annuity reserves for fixed annuity products are based entirely on insurers' chosen actuarial assumptions, provided that these assumptions produce reserves that meet statutory minimum standards.
- U.S. statutory requirements set the minimum size of insurers' statutory policy reserves but do not specify any maximum limitations.
- U.S. statutory requirements give insurers complete discretion in choosing actuarial assumptions for some types of noncontractual reserves.
- For all types of annuity reserves in Canada, insurers have complete discretion in choosing actuarial assumptions.

Each insurer must adopt appropriate reserving practices based on its circumstances and its business objectives. Figure 11-2 summarizes the potential benefits and drawbacks of maintaining conservative reserves.

FIGURE 11.2

Conservative Reserves.

Conservative annuity reserves can lead to . . .

Benefits	**Drawbacks**
Greater protection against insolvency	Lower crediting rates for fixed annuities
Higher quality ratings	Higher charges for variable annuities
	Lower annuity contract sales
	Increased surplus strain

An insurer sometimes decides that reserves for an existing product are inadequate, and might then decide to increase its reserves to protect its quality rating or its solvency. In such a situation, the insurer can engage in ***reserve strengthening***—which is increasing the amount of its reserves. Reserve strengthening, which can serve a number of business purposes, is usually applied to a specific block of contracts. Insurers can strengthen reserves by using actuarial assumptions that are less favorable to the company than those used in the original reserve valuation. To strengthen annuity reserves, an insurer could recalculate the reserves using lower interest-rate or mortality-rate assumptions.

If reserves are too conservative, a U.S. insurer may obtain regulatory permission for ***reserve destrengthening***—reducing the amount of its reserves. However, insurers rarely destrengthen their contractual reserves.

Actuarial Assumptions and Annuity Reserves

Subject to regulatory limitations, an insurer chooses the values for the actuarial assumptions used in setting policy reserves. These actuarial assumptions include the assumed values for interest rates, mortality rates, and lapse rates on which the insurer bases its reserves and its product design. The insurer's chosen actuarial assumptions determine the level of the insurer's reserves.

U.S. GAAP generally does not permit insurers to change the original reserves or the original reserving assumptions for fixed annuity products. Furthermore, U.S. GAAP usually does not permit insurers to alter their reserving assumptions after a contract has been issued. However, recall that insurers can voluntarily strengthen their reserves if the original reserve assumptions turn out to be inadequate. Figure 11-3 summarizes some essential differences between actuarial assumptions used in U.S. statutory reserves and U.S. GAAP reserves.

Interest-Rate Assumptions

An interest-rate assumption represents the net investment earnings on a product, regardless of the source of those earnings. Although the investment earnings on fixed-rate annuity products are actually expressed as interest earnings, the investment earnings on variable annuity products may take other forms of earnings than interest. The interest-rate assumption reflects investment earnings after any administrative expenses of investing have been covered. The effect of the interest-rate assumption on the value of annuity reserves depends upon whether the product is in the accumulation period or the payout period.

- In the accumulation period, the higher the interest rate used to calculate annuity reserves, the higher the reserves will be. In general,

FIGURE 11.3

Actuarial Assumptions Used in U.S. Annuity Reserves.

The table below compares the U.S. statutory and U.S. GAAP treatments of various actuarial assumptions that affect annuity reserves.

	U.S. Statutory Annuity Reserves Use	U.S. GAAP Annuity Reserves Use
Mortality Tables	Valuation mortality tables having a built-in safety margin	Basic mortality tables, often the same as those used in pricing
Assumed Values	Specified conservative assumed values	Realistic assumed values, often the same as those used in product pricing models
Expense Assumptions	No expense assumptions	Realistic expense assumptions
Margin Assumptions (Provision for Adverse Deviation)	No margin assumptions, except for any safety margin built into the mortality rates	Some margin assumptions, where appropriate

for the accumulation period, the level of the interest rate used to calculate reserves is directly related to the reserve value.

- In the payout period, the higher the interest rate used to calculate annuity reserves, the lower the reserves will be. Generally, for the payout period, the level of the interest rate used to calculate reserves is inversely related to the reserve value.

Mortality-Rate Assumptions

For U.S. statutory annuity reserve valuations, insurers typically use the annuity mortality tables prescribed by the NAIC. If insurers meet all statutory limitations, however, they may choose other mortality assumptions. For annuity contracts in the payout period, the lower the mortality rates used to calculate annuity reserves, generally the larger the reserves will be. In other words, normally the assumed level of mortality rates for annuity contracts in the payout period and the level of total reserves are inversely related.

Contractual reserves are typically calculated using the mortality and interest-rate assumptions specified at contract issue, rather than the insurer's actual mortality and interest experience. However, the insurer can create additional voluntary reserves to strengthen its reserves.

Lapse-Rate Assumptions

As we discussed in Chapter 2, a lapse rate is a measure of the percentage of contracts that are voluntarily terminated in a given year. As discussed in Chapters 2 and 7, a lapse-rate assumption is a value assigned to the percentage of contracts that will be voluntarily terminated in future years for a given group of products. For our purpose of discussing aggregate annuity contract reserves, lapses can be considered the same as withdrawals of funds from a deferred annuity contract. Lapse-rate assumptions can affect only GAAP reserve valuations. U.S. statutory annuity reserve calculations are not permitted to include a lapse-rate assumption.

The level of total contractual GAAP reserves is normally inversely related to the level of the lapse-rate assumption applied in designing the product. In other words, for the accumulation period of most deferred annuity products, a higher lapse-rate assumption normally produces a lower annuity reserve. Figure 11-4 shows how specified changes in values of different actuarial assumptions can render a reserve larger or smaller.

FIGURE 11.4

Effects of Actuarial Assumptions on Annuity Reserves.

Actuarial Assumption	Reserve will be LARGER if the assumed value is	Reserve will be SMALLER if the assumed value is
• Interest rate—accumulation period	increased	decreased
• Interest rate—payout period	decreased	increased
• Mortality rate—payout period, if life contingencies are involved	decreased	increased
• Lapse rate—accumulation period, where withdrawals and surrenders are assumed, usual effect for GAAP reserves	decreased	increased

METHODS FOR ADDRESSING SURPLUS STRAIN

In an annuity product's first year, high costs of contract issue, sales commissions, and the creation of new reserves cause a negative first-year surplus. This negative surplus is an aspect of surplus strain. The approaches insurers use for spreading out the accounting impact of surplus strain differ for U.S. statutory and U.S. GAAP accounting. In brief, U.S. statutory accounting provides for adjusting contractual reserves to produce reserves known as modified reserves, but it does not provide for any adjustment to assets. Under U.S. GAAP, insurers spread out the impact of first-year expenses on surplus by means of an asset account known as deferred acquisition cost (DAC), without making any adjustment to reserve liabilities. Figure 11-5 summarizes our discussion of how statutory and U.S. GAAP reporting attempt to relieve the problem of surplus strain.

Modified Reserves for U.S. Statutory Reporting

A ***reserve valuation method*** is an approach for calculating reserve amounts. For U.S. statutory annuity reserve valuation, insurers can relieve surplus

FIGURE 11.5

Addressing Surplus Strain for U.S. Reporting Purposes.

	U.S. Reporting Basis	
	Statutory	**GAAP**
Adjustment Mechanism	Modified reserves	Deferred acquisition cost (DAC)
Balance Sheet Item Adjusted	Statutory reserves	GAAP assets

strain by using modified reserve valuation methods, which produce lower first-year statutory reserves than do unmodified level reserving methods. A ***modified reserve valuation method*** is a way of calculating reserves that permits an insurer to set a lower-than-level first-year statutory contractual reserve in recognition of the surplus strain from first-year expenses. The first-year reserve adjustment then affects the statutory reserve values for all subsequent years. A reserve developed using a modified reserve valuation method is known as a ***modified reserve***. It is important to note that modified reserve valuation methods are not designed to achieve reserve strengthening or destrengthening.

Deferred Acquisition Costs for U.S. GAAP

U.S. GAAP limits surplus strain by permitting insurers to spread out, in a process known as amortization, the reporting of annuity contract acquisition and issue expenses over several years. At the same time, in order to keep their GAAP accounts balanced, insurers must create an asset account called ***deferred acquisition cost (DAC)***. DAC is an asset account established to enable insurers to spread out the impact on surplus of first-year expenses such as acquisition expenses and issue expenses. Then, the negative impact on surplus is applied in subsequent years. Note that DAC is not a tool for achieving reserve strengthening or destrengthening.

Because of the presence of DAC, when analysts use GAAP financial statements to evaluate an insurer's strength, they typically adjust GAAP reserves for DAC to produce a measure known as net GAAP reserves. ***Net GAAP reserves*** equal the insurer's reported GAAP reserves minus DAC, as shown:

Net GAAP reserves = GAAP reserves – Deferred acquisition costs

Net GAAP reserves are similar to modified statutory reserves in that both net GAAP reserves and modified statutory reserves represent the insurer's contractual reserve liabilities modified by an allowance to reflect the high cost of first-year expenses.

RESERVE VALUATION METHODS

Insurers use several approaches for calculating annuity reserves. A product's actual net cash flows, representing the company's final realized profit or loss on the product, will be the same in the end regardless of the reserve valuation method chosen. However, the chosen reserve valuation method can have a pronounced effect on the timing of a product's reported earnings.

Most reserve valuation methods used in the United States produce net reserves. Net reserves do not directly provide for loading. A ***net reserve valuation method*** is a method of computing reserves that does not take into consideration the insurer's product-related expenses. Reserves developed using a net reserve valuation method are sometimes known as ***net reserves***. ***Gross reserve valuation methods***, which make provision for the insurer's product-related expenses, are used in Canada but are not used for reported reserves in the United States. Reserves developed using a gross reserve valuation method are sometimes known as ***gross reserves***.

Insurers in the United States use two approaches to net level reserve valuation methods—(1) the prospective method and (2) the retrospective method. As used in the United States, the retrospective and prospective methods always yield the same reserve amount when applied to the same valuation problem and when using the same actuarial assumptions. Typically, the prospective method is used for the payout period and the retrospective method is used for the accumulation period.

- A ***prospective reserve valuation method*** for estimating a value for a reserve liability looks at a contract's *future* cash flows—its premiums and payments on behalf of contract owners. For most individual immediate annuities, which have no future premiums, the prospective reserve is equal to the present value of future periodic income payments, as expressed in the formula:

  Prospective annuity reserve, payout period =
  Present value of future periodic income payments

  This prospective annuity reserve formula is problematic for (1) annuities in the accumulation period and (2) annuity benefit streams that are not fixed in amount.

- A ***retrospective reserve valuation method*** for setting a value for a reserve liability looks at a contract's *past* cash flows—its past premiums and benefits. For most individual deferred annuities, which have no past periodic income payments, the retrospective reserve is equal to the present value of accumulated premiums, as expressed in the formula:

  Retrospective annuity reserve, accumulation period =
  Present value of accumulated premiums

ANNUITY RESERVES IN THE UNITED STATES

The different authorities that set the standards for the accounting systems discussed at the beginning of this chapter also set the standards for annuity reserves in the United States. In this section, we will discuss the reserving standards that apply under U.S. statutory and U.S. GAAP approaches to accounting. Under both of these accounting systems, the treatment of annuity contract reserves differs according to whether the annuities are in the accumulation period or the payout period.

Statutory Annuity Reserves

State regulations derived from NAIC model laws set standards for statutory reserve valuation practices. Insurers must hold actual statutory annuity reserves at least as large as those calculated using the minimum statutory reserve requirements. The NAIC model law that sets annuity reserving standards covering both the accumulation phase and the payout phase is the ***Standard Valuation Law***. The model law was amended in 1980 and again in 1990, and the laws in effect in most states reflect these amendments. The Standard Valuation Law (1) specifies a required reserve valuation method and (2) limits permissible actuarial assumptions for use in reserve valuations. The reserve valuation method that the Standard Valuation Law specifies for statutory valuations is the ***Commissioners' Annuity Reserve Valuation Method (CARVM)***. CARVM is properly classified as a net premium reserve valuation method, a modified reserve valuation method, and a prospective reserve valuation method. The Standard Valuation Law and CARVM set the following limits on U.S. statutory reserves:

- Minimum reserves
- Maximum interest-rate assumptions
- Permissible range of assumptions as to mortality rates
- Permissible mortality tables
- Permissible reserve valuation methods

The 1990 amendments to the Standard Valuation Law require insurers to file an actuarial opinion and memorandum verifying that an insurer's reserves and related actuarial items make adequate provision for the insurer's future cash flows required to cover expected contractual obligations and expenses. This requirement means that each affected insurer must perform extensive cash-flow testing. Under these amendments, insurers must meet statutory minimum standards for required reserves, but also could be required to hold added reserves if the company's appointed actuary believes the added reserves are needed.

Reserves During the Accumulation Period

For statutory annuity reserves in the United States, the Standard Valuation Law and CARVM set the required minimum reserve valuation formulas and set restrictive limits on the values permissible for the actuarial assumptions used in reserve valuations. CARVM requires insurers to calculate the excess of future benefits over future premiums for each potential benefit payment outflow under a deferred annuity contract. However, future premiums for most annuity types are equal to zero, so CARVM essentially requires the insurer to find only the values of future benefit payment outflows. Under CARVM, the minimum required statutory reserve for an annuity product in the accumulation period is equal to the largest of the calculated values for the various potential benefit payment outflows. Five types of potential benefit payment outflows for annuities in the accumulation period include the

1. Cash surrender value
2. Survivor benefit upon death of the annuitant
3. Periodic annuity income payments calculated as of the scheduled maturity date
4. Periodic annuity income payments calculated as of a date earlier than the scheduled maturity date
5. Partial withdrawals of the account balance prior to the scheduled maturity date

For deferred annuity products having the potential for all of these types of cash outflows, insurers must perform as many as five separate valuations, one for each of the possible benefit payment outflows. Then insurers must establish a statutory reserve at least equal to the greatest of these required valuations. Conveniently, several of these potential benefit outflows are linked in value to a contract's accumulation value, so that the minimum annuity reserve generally is close in value to a contract's accumulation value. In many cases, CARVM enables insurers to apply the accumulation values of deferred annuity contracts as the reserve value.

Reserves During the Payout Period

When an annuity contract enters the payout period, no further premiums will be paid into it. Thus, during the payout period, the U.S. statutory annuity reserve equals the actuarial present value of future periodic income payments, as shown below:

Statutory annuity reserve, payout period =
Actuarial present value of future periodic income payments

For annuity contracts in the payout period, the insurer calculates the actuarial present value of future periodic income payments with reference to a legally recognized mortality table and a legally permitted interest rate, the annuitant's attained age, the periodic income payment amount, and any minimum benefit guarantees. At the beginning of the payout period for these contracts, the amount of each periodic income payment is set based on (1) the single premium amount used to purchase the annuity and (2) an annuity conversion cost factor (or annuity purchase cost factor) for the annuitant's attained age. Under CARVM, reserve valuations for supplementary contracts and immediate annuities involving life contingencies apply the mortality and interest assumptions that were used in calculating these annuity conversion cost factors. Under CARVM, insurers do not need to value several different potential benefit streams for these contract types.

GAAP Annuity Reserves

As we discussed earlier in this chapter, U.S. GAAP standards for annuity reserving are set by the Financial Accounting Standards Board (FASB), with influence from the Securities and Exchange Commission (SEC). Under GAAP, insurers may use whatever mortality- and interest-rate assumptions reflect their best reasonable estimates. U.S. GAAP addresses surplus strain by the amortization of deferred acquisition costs (DAC). DAC is an asset account, and as such it does not affect the reserve liability calculation.

U.S. GAAP annuity reserves differ depending on whether an annuity product is in its accumulation period or its payout period.

- During an annuity product's accumulation period, the U.S. GAAP annuity reserve is essentially equal to the product's accumulation values.
- During an annuity product's payout period, the U.S. GAAP annuity reserve—like the statutory reserve for the payout period—is equal to the actuarial present value of future periodic income benefits.

Figure 11-6 summarizes the typical applications of minimum annuity reserve requirements for insurers in the United States.

FIGURE 11.6

U.S. Minimum Annuity Reserve Requirements.

	Statutory Reserve	GAAP Reserve
Accumulation Period	The largest of the calculated values for the various potential benefit payment outflows	Typically the product's accumulation values
Payout Period	The actuarial present value of future periodic income payments	The actuarial present value of future periodic income payments

Annuity Reserves in Canada

The methods used to calculate Canadian GAAP annuity reserves differ from the methods used to calculate the similar U.S. GAAP reserves. With Canadian GAAP, unlike with U.S. GAAP, an annuity's reserve during the accumulation period is not based on the customer's account value. Instead, insurers in Canada use scenario analysis, discussed earlier in Chapters 7 and 8, to predict the nature and amount of future benefits. Insurers then use the results of scenario analysis to calculate the present value of predicted future benefits. In brief, insurers in Canada

- Must use the policy premium method of reserve valuation
- Must use scenario analysis in setting contractual reserves for nonparticipating products
- Can change their actuarial assumptions every year to reflect their emerging experience and their new expectations for the future, and thus can destrengthen or strengthen reserves as needed without obtaining regulatory permission
- Must submit a qualified valuation actuary's formal certification that the reserve valuation conforms to professional standards of actuarial practice set by the Canadian Institute of Actuaries (CIA)

Policy Premium Method

The ***policy premium method (PPM)***, used by insurers in Canada, is a type of prospective gross level reserve valuation method. The PPM annuity reserve is equal to the difference between the present value of future benefits and the present value of future premiums. The following points about the PPM formula are noteworthy:

- The PPM formula includes a provision for loading. Thus, the value of future benefits under the PPM formula includes estimated future maintenance expenses and future excess interest credits.
- Canadian GAAP provides for future premiums for flexible premium contracts to be estimated using scenario analysis. The estimated future premiums are then used with the PPM to calculate policy reserves for these products.
- As we discussed earlier in this chapter, the PPM formula's reference to future premiums is irrelevant for single premium annuity contracts—SPIAs and SPDAs.

Scenario Analysis for Reserves

Insurers in Canada must use scenario analysis in developing reserves for nonparticipating annuity products. In scenario analysis for reserve valuation, an analyst develops numerous reserve calculations, or scenarios, for each product. Each scenario reflects a different set of actuarial assumptions for interest rates, mortality rates, and persistency rates. Guidelines provided by the CIA help insurers select the sets of actuarial assumptions used in scenario analysis for reserve valuations.

Scenario analysis helps insurers identify a likely range of values for a product's future experience. Insurers can then use this information to calculate a range of values for the reserves they need to maintain in order to safeguard their contractual obligations. Given a range of possible values for their reserves, insurers are expected to use conservative reserving practices and so are expected to select a reserve value near the high end of the identified range.

Before we proceed to our discussion of nonforfeiture values for deferred annuities, read Figure 11-7 to review definitions of some important types of reserves.

FIGURE 11.7

Reserve Types.

The following table summarizes the definitions of reserves that we have discussed in this chapter. These definitions are not mutually exclusive. For example, a specified reserve could properly be described as a contractual reserve, a modified reserve, a U.S. statutory reserve, and a net reserve.

Contractual reserves	Liabilities that identify the amount that, together with future premiums and interest earnings, represents the expected amount of future benefits payable on an insurer's in-force business
Noncontractual reserves	Reserves that are not contractual, including contingency reserves, asset fluctuation reserves, and supplemental reserves
Contingency reserves	Voluntary, noncontractual reserves that supply added reserve protection against various special categories of risk
Asset fluctuation reserves	Noncontractual reserves that are designed to absorb short-term fluctuations in the gains and losses affecting an insurer's invested assets
Supplemental reserves	Reserves established for the purpose of strengthening required reserves, usually on a voluntary basis
U.S. statutory reserves	Reserves established and reported according to the reporting requirements applicable to insurers operating in the United States
U.S. GAAP reserves	Reserves established and reported according to generally accepted accounting principles (GAAP) established by the Financial Accounting Standards Board for insurers operating in the United States
Internal reserves	Reserves—also known as modified GAAP reserves—established for an insurer's internal accounting purposes, and intended for use in management decisions, but not for publication
Tax reserves	Reserves established according to the requirements for tax reporting
Modified reserve	A reserve developed using a modified reserve valuation method
Net GAAP reserve	The insurer's reported GAAP reserves minus deferred acquisition costs
Net reserve	A reserve that does not take into consideration the insurer's expenses of issuing and supporting a contract, sometimes known as loading
Gross reserve	A reserve that takes into consideration the insurer's expenses of issuing and supporting a contract, sometimes known as loading

Nonforfeiture Values for Deferred Annuities

Any annuity contract has an accumulation value, also known as an account value. Insurers are required to provide cash surrender benefits for the accumulation period of deferred annuities in the United States. Canadian law does not require insurers in Canada to provide cash surrender values, although many insurers provide cash surrender values voluntarily. In the United States, insurers are not required to provide cash surrender benefits for annuities once the payout period begins. Currently, for the payout phase of contracts with life contingencies, annuity contracts typically do not permit cash surrenders. However, this feature of the payout phase seems to be extremely unattractive to deferred annuity customers, who are overwhelmingly reluctant to annuitize a deferred annuity contract. Insurers are responding to customer concerns by designing an annuity contract that offers the contract owner access to contract values once the payout phase has begun. Insight 11-1 discusses two adaptations that insurers have developed to address the reluctance of contract owners to annuitize.

During an annuity contract's accumulation period, the accumulation value is the amount paid for the contract minus load charges, plus investment

INSIGHT 11.1

Addressing Reluctance to Annuitize.

Most owners of deferred annuity contracts currently choose to withdraw their accumulation value in a lump sum upon a contract's maturity, partly out of reluctance to lose control over their account value as would happen under traditional annuity payout options. Insurers thus are offering arrangements that give annuity owners more flexibility than was available in the past.

Systematic Withdrawal Plans

Under one variable contract's systematic withdrawal program, the following conditions apply to the contract's subaccount values:

1. A series of automatic withdrawals are made at regular intervals on an annual, semiannual, quarterly, semi-monthly, or monthly basis.
2. A set dollar amount or a set percentage of contract accumulation value is withdrawn at each withdrawal date.
3. The minimum automatic withdrawal amount is $100.
4. A surrender charge applies to each withdrawal made while contract surrender fees would normally apply.
5. The withdrawal amount and any surrender charge is deducted from the contract's Fixed Account and Variable Subaccounts on a pro-rata basis.

Commutation Rights

In an annuity contract's payout period, a ***commutation right*** states that an annuity contract owner can withdraw a lump sum from the contract's remaining principal and from any growth of the principal of a variable contract, even while the contract owner is receiving annuity payments. If the contract owner exercises the commutation right, the withdrawal will reduce the present value of the contract and will accordingly reduce the amount of future annuity payments. Insurers sometimes offer a commutation right for annuities under settlement options that do not involve life contingencies.

earnings, less the amount of any partial withdrawals and lapse charges. The entire accumulation value of an annuity contract is generally available to the contract owner to purchase periodic annuity income benefits when the contract matures. Until a contract has been in force for a substantial number of years, however, withdrawals from or surrenders of the accumulation value often are subject to a surrender charge or penalty for withdrawal. The types of surrender charges or penalties vary considerably from one contract to another. Although surrender charge percentages are not directly related to the actual costs the insurer has incurred under the contract, the existence of any surrender charges is an attempt by the insurer to recover at least a portion of its excess expenses.

Deferred annuity contract owners can withdraw all or part of the funds from an annuity contract, by means of surrender or partial withdrawal, as follows:

- A ***surrender*** involves withdrawing the annuity contract's entire accumulation value, subject to an administrative fee and surrender charges, and thereby terminating the contract.
- A ***withdrawal***, also known as a *partial withdrawal* or *partial surrender*, of deferred annuity contract values occurs when a contract owner exercises the option to remove some, but not all, funds from the accumulation account. The withdrawal may be subject to an administrative charge and surrender charges.

A sample accumulation value provision, with surrender charge table, appears in Figure 11-8.

Cash Surrender Values in the United States

Insurers must provide nonforfeiture benefit provisions in deferred annuities during the accumulation period. A nonforfeiture benefit provision, required in individual deferred fixed annuity contracts, states that if the contract owner terminates the contract during the accumulation period, then the contract owner will receive a lump sum cash settlement in place of a future periodic income payment. The general formula for a deferred annuity cash surrender value is

Cash surrender value, deferred annuity =
Accumulation value – Any applicable surrender charge

For individual deferred annuity products in the United States, insurers must make available to a contract owner whose contract is surrendered a cash payment in the amount of the contract's accumulation value less any surrender charge. This payment is called the *surrender value, cash surrender value,* or *nonforfeiture value*. In the United States, regulations affecting deferred annuity minimum cash values are described in the ***Model Standard Nonforfeiture Law for Individual Deferred Annuities***. Most states

FIGURE 11.8

Sample Accumulation Value and Surrender Provisions, Deferred Annuity Contract.

Method of Determination

The Accumulated Value as of any date will be the sum of all Net Premium Payments plus interest to that date and reduced by the following:

1. All sums that have been withdrawn, including any withdrawal charges
2. All unpaid premium taxes

Interest Credits

Interest will be credited from the day the Premium Payments are received at our Home Office. The guaranteed annual interest rate is as follows:

Contract Years	Annual Interest Rate
1 and 2	5.5%
3 through 10	4.0%
after 10	3.5%

At our discretion a greater effective annual rate of interest may be credited at any time over and above the guaranteed interest rate.

Annual Report

Each contract year we will inform you of the accumulated value. Unpaid premium taxes will not be reflected in the Accumulated Value on the report.

Application of Accumulated Value

Unless an Optional Settlement has been elected in advance of the Annuity Starting Date, then on the Annuity Starting Date we will apply the Accumulated Value under the option to provide a Monthly Annuity during the lifetime of the Annuitant for at least 10 years.

Withdrawal Charges

While this contract has Accumulated Value, before the Annuity Date or on the death of the Annuitant, you may (in writing) elect to withdraw part or all of such value. If all of the contract value is withdrawn, we will consider this contract terminated. Any withdrawal in excess of 6% of the Accumulated Value in a contract year will necessitate a withdrawal charge as follows:

Table of Surrender Charges

Contract Year	Surrender Charge Percentage	The column below shows the actual surrender charges that would result for a termination of a deferred annuity contract having a $100,000 accumulation value.
Year 1	7 percent	$7,000
Year 2	6 percent	$6,000
Year 3	5 percent	$5,000
Year 4	4 percent	$4,000
Year 5	3 percent	$3,000
Year 6	2 percent	$2,000
Year 7	1 percent	$1,000
8 & over	0	0

have adopted laws based on this model law. The laws in most states describe the minimum nonforfeiture values that insurers must set for individual deferred annuities. Insurers may pay higher cash surrender values than those derived from the model law, but not lower. For competitive reasons, some insurers decide to award cash values that are substantially higher than those required by law.

Cash Surrender Values in Canada

Canadian insurance regulations do not address issues related to cash surrender values for insurance and annuity products. However, most insurers in Canada voluntarily provide cash surrender values for deferred annuity products. Although Canadian law does not address how voluntary cash surrender values should be calculated, annuity cash surrender values are generally set to equal the contract's accumulation value minus a surrender charge. In Canada, annuity surrender charges are typically smaller than those in the United States, reflecting the generally lower commissions paid to agents for annuity sales in Canada.

Key Terms and Concepts

contractual reserve
noncontractual reserve
contingency reserve
asset fluctuation reserve
supplemental reserve
statutory accounting records
GAAP accounting records
internal accounting records
tax accounting records
insurance rating agency
quality rating
reserve strengthening
reserve destrengthening
reserve valuation method
modified reserve valuation method
modified reserve
deferred acquisition cost (DAC)
net GAAP reserve
net reserve valuation method
net reserve
gross reserve valuation method
gross reserve
prospective reserve valuation method
retrospective reserve valuation method
Standard Valuation Law
Commissioners' Annuity Reserve Valuation Method (CARVM)
policy premium method (PPM)

commutation right
surrender
withdrawal
Model Standard Nonforfeiture Law for Individual Deferred Annuities

REFERENCES

Committee on Life Insurance Company Valuation Principles. *The Valuation Actuary Handbook*. Itasca, IL: Society of Actuaries, 1987.

Tullis, Mark A., and Polkinghorn, Philip K. *Valuation of Life Insurance Liabilities*. 2nd ed. Winsted, CT: ACTEX Publications, 1992.

CHAPTER 12

Pension Plans

After studying this chapter, you should be able to

- Recognize and distinguish among coverage, eligibility, and participation with respect to pension plans
- Compare a defined benefit pension formula and a defined contribution pension formula
- Describe important actuarial cost methods used for pension plans
- Distinguish between allocated and unallocated funding for pension plans
- Describe insured, combination, and trusteed pension plans
- Recognize important insured product types used for funding pension plans

Our discussion to this point in the textbook has focused entirely on individual annuities, which provide retirement income on an individual basis. We now turn our attention to private pension plans, which provide retirement income to members of groups. We begin by discussing the important elements of a pension plan—plan provisions, plan benefits, and arrangements for plan administration. Next, we consider how actuaries calculate the contribution amounts needed for funding pension plans. Finally, we review various arrangements for investing plan assets through life insurance companies, banks, and trust companies.

For purposes of our discussion, a ***pension plan*** is a group benefit plan that provides retirement income. The entity that maintains a pension plan is the ***pension plan sponsor***. Private pension plans are sponsored through an organization—such as an employer, a labor union, or a trade association. *Private* pension plans may be contrasted with *public* pension plans, such as Social Security, which are sponsored by government bodies. In this chapter, our discussions relate primarily to private employer-sponsored plans.

The group members who are covered by pension plans are referred to as ***pension plan participants***. In 1997, more than 50 million people in the United States participated in retirement plans other than Social Security.[1] Finally, ***pension plan beneficiaries*** are all individuals who receive benefits under pension plans, though they may not be current or former plan participants. Pension plan beneficiaries can include dependents, spouses, and survivors of plan participants.

Private pension plans in Canada and the United States usually are designed to qualify for favored tax treatment. Pension plans that meet the requirements for favored tax status are known as ***registered pension plans*** in Canada and as ***qualified pension plans*** in the United States. Although Canadian and U.S. regulation of pension plans differ in many respects, the different sets of regulations generally address the same issues. For a few details of the requirements that pension plans must meet in order to obtain registered or qualified tax status, see Insight 12-1. Most details of these requirements, however, are beyond the scope of this text.

INSIGHT 12.1

U.S. Federal Regulation Affecting Qualified Pension Plans.

In the United States, most employer-employee benefit plans must comply with both the *Internal Revenue Code* and the federal *Employee Retirement Income Security Act (ERISA)*.[1] A qualified plan can be specifically defined as one that the Internal Revenue Service approves because the plan meets all applicable requirements. ERISA is designed to ensure that certain minimum plan requirements are included in employee benefit plans. ERISA also provides the majority of pension plan legislation in the United States. For ERISA purposes, a pension plan is any plan, fund, or program that is established or maintained by an employer or by an employee organization that (1) provides retirement income to employees or (2) results in a deferral of income by employees for periods extending to the termination of employment or beyond.

ERISA requires retirement plans to be established and maintained in accordance with a written plan document that describes the benefits provided, how the plan will be funded, and the procedure that will be followed to amend the plan. Plan participants and beneficiaries who are receiving plan benefits must be provided with a summary plan description that is understandable by the average plan participant and that reasonably apprises participants and beneficiaries of their rights and obligations under the plan.

ERISA and the federal tax laws spell out the requirements a plan must meet in order to qualify for favorable federal tax treatment. A group retirement plan must have been established in the United States by an employer for the exclusive benefit of its employees or the beneficiaries named by those employees. The plan also must comply with regulatory standards that impose a variety of requirements designed to protect plan participants. Some of the requirements imposed on qualified plans include minimum participation requirements, minimum vesting requirements, nondiscrimination requirements, and distribution requirements. These are general requirements imposed on all qualified pension plans. In many cases, other requirements vary depending on the type of plan. Any retirement plan generally can be classified as either a defined benefit or a defined contribution plan. Specific rules often are imposed on defined benefit pension plans while different rules are imposed on defined contribution pension plans, reflecting variations in how the plans operate.

In Canada, the federal government and all the provincial governments have each enacted a *Pension Benefits Act* that governs the terms and operation of private pension plans.

Source: Harriett E. Jones, *Regulatory Compliance: Companies, Producers, and Operations* (Atlanta: LOMA,1998), 256–57. Adapted with permission of the publisher.

PENSION PLAN PROVISIONS

As a first step in pension plan design, the pension plan sponsor must decide upon the type of plan to establish and the terms of that plan. The ***pension plan document*** is a detailed legal agreement establishing the existence of a pension plan and specifying the rights and obligations of various parties to the pension plan. This document must be made available to plan participants for inspection upon request. The plan document contains a number of provisions which specify the

- Eligibility requirements that employees (or other group members) must meet in order to participate in the retirement plan
- Retirement benefits that plan participants will receive
- Arrangements for plan administration

The major elements of plan design, all specified in the plan document, include (1) the plan's structure as to plan benefits and coverage,

(2) arrangements for plan administration and the designation of an administrator for the plan, and (3) the selection of an investment arrangement for plan assets.

Eligibility and Coverage Provisions

Eligibility requirements are rules used to determine which members of a sponsoring organization may participate in a pension plan. In most cases, the sponsoring organization is an employer and the members are employees. Pension plan ***eligibility*** refers to a person's qualification as a member of a group that has been identified for plan participation. The most common types of eligibility requirements are based on a minimum age and a minimum length of service. Eligibility requirements may be based on classifications of employees. For example, a plan can specify that it covers all full-time salaried employees of the sponsoring employer, provided they are at least 21 years old and have at least one full year of service with the employer. Eligibility requirements may also be based on the location of the work site.

The concept of eligibility is related to the concepts of participation and coverage. A person may meet a pension plan's eligibility requirements but may choose not to participate in the plan. Thus, all plan participants are members of a covered group, but not all members of covered groups elect to participate in the plan. Pension plan ***participation*** refers to the inclusion of an individual as a member in a pension plan. On the other hand, a pension plan's ***coverage*** identifies the scope of individuals eligible for membership in the plan and is defined in terms of a specified group or groups. Individuals who are members of covered groups are eligible for plan membership. In the United States, the setting of a maximum age for participation is not permitted. Other eligibility requirements are limited by regulation.

Provisions Describing Retirement Benefits

A pension plan's ***benefit formula*** describes the plan sponsor's financial obligation to plan participants. The benefit formula has three main components: (1) the benefit amount, (2) the age at which benefits will begin, and (3) the form of annuity the benefit will take. In brief, the specification of a benefit amount can take the form of a promise to (1) pay a specified benefit to participants or their beneficiaries or (2) contribute a specified amount to the plan on behalf of participants. These two main types of pension benefit formulas are known respectively as defined benefit and defined contribution pension formulas. A pension plan structured according to a defined benefit pension formula is referred to as a defined benefit plan. Similarly, a pension plan structured according to a defined contribution pension formula is referred to as a defined contribution plan. Figure 12-1 shows, for the United States, defined contribution and defined benefit plans by number of participants and by amount of assets.

FIGURE 12.1

Contributions to Defined Benefit and Defined Contribution Plans.

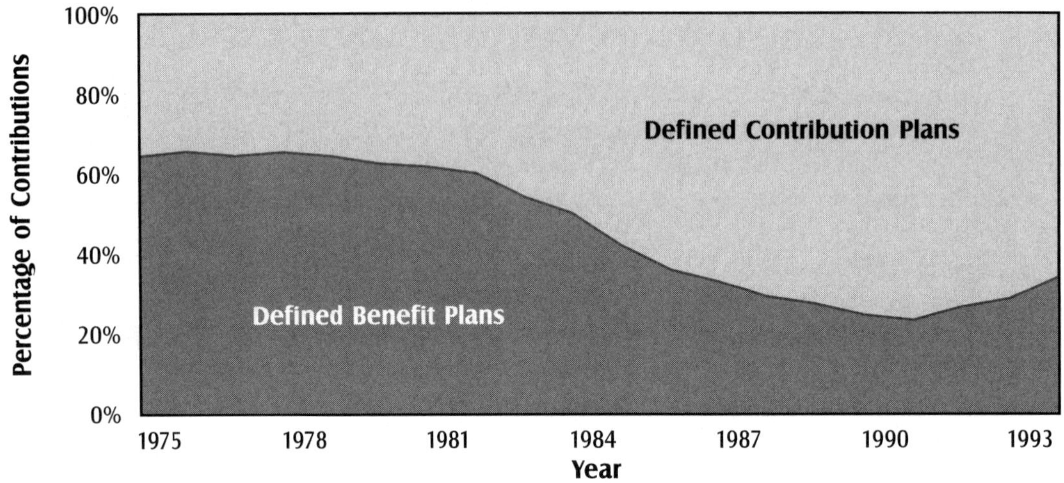

Source: ACLI, *1997 Life Insurance Fact Book* (Washington, D.C.: American Council of Life Insurance, 1997), 24.

Defined Benefit Pension Formulas

A ***defined benefit pension formula*** specifies the benefit amount the plan sponsor promises to provide to each plan participant at retirement. For defined benefit plans, the plan sponsor is obligated to deposit enough assets into the plan to provide the promised benefits. Although defined benefit formulas vary, a common defined benefit formula promises to pay a specified percentage of the participant's compensation per year of employment with the plan sponsor. Pension plans use a variety of approaches to measure both level of compensation and years of employment. For example, the level of compensation used to determine a benefit amount could be the participant's average salary for the last five years of service. In defined benefit formulas, the plan document must clearly specify how to measure the participant's compensation and years of employment. Figure 12-2 gives examples of common defined benefit pension formulas.

To the plan participants, the defined benefit formula has the advantage of providing a benefit amount that is determinable in advance. To the plan sponsor, one drawback of the defined benefit formula is that the plan sponsor cannot predict the dollar amount of its obligation to the plan for any given year in the future. This drawback carries with it the difficulty of trying to fund the pension plan and invest its assets over the long term. Another drawback is that regulatory reporting requirements for defined benefit plans in the United States are particularly costly and administratively burdensome. Since about 1972, most new pension plans have been designed with a defined contribution formula. However, many defined benefit plans remain in effect.

FIGURE 12.2

Examples of Defined Benefit Pension Formulas.

Flat Amount	Every plan participant receives the same benefit amount upon retirement, such as $150 per month.
Flat Amount per Year of Service	Plan participants receive a flat amount for each year of service with the employer. For example, if the flat amount is $20 per month for each year of service, a plan participant who has been employed for 20 years at retirement will receive a retirement benefit of $400 per month.
Flat Percentage of Earnings	Each plan participant will receive a specified percentage of earnings as a retirement benefit, regardless of years of service. The formula must specify the exact percentage and define the earnings that will be counted. The percentage specified usually ranges from 20 to 40 percent. *Earnings* may be the final year's earnings or a career average of earnings over a specified period of years. For example, suppose a plan specifies that each plan participant will receive 30 percent of final pay as a retirement benefit. Then, a plan participant earning $3,000 per month at retirement would receive a monthly retirement benefit of $900.
Percentage of Earnings per Year of Service	Plan participants receive a retirement benefit equal to a specified percentage of earnings for each year of their participation in the pension plan. *Earnings* may be the final year's earnings or a career average of earnings over a specified period of years. As an example, suppose a plan provides that participants will receive 1 percent of their final earnings for each year employed with the plan sponsor. A participant who has been employed for 20 years and who is earning $3,000 per month at the time of retirement will receive a monthly benefit of $600, calculated as 20 years x $3,000 salary x 1 percent.

Source: Dan M. McGill and Donald S. Grubbs, Jr., *Fundamentals of Private Pensions,* 6th ed. (Homewood, IL: Irwin, 1989), 105–11.

Defined Contribution Pension Formulas

For a given pension plan, a ***contribution*** is a payment to fund the plan's benefits. A ***defined contribution pension formula*** states the annual contribution the plan sponsor will pay into the plan on behalf of each plan participant. The amount of a participant's eventual benefit at retirement reflects the accumulated value of contributions made on behalf of the participant, including investment earnings on the contributions. Figure 12-3 gives examples of defined contribution pension benefit formulas.

Under a defined contribution formula, the plan sponsor's contribution amount can reasonably be estimated in advance. A drawback of the defined contribution plan to the participant is that the amount of the actual retirement benefit cannot be accurately predicted very far in advance of the retirement date. The amount of the actual retirement benefit depends heavily upon two important factors: (1) the amount of the plan sponsor's contributions and (2) the strength of the fund's investment earnings over a period of many years.

Defined contribution plans must keep an individual record for each plan participant. A participant's account can be increased by the amounts of

FIGURE 12.3

Examples of Defined Contribution Pension Benefit Formulas.

Money Purchase Pension Plans	The plan sponsor makes periodic contributions according to a predetermined formula. For example, contributions may be set at 5 percent of an employee's annual salary, to be contributed annually. For a plan participant earning $30,000 per year, the plan sponsor would contribute $1,500 annually to the plan.
Target Benefit Plans	A benefit formula, such as those used in defined benefit plans, is used to calculate a target benefit. The plan sponsor then computes the years to retirement for each plan participant and contributes a level annual amount that, along with investment earnings, would result in achieving the target benefit. There is no guarantee, however, that the target benefit will be achieved. For example, the target benefit on behalf of a plan participant is calculated to be $500 per month. The plan participant has 20 years before retirement. The plan sponsor has determined that a lump sum of $60,000 at the participant's retirement will be needed to provide the monthly benefit of $500; the plan sponsor contributes a flat amount annually for each of the 20 years until the participant retires, with the expectation that the contributions plus accumulations of interest will grow to equal the required sum.
Negotiated Contribution Plans	These plans are usually the result of collective bargaining and include multiple employers. Each employer's contributions on behalf of plan participants are determined with reference to earnings, hours of work, or a measure of productivity, with respect to each plan participant they employ. However, all contributions are pooled—rather than made to an individual account. Each plan participant then receives benefits according to a scale of benefits, such as a flat monthly benefit for each year of service.

Source: Dan M. McGill and Donald S. Grubbs, Jr., *Fundamentals of Private Pensions,* 6th ed. (Homewood, IL: Irwin, 1989), 114–16.

(1) contributions, (2) investment earnings, and, in some cases, (3) forfeitures of nonvested contributions that arise when nonvested participants leave the plan. ***Forfeitures*** are the account balances abandoned by plan participants who leave the plan before they have a right to keep those benefits. In some defined contribution plans, these forfeited account balances are distributed among the remaining plan participants; in other cases, however, forfeitures are applied to offset future contributions from the plan sponsor. In defined contribution plans, each participant's account may be charged for a share of the plan's operating expenses, including general administrative expenses, investment costs, legal fees, and start-up expenses for plan installation. Figure 12-4 summarizes the effects of various events on the accounts of participants in defined contribution plans.

Vesting Provisions for Pension Benefits

Pension plans must specify the circumstances in which a plan participant has a nonforfeitable right to the benefits funded by employer contributions. ***Vesting*** can be defined as the participant's right to keep all or part of her accrued pension benefit even if she retires early, leaves her job, or ends her association with the plan sponsor. A participant is vested when she has the right to receive partial or full benefits under the plan even if she terminates employment prior to retirement. Qualified or registered plans must provide

FIGURE 12.4

Effects of Various Events on Defined Contribution Plan Accounts.

Event	Increase	Decrease
Contributions	X	
Investment earnings	X	
Some forfeitures	X	
General administrative expenses		X
Investment costs		X
Investment losses		X

that each participant is immediately vested in the accrued benefit funded by her own contributions; additionally, a participant's right to such benefits is nonforfeitable.

Vested pension benefits are said to be ***portable*** if they can be moved from one pension plan to another. In the United States, plan sponsors may permit terminating employees to withdraw their vested benefits from a pension plan, but portability is not required. For registered pension plans in Canada, vested plan benefits must be portable.

Provisions for Payment of Pension Benefits

A pension plan document must describe arrangements for the payment of plan benefits. Two important elements of these arrangements are the normal annuity form and the normal retirement age. The ***normal annuity form*** is the form of annuity that the distribution of benefits is assumed to take for the purposes of all actuarial valuations of the plan or of a participant's expected future benefits. Pension plans usually permit retiring plan participants to elect a form of annuity other than the normal annuity form. Any form of benefit other than the normal annuity form is set to be actuarially equivalent to the benefit that would be payable under the normal annuity form. The normal annuity form is generally designated as the single life annuity, so that all elective annuity forms are calculated to be actuarially equivalent to the single life annuity. Some plans, notably qualified defined benefit pension plans, must provide a joint and survivor form of annuity as the normal annuity form for married pension plan participants, with the benefit amount actuarially reduced from the single life annuity basis.

Pension rules for determining when a plan participant can elect to begin receiving plan benefits usually set requirements of a specified minimum age, plus the completion of a minimum number of years of service. In the United States, any other requirements for beginning the distribution of retirement income benefits are rare, although additional requirements are permitted.

Some important pension plan provisions relate to the age of retirement. The ***normal retirement age*** for a pension plan is defined as the earliest age at which eligible participants in a pension plan can retire with full benefits. Age 65 is traditionally set as the normal retirement age. ***Early retirement*** is an eligible participant's retirement before the normal retirement age, subject to minimum age and service requirements and subject to a reduced pension income benefit.

Late retirement is an eligible participant's retirement from employment later than the normal retirement age. A late retiree would continue to accrue benefits until actual retirement and thus could qualify to receive an increased pension income benefit. In some cases an eligible participant elects to retire later than the normal retirement age because of entrance into the retirement plan at a late age, for example, older than 55. Late entrance into a plan can pose a problem for the plan participant in meeting a minimum service requirement. In such cases, late retirement can allow the participant to meet a minimum service requirement or otherwise to accrue a larger benefit than he would have been eligible to receive at age 65.

Provisions Describing Plan Administration

The pension plan document must also name someone who is responsible for managing the operation of the benefit plan. A ***fiduciary*** is a person or other legal entity who holds a special position of trust or confidence when handling the business affairs of another and who must put the other's interest above his or her own. Examples of fiduciaries include pension plan trustees, executors of wills and estates, receivers in bankruptcy actions, and administrators of the affairs of minors. Examples of pension plan fiduciaries include plan trustees, plan administrators, and plan investment advisors. In general, a fiduciary must fulfill specified duties for the trust beneficiaries, including a duty to manage the assets wisely and a duty to refrain from misusing the funds for personal gain. Pension plan fiduciaries must also meet detailed standards of care and must, above all, act solely for the benefit of plan participants. A plan fiduciary can be held personally liable for the amount of any losses that result from a failure to carry out a fiduciary duty, and may, in some cases, be subject to criminal penalties for failing to carry out fiduciary duties.

The plan sponsor usually names a ***plan administrator*** who has fiduciary responsibility for a variety of aspects of the plan's operation. The plan administrator for an employer-sponsored plan, for example, must maintain employment service records on all participants. These records ensure that the plan's eligibility and vesting requirements are met. Other records are also needed to document the amount of benefits payable to participants. The plan administrator uses these records to prepare all required reports for governmental agencies and to provide the plan participants with information about the plan.

The services of various professionals are often employed in the course of operating a pension plan. For example, actuarial services are typically required to set the amount of annual contributions needed to fund a defined benefit pension plan. The plan administrator may also need to obtain the services of accountants, attorneys, and other consultants. The plan administrator is responsible for hiring these professionals.

In the United States, a qualified pension plan must be established and maintained in accordance with a written pension plan document describing the plan's benefits, funding arrangements, and the procedure required for amending the plan. Regulations for qualified plans in the United States require the plan sponsor to provide to each plan participant a written disclosure document, known as a ***summary plan description***. In addition, the plan sponsor must keep in its office—for disclosure purposes and available for inspection upon request—at least one copy of the complete pension plan document discussed earlier in this chapter. Figure 12-5 specifies information that must be disclosed in a summary plan description, accurately reflecting information in the plan document.

FIGURE 12.5

Disclosures in a Summary Plan Description.

The contents of a summary plan description reflect the contents of the pension plan document, including

- The name and address of the plan administrator
- The individual or organization designated in the plan description as being responsible for ensuring the plan complies with applicable requirements
- The names and addresses of plan trustees, if any
- The identity of any organization that administers plan benefits
- The plan's source of financing
- The plan's eligibility requirements
- A description of the provisions regarding vesting of pension benefits
- A description of circumstances that may result in disqualification, ineligibility, or denial or loss of benefits
- The procedures to be followed in presenting claims for plan benefits
- The remedies available for appealing claims that are denied
- The date of the end of the plan year and whether the plan's records are kept on a calendar-year, policy-year, or fiscal-year basis

Source: Harriett E. Jones, *Regulatory Compliance: Insurance and Annuity Products* (Atlanta: LOMA,1998), 221–22. Adapted with permission of the publisher.

FINANCIAL ASPECTS OF PENSION PLANS

Financial management of pension plans focuses on balancing plan assets and plan liabilities. How a plan sponsor achieves this balance largely depends upon whether the plan is a defined benefit or a defined contribution plan.

A pension plan's assets consist of the contributions to fund the plan, plus the investment earnings on the contributions, less benefit payments, and less expenses. In a healthy economic environment, the investment earnings are expected to create positive outcomes by (1) increasing the benefits for participants in a defined contribution plan or (2) decreasing the contributions required from the plan sponsor of a defined benefit plan.

Pension plan liabilities represent the current value of accrued benefits for plan participants. For defined benefit plans, these plan liabilities represent a binding obligation that the plan sponsor must fund. Thus, the estimated amount of unfunded plan liabilities affects the amount of required current contributions to the plan. For defined contribution plans, the value of the assets attributed to each participant sets the amount of benefits that the plan will later be able to provide to each participant. Although the sponsor of a defined contribution plan has no formal commitment to fund a stated amount of pension benefit, the plan sponsor often sets a target level of benefit to provide to plan participants. Because both the assets and liabilities of pension plans are complex to value and are crucial to creating a sound pension plan, both assets and liabilities are subject to regular formal valuations. Figure 12-6 presents several purposes for pension plan valuations.

FIGURE 12.6

Purposes for Valuations of Pension Plans.

Valuations of pension plans are commonly undertaken for the following purposes:

- To estimate the long-term cost of a pension plan or any proposed changes in the plan
- To find the level of benefits that can be funded from a series of stipulated contributions
- To find the level of contributions needed to fund a given set of benefits
- To find the proper charge to be made against the plan sponsor's operating revenues for expense accounting purposes
- To find the maximum contribution that the plan sponsor can deduct in any one year for U.S. federal income tax purposes
- To find the minimum annual contribution to the plan under U.S. federal law
- To prepare actuarial reports required under U.S. federal law
- To establish plan costs and liabilities for use in corporate mergers and other changes of corporate affiliation
- To provide a basis for allocating the assets of a terminated plan among interested parties
- To provide a basis for informing plan participants about the funded status of their benefits

Source: Dan M. McGill and Donald S. Grubbs, Jr., *Fundamentals of Private Pensions,* 6th ed. (Philadelphia: Pension Research Council, Wharton School of the University of Pennsylvania, 1989), 240. Adapted with permission.

Valuation of Pension Plan Assets

Plan sponsors must regularly obtain valuations of pension plan assets, in part because laws require regular reporting and disclosure of the value of pension plan assets. Also, such asset valuations provide a basis for measuring the overall rate of return being earned on the investment portfolio. For publicly traded stocks and bonds, an asset valuation is a relatively straightforward process in which analysts record the assets' market values on a specified date. However, pension funds often hold assets—such as private placement bonds, annuity contracts, and real estate—for which a market value is not readily available. For some types of assets, analysts must estimate a fair market value.

Actuarial valuations of any group benefits may be closed group or open group valuations, and such valuations may focus on either accrued benefits or prospective benefits.

- A ***closed group valuation***, also known as a *static valuation*, is a pension plan valuation that takes into account only the benefits of persons currently affiliated with the plan as active participants, terminated vested participants, retired participants, or beneficiaries.
- An ***open group valuation***, also known as a *dynamic valuation*, takes into account the benefits of (1) the current group of participants and also (2) hypothetical participants who may enter the plan during some limited future period.[2]

According to a plan's prospects for continuing to operate, actuarial valuations for group plans may be classified as either plan continuation valuations or plan termination valuations.

- A ***plan continuation valuation*** is a pension plan valuation based on the assumption that the plan will continue in operation.
- A ***plan termination valuation*** is a pension plan valuation based on the assumption that the plan is being terminated as of the valuation date.[3]

Funding Requirements for Defined Contribution Pension Plans

As we saw earlier, the funding for defined contribution plans is known in advance, but the benefit levels are not known in advance. Determining the annual contribution amount for funding a defined contribution plan is relatively straightforward. The amount of annual contribution that an employer must make to fund a defined contribution pension plan is equal to the amount specified by the plan's contribution formula. Defined contribution plans accumulate contributions and investment earnings and then deliver to participants whatever level of benefits can be purchased with the funds accumulated on their behalf at retirement age. The valuation of plan liabilities is a relatively straightforward process for defined contribution plans, because the sum of the assets attributed to plan participants is the value of plan liabilities.

FUNDING REQUIREMENTS FOR DEFINED BENEFIT PENSION PLANS

The process of estimating the annual contribution amount for funding a defined benefit plan is much more complex than is the process for a defined contribution plan. As a first step in planning for a defined benefit pension plan, the plan sponsor must find the pension plan's cost of benefits—sometimes known as plan benefit obligations or plan benefit liabilities. For defined benefit pension plans, the amount of a participant's benefit can be projected in advance, but the cost of plan benefits cannot be known exactly and so must be estimated. Also, the plan sponsor for a defined benefit plan must establish a reasonable plan for funding that future obligation. For defined contribution pension plans, these steps are not needed.

For each defined benefit pension plan, the plan sponsor must decide upon the actuarial cost method to apply in measuring the required contributions to fund the plan and in setting a value upon the plan liabilities. An ***actuarial cost method***, also known as an *actuarial funding method* or a *pension plan valuation method*, is a formal approach used for preparing valuations of defined benefit plan liabilities. More specifically, under an actuarial cost method, the actuaries allocate the cost of a defined benefit plan to specific future periods. Because the plan liabilities are actually the plan sponsor's financial obligations, the plan sponsor must make annual contributions that will enable the plan sponsor to meet the plan's future obligations.

An ***actuarial valuation of pension plan benefits*** is the outcome or process of finding the actuarial present value of a defined benefit plan's future benefit payments as of a specified valuation date. This dollar value includes all types of plan benefits for all plan participants. Plan sponsors regularly obtain these valuations to determine the proper level of contributions to the plan and for other purposes.

Characteristics of the pension plan that affect the valuation of plan benefits include (1) characteristics of the plan population, including compensation levels of plan participants, (2) the level of benefits provided under the plan, and (3) the investment returns on plan assets. A plan valuation is also affected by elements that are not characteristics of the plan or its population. For several reasons, the results of different valuations of the same plan can vary considerably. Variations are possible because many different legitimate values are available for the array of actuarial assumptions required. Also, the methods used to develop the valuation of plan liabilities can vary, depending on the purpose for the valuation. Three important factors that affect the outcome of a valuation are (1) the characteristics of the plan population, (2) the actuarial cost method used for the valuation, and (3) the actuarial assumptions used for preparing the plan valuation.

Characteristics of the Plan Population

The characteristics of the plan population strongly influence the outcome of the actuarial valuation of plan liabilities. Important population characteristics include the plan's number of participants, compensation levels of participants, distribution of male and female participants, distribution of participants by age, and distribution of participants by years of service.

Actuarial Cost Methods

An actuarial cost method serves as a budgeting tool for helping to ensure that a pension plan is adequately and systematically funded. Different actuarial cost methods produce different patterns for assigning plan costs to specified plan years. Thus, an actuarial cost method strongly influences a plan sponsor's actual pattern of contributions to fund a defined benefit pension plan. Ultimately, however, the plan's realized net cash flows will be the same regardless of the valuation method chosen.

Cost Allocation Cost Methods

Cost allocation cost methods focus on calculating the actuarial present value of the total benefits to be paid and then assign a portion of the calculated value to each plan year. Cost allocation cost methods focus on the cost of benefits at retirement age. Under these methods, projected benefits at retirement age are estimated with or without assumed salary increases. Then the actuarial present value of the projected benefits is computed as of a specified date. Next the plan cost is determined by allocating this present value among plan years. Under a cost allocation cost method, the benefits themselves are not allocated to participants.

Cost allocation cost methods can be further classified as either individual level cost allocation methods or aggregate level cost allocation methods.

- ***Individual level cost allocation methods***, also known as *individual level-premium cost methods*, involve (1) measuring costs for individual participants and (2) summing the individual costs to obtain costs for the plan as a whole.
- ***Aggregate level cost allocation methods***, also known as *aggregate level-premium cost methods*, measure costs directly for the entire plan without attribution to individual plan participants.

Benefit Allocation Cost Methods

Benefit allocation cost methods allocate plan benefits among the various plan years and then derive the actuarial present value of the benefits. Specifically, a benefit allocation cost method first requires assigning plan participants' benefits to specific plan years; then, the method requires finding the actuarial present values of the benefits; finally, the method requires summing the resulting actuarial present values to produce costs and liabilities for the plan as a whole.

FUNDING ARRANGEMENTS FOR PENSION PLANS

For each pension plan, the sponsor must choose a funding vehicle. A ***funding vehicle*** is an arrangement for investing a pension plan's assets. Examples of funding vehicles include annuities, life insurance contracts, and mutual funds. The possible approaches to funding pension plans address whether a plan will be funded using insurance company pension products or other options. The three main categories of funding vehicles are (1) trusteed plans, (2) combination plans, and (3) fully insured plans. Figure 12-7 illustrates the share of market in insured and trusteed pension plans.

- A ***trusteed pension plan***, also known as an *uninsured plan* or a *self-administered plan*, is a pension plan that is funded through a trust arrangement.
- A ***combination pension plan,*** or a *split-funded plan*, is a pension plan that is funded using a combination of insured and uninsured funding.
- A ***fully insured pension plan*** is a plan that is funded exclusively through insured pension products.

FIGURE 12.7

Share of Market in Insured and Trusteed Pension Plans.

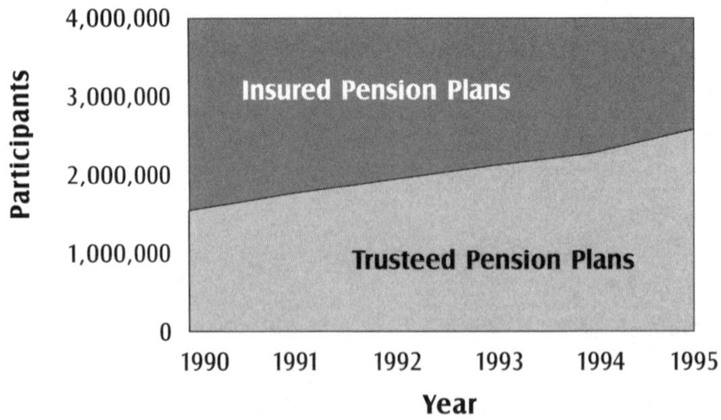

Source: ACLI, *1998 Life Insurance Fact Book* (Washington, D.C.: American Council of Life Insurance, 1998), 29.

Funding Arrangements with Banks or Trust Companies

Under a typical trusteed pension plan, contributions are paid into a trust. The trust holds the pension plan's assets, invests the assets, and pays benefits according to the plan's provisions and the terms of the trust. A ***trust*** is a legal entity that provides for ownership of property by one legal entity, known as the ***trustee***, for the benefit of another, known as the ***trust beneficiary***. (A trustee is an example of a fiduciary, as discussed earlier in this chapter.) The trustee receives title to the property but does not have the right to benefit personally from that property. The trustee has a legal obligation to manage the property and invest its assets solely for the benefit of the trust beneficiary. Because the trustee is required to manage the assets with care, the trustee may be personally liable for any expenses or lost profits that might arise from a breach of duty. A ***trust agreement*** is a legal document specifying the rules to be followed by a trustee in administering the assets of a trust. The trust agreement may limit investment of trust assets to specified types of securities or may provide for the distribution of the trust principal or earnings to a trust beneficiary only under specified circumstances.

A plan sponsor may appoint a financial institution, such as a bank or trust company, to handle some tasks associated with providing a pension plan. For example, when a plan sponsor appoints a bank or trust company to act as the plan's asset manager, the financial institution will collect contributions from the plan sponsor, invest new contributions, oversee the assets, and provide legally required reports to the plan sponsor. When a plan sponsor also appoints the bank or trust company to act as the pension plan's trustee, the financial institution also disburses benefit payments to plan participants. For a very large pension plan sponsor, an in-house pension staff sometimes administers a pension trust.

Pension Products Offered by Life Insurers

Funding arrangements offered by life insurance companies can provide plan sponsors with protection against specified financial and mortality risks. Thus, these arrangements are attractive to many plan sponsors. These products can be classified according to whether they are allocated or unallocated.

- An ***allocated funding contract*** is a pension funding contract in which all of the plan sponsor's contributions are credited to individuals in a manner that gives the participants a legally enforceable claim to the benefits attributable to those contributions. In practice, only contractual agreements issued by life insurance companies can qualify as allocated funding vehicles.
- An ***unallocated funding contract*** is one in which some or all of the contributions are held in a pooled account and are not attributed to

> individuals until the time arrives for the disbursement of benefits. Under an unallocated group annuity contract, payments made to the insurer by the plan sponsor are not immediately applied to the purchase of annuities but instead are credited to an account specified under the group contract.

A ***group annuity*** is a funding arrangement that provides annuities at retirement to a group of people under a master contract. A group annuity is usually issued to pension plan trustees for the benefit of plan participants. Individual participants hold individual certificates as evidence of their annuity benefits.

Types of unallocated group annuity contracts include group deferred annuity contracts, deposit administration contracts, immediate participation guarantee (IPG) contracts, and guaranteed interest contracts (GICs). Insurers also offer individual contracts used for funding individual policy pension trusts.

In the next few pages we will examine the insurance company products that serve as funding vehicles for pension plans.[4]

Group Deferred Annuity Contracts

Under a ***group deferred annuity***, a life insurance company issues a master policy to the plan sponsor and issues certificates to each individual plan participant before retirement. Each year, the insurer uses the contributions made on behalf of each plan participant to purchase a single premium deferred annuity for that plan participant. When a plan participant retires, these deferred annuities will provide the benefit payments promised under the plan. The total benefit amount paid to a retiree is equal to the sum of the deferred annuities purchased each year. Group deferred annuities are a type of unallocated group annuity contract.

Plan sponsors use contributions to purchase group deferred annuities in the years prior to a plan participant's retirement. Thus, group deferred annuities require premium payments and are examples of fully insured products. Very few group deferred annuity contracts have been issued in recent years, because pension plan sponsors have increasingly turned to contracts that provide greater flexibility in terms of contributions and greater participation in investment experience.

Deposit Administration Contracts

Under a ***deposit administration pension funding contract***, the plan sponsor places—or *deposits*—plan assets with the insurance company, and the assets are invested along with the insurer's general investment account. Whenever a plan participant retires, the insurer withdraws funds from the plan's general account assets to purchase an immediate annuity for the retiree. The insurer usually provides the plan sponsor with guarantees against investment loss, as well as a guaranteed minimum investment return. Further, the insurer usually guarantees, in advance, the price of the immediate annuity to be purchased at a plan participant's retirement. When the immediate annuity is purchased, the insurance company also guarantees the amount of the periodic annuity benefit that will be paid to plan participants. A deposit administration contract is an unallocated type of group annuity contract. Deposit administration contracts are suited for use with defined benefit or defined contribution plans.

Immediate Participation Guarantee Contracts

When a plan sponsor enters into an ***immediate participation guarantee (IPG) pension funding contract***, the insurance company places the plan assets in an investment account in the name of the plan sponsor. An IPG contract is designed to allow the pension plan assets to share in the actual experience of the gains or losses relating to the activities of investing and paying benefits from the pension plan's account. IPG contracts neither guarantee a minimum investment return nor provide full guarantees against investment loss. Many IPG contracts, however, guarantee that the plan sponsor will not share in losses greater than a stated amount. When a plan participant retires, the plan sponsor may withdraw funds to purchase an immediate annuity for that retiree or the monthly retirement benefit may be paid directly from the investment account to the retiree. An IPG is an unallocated funding vehicle.

Separate Account Pension Funding Riders

A separate account pension rider is generally used as an addition to a deposit administration or an immediate participation guarantee contract. Under a ***separate account pension rider***, the insurance company invests the pension plan sponsor's contributions in the insurance company's separate account investment portfolios. Our discussions in this text have mentioned that, for life insurance companies, a separate account is a type of asset account for holding certain investments separately from the investments in the insurer's general account. An insurer's separate account permits broader choice in the selection of asset types than is permitted for the general account. Thus, separate account investments are often used in connection with pension contracts. Separate account arrangements are normally included in a deferred annuity contract or an IPG contract through a rider.

Separate account pension riders usually do not make any guarantees regarding investment returns or even preservation of the invested principal. At the time of a plan participant's retirement, the plan sponsor is permitted to purchase an immediate annuity from the insurer. However, the plan sponsor is not required to purchase such an annuity.

For a separate account pension rider, the insurance company keeps records of pension plan assets under an administrative account set up in the name of the plan sponsor. Then, the plan sponsor has the option of investing the pension plan assets in a choice of the insurer's separate account portfolios. The insurer follows a different stated investment strategy for each separate account portfolio, and the plan sponsor chooses the portfolios in which the plan contributions are to be placed.

For example, suppose the Reliable Insurance Company has issued a separate account contract to the Lago Corporation. Last year, Reliable received a plan contribution of $2.5 million for Lago's investment account. Lago directed Reliable to invest the money in the separate account portfolios as follows:

Reliable Fund A	Common stock	30%	$750,000
Reliable Fund B	Corporate bonds	30%	$750,000
Reliable Fund C	Government bonds	20%	$500,000
Reliable Fund D	Real estate	20%	$500,000

Thus, the plan sponsor chooses not only the type of investments used for the pension but the level of risk it is willing to accept for the returns it expects to earn.

Guaranteed Investment Contracts (GICs)

Under a basic ***guaranteed investment contract (GIC)***, also called a *guaranteed interest contract* or a *guaranteed income contract*, the plan sponsor makes a single deposit for the insurer to hold for a specified period of time, such as five years. GICs generally have a specified maturity date and guarantee the repayment at the maturity date of the amounts deposited under the contract, plus the amount of credited interest, less withdrawals. Some GICs allow the sponsor to make monthly contributions rather than a single up-front deposit. The GIC guarantees that the insurer will pay at least a stated minimum interest rate during the contract period. The plan sponsor can choose for interest earned to be (1) accumulated until the GIC expires or (2) paid annually. When the GIC expires, the account balance—with any accumulated interest—is returned to the plan sponsor. Under an optional arrangement for benefit payments to plan participants, the plan sponsor can choose to have the principal and interest paid out in installments. Like separate account contracts, GICs permit but do not require the plan sponsor to purchase an immediate annuity at the time of a plan participant's retirement. GICs are an unallocated type of group annuity contract.

Individual Policy Pension Trusts

An ***individual policy pension trust*** is a type of allocated pension plan funding arrangement. Plan trustees administer the plan on behalf of a small group, and the trustees purchase individual level premium annuity contracts for each member of the plan.

KEY TERMS AND CONCEPTS

pension plan
pension plan sponsor
pension plan participant
pension plan beneficiary
registered pension plan
qualified pension plan
pension plan document
eligibility requirement
eligibility
participation
coverage
benefit formula
defined benefit pension formula
contribution
defined contribution pension formula
forfeiture
vesting
portable
normal annuity form
normal retirement age
early retirement
late retirement
fiduciary
plan administrator
summary plan description
closed group valuation
open group valuation
plan continuation valuation
plan termination valuation
actuarial cost method
actuarial valuation of pension plan benefits
individual level cost allocation methods
aggregate level cost allocation methods
funding vehicle
trusteed pension plan
combination pension plan
fully insured pension plan
trust
trustee
trust beneficiary
trust agreement
allocated funding contract
unallocated funding contract
group annuity
group deferred annuity
deposit administration pension funding contract

immediate participation guarantee (IPG) pension funding contract
separate account pension rider
guaranteed investment contract (GIC)
individual policy pension trust

ENDNOTES

1. ACLI, *1998 ACLI Fact Book* (Washington, D.C.: American Council of Life Insurance, 1998), 28.
2. Dan M. McGill and Donald S. Grubbs, Jr., *Fundamentals of Private Pensions,* 6th ed. (Homewood, IL: Irwin, 1989), 241.
3. Ibid.
4. Harriett E. Jones and Dani L. Long, *Principles of Insurance: Life, Health, and Annuities*, 2nd ed. (Atlanta: LOMA, 1999), 333–34.

GLOSSARY

Aa

absorption costing. *See* **full costing**.

accumulated value. *See* **future value (FV)**.

accumulation period. For a deferred annuity contract, the time period between the issue date and either the date that the payout period begins or the date that the contract's surrender value is paid; during the accumulation period, the accumulation value of the annuity account grows. [1]

accumulation value. For a deferred annuity contract, the amount paid for the annuity plus interest earned, less the amount of any withdrawals or fees. [1]

acquisition expense. Any of the costs that an insurer incurs related to obtaining and issuing new annuity business. [9]

actuarial assumption. Estimated value for any of the important elements of insurance and annuity product design, including the product's assumed investment earnings, assumed costs of providing benefits, and various assumed values for company expenses. [2]

actuarial cost method. A formal approach used for preparing valuations of defined benefit pension plan liabilities in order to ensure that the plan is adequately and systematically funded. Also known as *actuarial funding method* or *pension plan valuation method*. [12]

actuarial funding method. *See* **actuarial cost method**.

actuarial memorandum. A document, included in the form filings for an annuity contract, showing that the contract in question complies with all state insurance laws and regulations regarding the mathematical soundness of the contract. [2]

actuarial opinion and memorandum (AOM). A formal written statement prepared by an insurer's appointed actuary, attesting that the actuary has analyzed the insurer's projected cash flows under the required scenarios and that, in the actuary's opinion, the insurer's reserves make adequate provision for the insurer to meet future obligations to customers, given the assets backing the reserves. [8]

actuarial valuation of pension plan benefits. The outcome or process of finding the actuarial present value, as of a specified valuation date, of a defined benefit plan's future benefit payments. [12]

actuary. An expert in the mathematics of insurance, annuities, and financial instruments. *See also* **product actuary**, **valuation actuary**, and **appointed actuary**. [1]

adjustment methods provision. In an annuity contract, a written statement describing the steps the insurer will take to correct any material misstatement of age or sex. *See also* **misstatement of age or sex provision**. [2]

administrative charge. For variable annuity accounts, a specified percentage deducted on periodic valuation dates from the assets in the investment subaccounts. [2]

adverse deviation. Regarding a company's experience with a product, a difference between actual and assumed product values that produces a decrease in actual product profitability relative to assumed product profitability. *Contrast with* **favorable deviation**. [2]

aggregate level cost allocation methods. Pension plan valuation methods that measure costs directly for an entire pension plan without attribution to individual plan participants. Also known as *aggregate level-premium cost methods. Contrast with* **individual level cost allocation methods**. [12]

aggregate level-premium cost methods. *See* **aggregate level cost allocation methods**.

allocated funding contract. A type of pension plan contract in which all of the plan sponsor's contributions are credited to individuals in a manner that gives the participants a legally enforceable claim to the benefits attributable to those contributions. *Contrast with* **unallocated funding contract**. [12]

ALM. *See* **asset/liability management**.

annual administration charge. In fixed deferred annuities, a stated, flat dollar amount automatically deducted from the customer's annuity account value each year. [2]

annuitant. The person whose lifetime is used in determining the benefits payable under an annuity contract. [1]

annuitization period. *See* **payout period**.

annuity (actuarial definition). For purposes of the mathematics used in finance, any series of equal payments made over equally spaced time periods. [5]

annuity certain. A type of annuity contract that has no life contingencies—that is, periodic income benefits are payable under such an annuity whether the annuitant lives or dies. [1]

annuity contract. A legally enforceable written agreement under which an insurance company promises to make a series of periodic payments to a named person, starting on a specified date, in exchange for a premium or series of premiums paid to the insurer. [1]

annuity conversion cost. Amount paid by the owner of a deferred annuity contract to obtain a specified dollar amount of periodic income payment upon annuitization of the contract. *Contrast with* **annuity purchase cost**. [2]

annuity due. A stream of periodic payments for which the payment occurs at the beginning of each payment period. Also known as *annuity in advance*. *Contrast with* **ordinary annuity**. [5]

annuity immediate. *See* **ordinary annuity**.

annuity in advance. *See* **annuity due**.

annuity in arrears. *See* **ordinary annuity**.

annuity mortality table. A chart that shows the projected rates of death and survival rates for a population of annuitants only. [10]

annuity purchase cost. Amount paid by the owner of an immediate annuity contract to obtain a specified dollar amount of periodic income payment upon annuitization of the contract. *Contrast with* **annuity conversion cost**. [2]

AOM. *See* **actuarial opinion and memorandum**.

appointed actuary. A professionally qualified expert in the mathematics of insurance who has been duly appointed by an insurer's board of directors to render an official *Actuarial Opinion and Memorandum* as to the insurer's financial condition. [2]

asset fluctuation reserve. Noncontractual reserve designed to absorb short-term changes in the gains and losses affecting an insurer's invested assets. [11]

asset/liability management (ALM). The activity that coordinates the administration of an insurer's obligations to customers with the administration of the insurer's investment portfolios so as to achieve the best possible financial effects. [4]

asset portfolio. For a life and annuity insurance company, the investment portfolio in which the company holds securities and other assets. [4]

asset risk. *See* **C-1 risk**.

assets. All things of value owned by a legal entity; for an insurance company, typical assets include cash, investments in stocks, bonds, mortgages, and real estate, and office buildings and equipment. [2]

asset share. For an annuity product at a given time, the net amount of cash that the product has accumulated per unit of annuity premium. [7]

asset-share model. A mathematical simulation model that insurance companies use to illustrate how a product's assets, liabilities, and surplus would change from year to year under given sets of conditions. [7]

assignment provision. In an annuity contract, a written statement granting the contract owner the right to temporarily or permanently transfer ownership of the contract. [2]

Bb

back-end load. *See* **surrender charge**.

back load. *See* **surrender charge**.

back-load annuity. A type of deferred annuity that has a relatively low minimum initial premium requirement and imposes surrender charges from the outset and for several years thereafter. *Contrast with* **front-credit annuity**, **front-load annuity**, and **no-load annuity**. [2]

bailout provision. In an annuity contract, a written statement giving the contract owner the right to surrender the annuity contract, usually without a surrender charge, if renewal interest rates on a fixed annuity fall below a pre-established level. Also known as *escape clause* or *cash-out provision*. [2]

basic accounting equation. Mathematical formula which states that assets equal the sum of liabilities and owners' equity; forms the basis of a balance sheet. [2]

basic mortality table. A chart showing mortality rates with no safety margin built into the rates. Insurers use basic mortality tables for technical design of annuity products. [10]

basis point. For an insurer, term used to refer to increments of one-hundredth of a percent (0.01 percent) of the interest margin. [7]

beneficiary. For an annuity contract, the person named to receive any proceeds payable after the annuitant's death. [1]

benefit formula. A statement that describes a pension plan sponsor's financial obligation to plan participants. *See also* **defined benefit pension formula** and **defined contribution pension formula**. [12]

bond. A debt certificate issued by a borrower who promises to repay the borrowed sum, to pay interest at a rate specified on the bond according to a specified schedule, and to repay the debt by a specified maturity date. [3]

breakeven point. For an annuity product, the point in time when the product's cumulative earnings equal its initial investment. [7]

budget. As part of the implementation process for a new product such as an annuity, a document that shows the costs associated with each activity in the implementation process and the anticipated revenue for the new product. [2]

bundled product structure. Product design in which an insurer presents a product to customers as a package of benefits, provided in exchange for a given sum of premium. *Contrast with* **unbundled product structure**. [9]

Cc

C-1 risk (asset risk). The risk that an insurer will lose money on its investments in stocks, bonds, mortgages, and real estate. *Contrast with* **C-2 risk (pricing risk)**, **C-3 risk (interest-rate risk)**, and **C-4 risk (general management risk)**. [4]

C-2 risk (pricing risk). The risk that an insurer's experience with mortality or expenses will differ significantly from expectations, causing the insurer to lose money on its product. *Contrast with* **C-1 risk (asset risk)**, **C-3 risk (interest-rate risk)**, and **C-4 risk (general management risk)**. [4]

C-3 risk (interest-rate risk). The risk that market interest rates might shift, causing an insurer's assets to lose value or its liabilities to gain value. *Contrast with* **C-1 risk (asset risk)**, **C-2 risk (pricing risk)**, and **C-4 risk (general management risk)**. [4]

C-4 risk (general management risk). The risk of losses resulting from an insurer's ineffective general business practices or from the need to pay a special assessment to cover another insurer's unsound business practices. *Contrast with* **C-1 risk (asset risk)**, **C-2 risk (pricing risk)**, and **C-3 risk (interest-rate risk)**. [4]

capital and surplus. *See* **owners' equity**.

capital budgeting tool. Any one of the numerous profitability measures that investors, such as insurance companies, use to evaluate investments of long-term funds. [6]

capital gain. *See* **price appreciation**.

CARVM. *See* **Commissioners' Annuity Reserve Valuation Method**.

cash-flow testing (CFT). The use of simulation modeling to project into a future period the cash flows associated with an insurance company's existing business, as of a given valuation date, and to compare the timing and amounts of asset and liability cash flows after the valuation date. *Contrast with* **dynamic solvency testing (DST)**. [8]

cash-out provision. *See* **bailout provision**.

CDSL. *See* **contingent deferred sales load.**

cede. The act of obtaining reinsurance on certain insurance business by transferring all or part of the risk to a reinsurer. [4]

ceding company. In a reinsurance agreement, the insurance company that purchases insurance from the reinsurer. [4]

CFT. *See* **cash-flow testing**.

closed group valuation. An assessment of the value of a pension plan that takes into account only the benefits of persons currently affiliated with the plan as active participants, terminated vested participants, retired participants, or beneficiaries. Also known as *static valuation*. *Contrast with* **open group valuation**. [12]

CMO. *See* **collateralized mortgage obligation**.

collateral. Assets pledged as security for a loan. [3]

collateralized mortgage obligation (CMO). A debt certificate secured by a pool of residential mortgage loans. [3]

combination pension plan. A type of pension plan that uses both insured and uninsured funding. Also known as a *split-funded plan*. *Contrast with* **trusteed pension plan** and **fully insured pension plan**. [12]

commission. An amount paid to compensate a sales producer. [2]

Commissioners' Annuity Reserve Valuation Method (CARVM). The net premium reserve valuation method that the Standard Valuation Law specifies for statutory valuations. [11]

commission rate. The percentage of premium or annuity account value specified for calculating the amount of a commission. [2]

common cost. *See* **indirect expense**.

commutation right. The ability of an annuity contract owner to withdraw a lump sum from the contract's remaining principal during the payout period. [11]

compound interest. The type of interest that is earned on both the principal and interest accumulated from earlier periods. *Contrast with* **simple interest**. [3]

compound value. *See* **future value (FV)**.

compound value interest factor. *See* **future value interest factor (FVIF)**.

compound value interest factor for an annuity. *See* **future value interest factor for an annuity (FVIFA)**.

comprehensive business analysis. In the development of individual annuity products, the activity in which the insurer prepares a number of studies designed to thoroughly analyze the feasibility of each product idea. [1]

confidence limit. An expression of the probability that a specific outcome will fall within a stated range. [7]

contingencies. Exposures to risk. [9]

contingency reserve. Voluntary, noncontractual reserve that supplies added reserve protection against various special categories of risk, usually related to the C-1 through C-4 risks. On an insurer's balance sheet, contingency reserves represent surplus, not liabilities. [11]

contingency risk. *See* **C risk**.

contingent deferred sales load (CDSL). For a variable annuity, an expense charge deducted from withdrawals and applied for recovery of sales expenses. [9]

contract form. For an individual annuity, the document that describes the legal agreement between the insurance company and the contract owner. [2]

contract owner. For an annuity contract, the person who exercises all rights and privileges in the contract during the lifetime of the annuitant. The contract owner may be someone other than the annuitant; however, the annuitant is automatically made the contract owner unless the applicant specifically requests to name another party as owner. [1]

contractual provision. A written statement in a contract that specifies the rights and duties of the parties to the contract. [2]

contractual reserve. Any of the liabilities that identify the amount that, together with future premiums and interest earnings, represents the expected amount of future benefits payable on an insurer's in-force business. Contractual reserves represent the insurer's obligations to customers. [11]

contribution. In pensions, a payment to fund a pension plan's benefits. [12]

corporate bond. A debt certificate issued by a corporation. [3]

cost accounting system. An accounting subsystem that accumulates expense data for the dual purposes of effective cost control and accurate pricing activities. [9]

cost accumulation. The process of capturing all of a company's costs and categorizing them in meaningful ways. [9]

cost allocation. The accounting process of assigning an indirect cost to a cost object according to a method or formula. Also known as *expense allocation*. [9]

cost allocation method. The procedure or formula used for assigning an indirect cost to a cost object such as a unit of product. [9]

costing. During technical design of an annuity product, the process used to set a product's expense assumptions. *See also* **marginal costing** and **full costing**. [9]

cost of benefits. For annuity product design, the value of contractually required benefits the product promises to pay. [2]

cost-plus approach. A method of annuity product design in which the insurer calculates the costs of developing, offering, and supporting a given product, then adds a small margin for error or profit, and thus calculates the annuity purchase cost or conversion cost charged to buyers. [2]

coverage. Regarding a pension plan, a term used to refer to the scope of individuals eligible for membership in the plan. Coverage is the result of the plan's specifying which group or groups of individuals are eligible to participate in the plan. [12]

crediting rate. For a fixed annuity contract, the interest rate applied to the customer's accumulation value. [2]

crediting-rate declaration. An insurance company's formal declaration of the crediting of a specified current interest rate on a specified product. [4]

credit risk. The possibility of poor financial performance on the part of a business; also, the possibility that a borrower (an individual or a business) could be late with payments or could entirely fail to pay its obligations. Also known as *default risk*. [4]

C risk (contingency risk). Areas of risk that the actuarial profession has identified as being vital to insurers. *See also* **C-1 risk (asset risk)**, **C-2 risk (pricing risk)**, **C-3 risk (interest-rate risk)**, and **C-4 risk (general management risk)**. [4]

currency risk. The risk arising from changes in currency exchange rates. [4]

Dd

DAC. *See* **deferred acquisition cost**.

death benefit provision. In an annuity contract, the written statement that describes how benefits will be paid upon the death of the contract owner or the annuitant. [2]

debenture. An unsecured corporate bond for which the borrower does not pledge any assets or income as security. [3]

debt. A loan. An amount owed. An investor's loan of funds to the debt issuer in return for the promised repayment of principal and payment of interest. [3]

default. A failure to meet a financial obligation. [4]

default risk. *See* **credit risk**.

deferred acquisition cost (DAC). An asset account that insurers create in order to keep their GAAP accounts balanced. Use of DAC allows insurers to spread out the impact on surplus of the first-year expenses connected with new products. [11]

deferred annuity contract. A type of annuity contract in which periodic income payments generally are scheduled to begin more than one period after the contract's issue date. *Contrast with* **immediate annuity contract**. [1]

defined benefit pension formula. A statement that specifies the benefit amount a pension plan sponsor promises to provide to each plan participant at retirement. *Contrast with* **defined contribution pension formula**. [12]

defined contribution pension formula. A statement that specifies the annual contribution a plan sponsor will pay into the pension plan on behalf of each plan participant. *Contrast with* **defined benefit pension formula**. [12]

dependent variable. In quantitative modeling, a modeling outcome, the value of which can change in response to changes in inputs to the model. *Contrast with* **independent variable**. [8]

deposit administration pension funding contract. A type of unallocated group annuity contract under which an insurer invests pension plan assets along with the insurer's general investment account. The insurer usually provides the plan sponsor with guarantees against investment loss, as well as a guaranteed minimum investment return. [12]

derivative. In investing, a financial security, such as a stock option, that derives its value from another security. [3]

direct costing. *See* **marginal costing**.

direct expense. For an insurance company, any of the costs incurred for or physically traceable to a specific annuity product. Also known as *traceable cost*. *Contrast with* **indirect expense**. [9]

discount. When a bond's market price is less than the bond's par value, the difference between the market value and the par value. *Contrast with* **premium**. [3]

discounted value. *See* **present value (PV)**.

discounting. The process of converting a future value to its present value. [6]

distribution. In marketing, the activities involved in making products available for sale to consumers. [1]

distribution system. In marketing, the network of organizations or individuals that performs all of the marketing activities needed to complete a marketing exchange process. Also known as *marketing channel*. [1]

diversifiable risk. *See* **nonsystematic risk**.

diversification. In the management of an investment portfolio, a technique for spreading risk by investing in different assets having different risk profiles. [4]

dividend. In investments, a share of earnings that a company pays to owners of its stock. [3]

DST. *See* **dynamic solvency testing**.

dynamic analysis of financial condition. *See* **dynamic solvency testing (DST)**.

dynamic capital adequacy testing. *See* **dynamic solvency testing (DST)**.

dynamic solvency testing (DST). The use of simulation modeling to project into a future period an insurance company's existing and future business, as of a given valuation date, and to compare the amounts of assets, liabilities, and owners' equity at various times after the valuation date. Also known as *dynamic analysis of financial condition* or *dynamic capital adequacy testing*. *Contrast with* **cash-flow testing (CFT)**. [8]

dynamic valuation. *See* **open group valuation**.

Ee

early retirement. In a pension plan, the election by an eligible participant to begin receiving plan benefits before the normal retirement age, subject to minimum age and service requirements and subject to a reduced pension income benefit. [12]

earnings. For an annuity product, the monetary amount that the product adds to the insurance company's capital and surplus in a given period; a measure of earnings takes into account non-cash items, such as a product's contributions to reserves. [6]

earnings statement. A basic form of financial statement which demonstrates that earnings equal the difference between revenues and expenses. As a format for a product testing model, the earnings statement approach views earnings as the amount that the product adds to owners' equity after expenses for the product are subtracted from product revenues. Also known as *income statement.* [2]

effective interest rate. Interest rate that includes the effects of compounding and is therefore greater than the corresponding nominal interest rate. *Contrast with* **nominal interest rate**. [3]

eligibility. Regarding a pension plan, a term used to refer to a person's qualification as a member of a group that has been identified for plan participation. [12]

eligibility requirement. Any of the rules used to determine which members of a sponsoring organization may participate in a pension plan. [12]

entire contract provision. In an annuity contract, a written statement specifying that only documents attached to or appearing in the contract are part of the contract. [2]

equity. In investing, an investor's ownership or share of ownership in an asset such as a business or property. [3]

escape clause. *See* **bailout provision**.

expected mortality. The number or rate of deaths that have been predicted to occur in a group of people at a given age according to a mortality table. Also known as *tabular mortality. Contrast with* **mortality experience**. [10]

expense allocation. *See* **cost allocation**.

expense charge. The portion of an annuity product's structure that is designed to reimburse the insurer for its operating expenses—specifically commissions, premium taxes, and general operating expenses. [2]

Ff

face value. For a bond, the sum the issuer of the bond borrows from the bond's initial purchaser. Also known as *maturity value. See also* **par value** and **principal**. [3]

favorable deviation. Regarding a company's experience with a product, a difference between actual and assumed product values that produces an increase in actual product profitability relative to assumed product profitability. *Contrast with* **adverse deviation**. [2]

feasibility study. In the new product design process, the evaluation a company makes in order to determine whether it has the capability to take a proposed product to market. [1]

fiduciary. A person or other legal entity who holds a special position of trust or confidence when handling the business affairs of another and who must put the other's interest above his or her own. [12]

fixed annuity contract. A type of annuity contract that guarantees the safety of the investment principal and specifies a minimum rate at which the contract's accumulation value will earn interest. [1]

fixed assumption. In an asset-share model, any value or formula for which the user cannot readily change the assumed value. Fixed assumptions reflect how the model's designer expects an annuity product to behave in the real world. *Contrast with* **user-defined assumption**. [7]

fixed payout. Offered by either a fixed or a variable annuity contract, a type of payout option under which periodic income benefit payments are guaranteed to remain the same throughout the payout period. [2]

flexible premium annuity. A type of annuity contract that is paid for in installments that may vary in timing and amount. [1]

flexible premium deferred annuity (FPDA) contract. A contract, purchased with a series of variable premium payments, that will begin making periodic income payments more than one annuity period after the contract's issue date. [1]

forecast. A projection of future values, events, or conditions; a forecast specifies an expected or most likely value for an unknown factor. [1]

forfeiture. Any pension plan account balance abandoned by participants who leave the plan before they have a right to keep those benefits. [12]

FPDA contract. *See* **flexible premium deferred annuity contract**.

free withdrawal amount. In many annuity contracts, the fractional portion of the annuity account value that the contract owner can withdraw without having to pay a charge. [2]

front-credit annuity. A type of deferred annuity that awards a bonus to the customer for signing on, but also imposes relatively high surrender charges from the outset and for several years thereafter. *Contrast with* **back-load annuity**, **front-load annuity**, and **no-load annuity**. [2]

front-end load. In an annuity product, a charge deducted from a premium at the time the customer pays that premium. Also known as *front load*. [9]

front load. *See* **front-end load**.

front-load annuity. A type of deferred annuity that imposes a significant load charge to the customer upon signing on, but has no surrender charges thereafter. *Contrast with* **back-load annuity**, **front-credit annuity**, and **no-load annuity**. [2]

full costing. A method for estimating product-related expenses in which both direct and indirect expenses are treated as product-related expenses. Also known as *absorption costing*. *Contrast with* **marginal costing**. [9]

fully insured pension plan. A type of pension plan that is funded exclusively through insured pension products. *Contrast with* **trusteed pension plan** and **combination pension plan**. [12]

funding vehicle. In pension planning, an arrangement for investing a pension plan's assets. *See* **trusteed pension plan**, **combination pension plan**, and **fully insured pension plan**. [12]

future value (FV). The amount that a sum of money is expected to be worth at a specified future date, given a stated rate of interest. Also known as *accumulated value* or *compound value*. *Contrast with* **present value (PV)**. [3]

future value interest factor (FVIF). A number that represents the future value of $1.00 at a given rate of interest for a stated number of periods. Also known as *compound value interest factor*. [5]

future value interest factor for an annuity (FVIFA). A number that represents the future value of a $1.00 annuity at a given rate of interest and for a stated number of periods. Also known as *compound value interest factor for an annuity*. [5]

future value interest factors for an annuity table. A chart that lists the future value of a $1.00 annuity for a variety of interest rates and a number of compounding periods.

future value interest factors table. A chart that shows the future value of $1.00 for various interest rates and a number of compounding periods. [5]

future value of an annuity. The amount that a series of equal payments earning a given rate of compound interest will accumulate by a given future date. [5]

future value of an annuity due (FVAd). The future value of an annuity in which the payment occurs at the beginning of each payment period. *Contrast with* **future value of an ordinary annuity (FVA)**. [5]

future value of an ordinary annuity (FVA). The future value of an annuity in which the payment occurs at the end of each payment period. *Contrast with* **future value of an annuity due (FVAd)**. [5]

FV. *See* **future value**.

FVA. *See* **future value of an annuity**.

FVAd. *See* **future value of an annuity due**.

FVIF. *See* **future value interest factor**.

FVIFA. *See* **future value interest factor for an annuity**.

Gg

GAAP accounting records. Designed as the basis for financial reporting to investors and the public at large, this set of financial records focuses on showing the company's financial stability along with its profitability. GAAP accounting records are prepared according to generally accepted accounting principles. *Contrast with* **statutory accounting records**. [11]

gender-based mortality table. *See* **sex-distinct mortality table**.

general account. For insurers, the portfolio of assets backing guaranteed products, such as traditional fixed-rate annuities. [3]

general and administrative expense. For an insurance company, any of the costs incurred as a result of undertaking normal business activities to generate sales of insurance and annuity products and to support annuity and insurance products. [9]

general management risk. *See* **C-4 risk**.

GIC. *See* **guaranteed investment contract**.

government bond. A debt certificate issued by a federal, state, county, city, or other local governmental unit. [3]

gross annuity cost. The present value of future periodic income payments, calculated with a specific provision for loading. *Contrast with* **net annuity cost**. [6]

gross annuity cost factor. An annuity cost factor that is calculated with a specific provision for loading and other expenses. *Contrast with* **net annuity cost factor**. [6]

gross reserve. Any reserve that makes provision for an insurer's product-related expenses. *Contrast with* **net reserve**. [11]

gross reserve valuation method. A method of computing reserves that makes provision for an insurer's product-related expenses. [11]

group annuity. A funding arrangement that provides annuities at retirement to a group of people under a master contract. *See also* **group deferred annuity**, **deposit administration pension funding contract**, and **immediate participation guarantee (IPG) pension funding contract**. [12]

group deferred annuity. A type of unallocated group annuity contract under which a life insurance company issues a master policy to the plan sponsor, issues certificates to each individual plan participant, uses the annual contributions for each plan participant to purchase a single-premium deferred annuity for that participant, and provides each retiree with a total benefit amount equal to the sum of the deferred annuities purchased each year. [12]

guaranteed income contract. *See* **guaranteed investment contract (GIC).**

guaranteed interest contract. *See* **guaranteed investment contract (GIC).**

guaranteed investment contract (GIC). A type of unallocated group annuity contract under which the pension plan sponsor makes a single deposit for the insurer to hold for a specified period of time. The contract guarantees a minimum interest rate and, when the contract expires, the insurer returns the account balance—with accumulated interest—to the plan sponsor, unless the plan sponsor purchases an immediate annuity from the insurer. Also known as a *guaranteed interest contract* or a *guaranteed income contract*. [12]

guaranteed minimum payout annuity. A type of annuity contract that promises to pay a specified minimum dollar amount or a specified minimum number of payments. The minimum payout can take the form of a lump sum or installments. [1]

Ii

idea generation. In the development of new products, the activity in which the insurer gathers ideas for new product concepts that will meet the needs of the company and of specific segments of the market for annuities. [1]

idea screening. In the development of new products, the activity in which the insurer evaluates new product ideas quickly and inexpensively in order to select those ideas that deserve further investigation. [1]

immediate annuity contract. A type of annuity contract in which periodic income payments generally are scheduled to begin one period after the contract's issue date. *Contrast with* **deferred annuity contract.** [1]

immediate participation guarantee (IPG) pension funding contract. A type of unallocated group annuity contract under which an insurer places pension plan assets in an investment account in the name of the plan sponsor, so that the pension plan assets share in the gains or losses relating to the activities of investing and paying pension benefits. The contract does not guarantee a minimum investment return or provide full guarantees against investment loss. [12]

income statement. *See* **earnings statement**.

incontestability provision. In an annuity contract, a written statement limiting the time, typically to two years, in which the issuer may contest the validity of the contract or a benefit on the ground of a material misrepresentation in the application. [2]

independent variable. In quantitative modeling, a modeling input that a model's user can change in order to observe any effect on the model's outcomes. *Contrast with* **dependent variable**. [8]

indirect expense. For an insurance company, any cost that cannot be traced to or is not incurred for one specific product. Also known as *common cost*. *Contrast with* **direct expense**. [9]

individual level cost allocation methods. Pension plan valuation methods that measure costs for individual participants and sum the individual costs to obtain costs for the plan as a whole. Also known as *individual level-premium cost methods*. *Contrast with* **aggregate level cost allocation methods**. [12]

individual level-premium cost methods. *See* **individual level cost allocation methods**.

individual policy pension trust. A type of allocated pension plan funding arrangement under which plan trustees purchase individual level premium annuity contracts for each member of the plan. [12]

inflation risk. The risk that the overall level or prices in the economy will increase so that returns from an investment would not keep pace with losses in the purchasing power of currency. [4]

initial investment. For a new annuity product, the amount of capital and surplus that an insurer must invest to establish the new product. [6]

installment premium annuity. A type of annuity contract that is paid for in installments. [1]

insurance rating agency. An independently owned, private organization that evaluates the financial condition of insurers and provides information to potential customers of and investors in insurance companies. [11]

intangible asset. A thing of value that represents ownership of a legal right or another nonphysical resource. *Contrast with* **tangible asset**. [3]

interest. The fee an institution or an individual pays for the use of someone else's money. [3]

interest margin. For a fixed annuity contract, the investment earnings on the company's assets less the interest credited to the annuity accumulation value. [2]

interest rate. The percentage by which an amount of money is multiplied to derive the amount that is paid for the use of that money; often expressed in decimal form. [3]

interest-rate risk. The uncertainty arising from fluctuations in market interest rates. *See also* **C-3 risk**. [4]

interest-sensitive cash-flow testing. A means of analyzing the effects of various interest-rate scenarios on cash flows by incorporating many types of internal and external forecasts. [8]

intermediate term. A term used to describe the longevity of an investment. In the United States, intermediate-term investments may be defined as covering periods from 1 to 10 years, whereas in Canada intermediate-term investments cover from more than 6 years to 10 years. *Contrast with* **short term** and **long term**. [3]

internal accounting records. A set of financial records used as the basis for financial reporting to company management, whose main interest is in having appropriate data for making sound decisions. Also known as *modified GAAP accounting records*. [11]

internal rate of return (IRR). For an annuity product, the percentage rate at which the product's earnings must be discounted, using present value techniques, in order to exactly repay the insurer's initial investment in the product. Also known as *return on investment (ROI)*. [6]

investing. The practice of employing a principal sum of money in some manner that generates earnings so that the principal sum will increase in value. [3]

investment expense. For an insurance company, any of the costs associated with investing the company's general account and separate account assets. [9]

investment management charge. In fixed deferred annuities, an unstated charge collected by the insurer to compensate for the expenses of investing. [2]

investment principal. *See* **principal.**

IPG pension funding contract. *See* **immediate participation guarantee pension funding contract**.

IRR. *See* **internal rate of return**.

Jj

joint and survivor annuity. A type of annuity contract that covers more than one life and pays benefits until both covered people die. [1]

joint life annuity. A type of annuity contract that covers more than one life and pays benefits until one of the covered people dies. [1]

Ll

lapse rate. For a specified group of contracts, a measure of the percentage of contracts that are surrendered in a given year. [2]

lapse-rate assumption. For a given group of contracts, the value assigned to the percentage of contracts that will be surrendered in a specified future year. [2]

late retirement. In a pension plan, the election by an eligible participant to begin receiving plan benefits later than the normal retirement age. [12]

level premium annuity. A type of annuity contract that is paid for in equal installments. [1]

liabilities. A company's debts and future obligations; liabilities of insurance companies tend to consist of limited debts and vast reserves for future contractual obligations. [2]

liability portfolio. For a life and annuity insurance company, the collection of products, which represent obligations to consumers. [4]

life annuity. A type of annuity contract under which benefits are payable for only so long as the annuitant lives. [1]

life expectancy. The number of years of life remaining for a group. [10]

life with period certain annuity. A type of annuity contract that promises to make benefit payments either until the death of the annuitant or until the end of a specified period, whichever is later. [1]

line diagram. *See* **time line**.

liquidity. The ease with which an asset can be converted into cash for an approximation of its true value. [3]

loan provision. In many qualified individual annuities, a written statement allowing the contract owner to obtain a loan against the annuity balance. [2]

long term. In investing, refers to the longevity of an asset. In both the United States and Canada, long-term investments last for a period greater than 10 years. *Contrast with* **short term** and **intermediate term**. [3]

Mm

M&E charge. *See* **mortality and expense risk charge.**

maintenance expense. For an insurance company, any of the product-related expenses that arise once a contract is in force. Also known as *renewal expense*. [9]

margin. *See* **profit**.

marginal costing. A method for estimating product-related expenses so that only direct expenses are treated as product-related expenses. Also known as *variable costing* and *direct costing*. *Contrast with* **full costing**. [9]

market analysis. In the new product design process, a study of all factors that might affect sales of a product. [1]

marketing channel. *See* **distribution system**.

marketing committee. A senior management group whose function is to provide overall guidance and control of the product development process, review new product designs, and approve the further development of each new product design, reject it, or call for product redesign. [1]

marketing plan. The actions that a company will take in order to reach potential customers and meet their needs. The specific strategies in a market plan cover the concepts of product, price, distribution, and promotion. [1]

market risk. The risk arising from movements in the direction of an entire market, such as the stock market, the bond market, or the real estate market. [4]

maturity date. In investing, the date on which a borrower must repay the amount originally borrowed. [3]

maturity value. *See* **face value.**

minimum death benefit guarantee. Statement included in variable annuities specifying that, if the contract owner dies before the annuity payments begin, the named beneficiary will receive a benefit equal to the greater of (a) the total amount of premium payments made for the annuity, less any withdrawals made, or (b) some enhanced value established as of the time of the contract owner's death. [2]

misstatement of age or sex provision. In an annuity contract, a written statement specifying that, if the annuitant's age or sex was misstated, then the affected benefits will be adjusted to the appropriate level for the correct age or sex, given the premium amount paid. [2]

Model Standard Nonforfeiture Law for Individual Deferred Annuities. Model regulation affecting deferred annuity minimum cash values in the United States. [11]

modified GAAP accounting records. *See* **internal accounting records**.

modified reserve. A reserve an insurer develops using a modified reserve valuation method. [11]

modified reserve valuation method. A way of calculating reserves that permits an insurer to set a lower-than-level first-year statutory contractual reserve in recognition of the surplus strain from first-year expenses. [11]

mortality and expense risk charge (M&E charge). For variable annuity accounts, a specified percentage deducted on periodic valuation dates from the assets in the investment subaccounts. [2]

mortality experience. The number or rate of deaths that actually occur in a given group of people. *Contrast with* **expected mortality**. [10]

mortality margin. For an annuity product, the excess of the insurer's actual mortality experience over the assumed mortality used in rate making for the product. [10]

mortality rate. The percentage rate at which death occurs among a defined group of people of a specified age and sometimes of a specified gender. [2]

mortality table. A chart that shows the expected death rates among a particular group of people at given ages—that is, the percentage of people in each age group who are expected to die in a particular year. [2]

mortality table with projection. A chart showing mortality rates that an insurer has modified by multiplying them by a chosen percentage. *Contrast with* **static mortality table**. [10]

mortgage. A loan secured by a pledge of specified real property. [3]

Nn

net annuity cost. The present value of future periodic income payments, calculated without any specific provision for loading. *Contrast with* **gross annuity cost**. [6]

net annuity cost factor. An annuity cost factor that is calculated on a net basis without any loading for commissions and other expenses. *Contrast with* **gross annuity cost factor**. [6]

net cash flow. For an annuity product, the total cash inflows generated from premiums, investments, and other sources minus the total cash outflows generated for commissions, expenses, benefit payments, etc. [6]

net GAAP reserve. A reserve that is equal to an insurer's reported generally accepted accounting principles reserves minus its deferred acquisition costs. [11]

net reserve. Any reserve that is developed without taking into consideration an insurer's product-related expenses. *Contrast with* **gross reserve**. [11]

net reserve valuation method. A method of computing reserves that does not take into consideration an insurer's product-related expenses. [11]

new money method. For a deferred annuity, a method of crediting interest under which a current interest rate is in effect at the time of each premium payment, so that different interest rates are credited to various portions of the money in the annuity account. *Contrast with* **portfolio method**. [2]

new product implementation. In the development of individual annuity products, the activity in which the insurer obtains appropriate regulatory approval, plans marketing promotions, trains the sales force, and begins to sell a new product. [1]

no-load annuity. A type of deferred annuity that has no front load and no surrender charges, but requires a relatively large initial premium of approximately $25,000. *Contrast with* **back-load annuity**, **front-credit annuity**, and **front-load annuity**. [2]

nominal interest rate. Interest rate that is quoted without the effects of compounding. Also known as *stated interest rate. Contrast with* **effective interest rate**. [3]

noncontractual reserve. Any type of reserve that is not contractual in nature. *See also* **contingency reserve**, **asset fluctuation reserve**, and **supplemental reserve**. [11]

nonforfeiture provision. In an annuity contract, a written statement specifying that, if the contract owner terminates the contract, an annuity benefit will still be payable based on the amount of premiums already paid. Also known as *surrender provision*. [2]

nonsystematic risk. A possibility of loss that is specific to an individual asset. Also known as *diversifiable risk* or *specific risk. Contrast with* **systematic risk**. [4]

normal annuity form. The method of benefit distribution that a pension plan document specifies will be used to assess the value of the plan or the value of a participant's expected future benefits. [12]

normal retirement age. For a pension plan, the earliest age at which an eligible participant can retire with full benefits. [12]

Oo

open group valuation. An assessment of the value of a pension plan that takes into account the benefits of the current group of participants and hypothetical participants who may enter the plan during some limited future period. Also known as *dynamic valuation. Contrast with* **closed group valuation**. [12]

ordinary annuity. A stream of periodic payments for which the payment occurs at the end of each payment period. Also known as *annuity immediate* or *annuity in arrears. Contrast with* **annuity due**. [5]

overhead expense. For an insurance company, any of the costs incurred during normal business operations and not directly associated with a specific product or service. [9]

owners' equity. The financial interests of a company's owners. For an insurance company, also known as *capital and surplus* or *surplus*. [2]

Pp

partial surrender. *See* **withdrawal.**

partial withdrawal. *See* **withdrawal**.

participation. Term used to refer to the inclusion of an individual as a member of a pension plan. Participation is the result of an eligible person's choice to become a plan member. [12]

par value. In investing, a security's nominal or face value. *See also* **face value** and **principal**. [3]

payback period. For an annuity product, the number of years that pass before the insurer's earnings from the product equal the insurer's initial investment in the product. [7]

payee. In an annuity contract, the person designated to receive all periodic income payments. Although the payee may be someone other than the contract owner or the annuitant, the owner is automatically made the payee unless there is a specific request to name another party as payee. [1]

payout option. An alternative arrangement for payment of periodic income payments to the contract's payee. Also known as *settlement option*. [6]

payout option provision. In an annuity contract, a written statement describing the payout options the insurer offers under the annuity contract. Also known as *settlement option provision*. [2]

payout period. Time specified in an annuity contract during which periodic annuity income benefits are payable to the contract's payee. Also known as *annuitization period*. [1]

pension plan. A group benefit plan that provides retirement income. [12]

pension plan beneficiary. The individual who receives benefits under a pension plan. Current or former plan participants, as well as dependents, spouses, and survivors of plan participants, can all be pension plan beneficiaries. [12]

pension plan document. A detailed legal agreement establishing the existence of a pension plan and specifying the rights and obligations of various parties to the pension plan. [12]

pension plan participant. Any group member who is covered by a pension plan. [12]

pension plan sponsor. The entity that establishes or maintains a pension plan. [12]

pension plan valuation method. *See* **actuarial cost method**.

period certain annuity. A type of annuity contract that promises to make benefit payments for at least a minimum number of periods, regardless of whether the covered person lives. [1]

periodic annuity payment factor. Number that shows, for annuitants at a given age, the periodic income payment amount that a contract owner can purchase for each $1,000 of single premium applied. [2]

periodic fee. An amount, generally intended to compensate an insurer for its administrative expenses, that must be paid at predetermined intervals, such as yearly or monthly. [9]

periodic income payment. For an annuity contract, the monthly, quarterly, semiannual, or yearly annuity payment made to the payee throughout the contract's payout period. [1]

personal property. Any property that is not real estate. *Contrast with* **real estate**. [3]

plan administrator. The person or legal entity who has fiduciary responsibility for a variety of aspects of the operation of a pension plan. [12]

plan continuation valuation. An assessment of the value of a pension plan that is based on the assumption that the plan will continue in operation. *Contrast with* **plan termination valuation**. [12]

plan termination valuation. An assessment of the value of a pension plan that is based on the assumption that the plan is being terminated as of the valuation date. *Contrast with* **plan continuation valuation**. [12]

policy premium method (PPM). A type of prospective gross level reserve valuation method that is used by insurers in Canada. The PPM annuity reserve is equal to the difference between the present value of future benefits and the present value of future premiums. [11]

population mortality table. A chart that shows rates of death for the general population, based on data from a population census. [10]

portable. The ability of vested pension benefits to be moved from one pension plan to another. [12]

portfolio. In investments, a collection of various assets usually assembled for the purpose of meeting a defined set of investment goals. [3]

portfolio method. For a deferred annuity, a method of crediting interest under which all money in the customer's annuity account is credited with one specified current rate of interest, regardless of when the money was placed in the account. *Contrast with* **new money method**. [2]

PPM. *See* **policy premium method**.

premium. When a bond's market price is greater than the bond's par value, the excess of the price over the par value. *Contrast with* **discount**. [3]

present value (PV). For a future amount of money, the amount that, if invested at a specified interest rate on a given date, would grow to equal that future amount. Also known as *discounted value. Contrast with* **future value (FV)**. [3]

present value interest factor (PVIF). A number that represents the present value of $1.00 discounted at an interest rate of *i* percent for *n* periods. [6]

present value interest factor for an annuity (PVIFA). A number that represents the present value of a $1.00 annuity at a given rate of interest and for a stated number of periods. [6]

present value interest factors for an annuity table. A chart that shows the present value of a $1 annuity for a variety of interest rates and a number of periods. [6]

present value interest factors table. A chart that shows the future value of $1 for various interest rates and a number of periods. [6]

present value of an annuity. The amount that must be invested now in order to provide for a specified, equally spaced series of equal future payments, given a specified interest rate and a specified number of periods. [6]

present value of an annuity due (PVAd). The amount that must be invested now in order to provide for a specified, equally spaced series of equal future payments made at the beginning of each payment period, given a specified interest rate and a specified number of periods. *Contrast with* **present value of an ordinary annuity (PVA)**. [6]

present value of an ordinary annuity (PVA). The amount that must be invested now in order to provide for a specified, equally spaced series of equal future payments made at the end of each payment period, given a specified interest rate and a specified number of periods. *Contrast with* **present value of an annuity due (PVAd)**. [6]

price appreciation. In stock investing, any increase in the price of stock shares. Also known as *capital gain*. [3]

pricing risk. *See* **C-2 risk**.

principal. For an investment, the sum of money originally invested; the amount upon which interest is calculated. For an annuity, the amount of money the purchaser pays as premiums. *See also* **par value** and **face value**. [3]

proceeds. In an annuity contract, any death benefit, usually in the amount of the contract's accumulation value, payable upon the death of the annuitant. [1]

product actuary. An expert in the mathematics of insurance who specializes in designing new insurance products. [1]

product design objective. For a proposed annuity product, any of the specifications that serve as guidelines during the technical design of the product; examples include the product's basic characteristics, benefits, limits on the contract amount, age limits for an annuitant, any special features, commission range, and the manner in which the insurer will provide annuity income payments. [1]

product development team. A specific type of project team that undertakes the development of a new product. [1]

product evaluation. In the development of individual annuity products, the activity in which the insurer monitors a new product's performance relative to the performance expectations built into the product's structure so corrective action can be taken, if necessary. [1]

profit. The amount by which the revenues from a product exceed the expenses associated with that product. Also known as *profit margin, margin,* and *spread*. [1]

profit margin. A popular measure of insurance product profitability that is the ratio of the present value of estimated profits to the present value of premiums. [5]

profit margin. *See* **profit**.

project schedule. A document that shows the activities that must be accomplished to complete a project, the time frames required for the completion of these activities, and the interrelationships among these activities. [2]

project team. A group of individuals who are assembled on a temporary basis for the purpose of completing a specified complex task or project. [1]

property. An asset that can be owned or possessed. *See also* **real estate** and **personal property**. [3]

proprietary mortality table. A chart developed by a single insurance company, based largely on the mortality rates the company has experienced with its own customers. *Contrast with* **published mortality table**. [10]

prospective reserve valuation method. A method of computing reserves that estimates a value for a reserve liability by looking at a contract's future cash flows—its premiums and payments on behalf of contract owners. For most individual immediate annuities, the prospective reserve is equal to the present value of future benefit payments. *Contrast with* **retrospective reserve valuation method**. [11]

prospectus. A document that offers a security for sale and contains most of the information presented in the security's registration statement. [2]

public mortality table. *See* **published mortality table.**

published mortality table. A chart showing mortality rates experienced by the insurance industry as a whole. Also known as *public mortality table. Contrast with* **proprietary mortality table**. [10]

PV. *See* **present value**.

PVA. *See* **present value of an ordinary annuity**.

PVAd. *See* **present value of an annuity due**.

PVIF. *See* **present value interest factor**.

PVIFA. *See* **present value interest factor for an annuity**.

Qq

qualified pension plan. Term used to identify a pension plan that meets the requirements for favored tax status in the United States. [12]

quality rating. An alphabetical grade or rating assigned to an insurance company by an insurance rating agency to indicate the level of the insurance company's financial strength, its ability to pay its obligations to customers, or its ability to pay its obligations to creditors. [11]

Rr

rate of return. Investment earnings expressed as a percentage relative to the invested principal. [3]

real estate. Land or anything attached to land. Also known as *real property. Contrast with* **personal property**. [3]

real property. *See* **real estate**.

refinance. Action taken by borrowers when they repay their debt before repayment is due, often in order to make new borrowing arrangements at lower interest rates. [4]

refund annuity. A type of annuity contract that promises a return of premiums paid if the covered person dies before recovering all premiums paid. [1]

registered pension plan. Term used to identify a pension plan that meets the requirements for favored tax status in Canada. [12]

reinsurance. A type of insurance that one insurance company purchases from another insurance company. [4]

reinsurer. In a reinsurance agreement, the insurance company that sells insurance to the ceding company. [4]

relevant cost. In the context of product loading, any cost that is important to include in the product design as an expense. [9]

renewal expense. *See* **maintenance expense**.

reserve. A liability amount representing an insurer's expected financial obligation under its contracts. [2]

reserve destrengthening. The action an insurer can take, after obtaining appropriate regulatory permission, to reduce the amount of its reserves. *Contrast with* **reserve strengthening**. [11]

reserve strengthening. The action of an insurer to increase the amount of its reserves for a specific block of contracts. *Contrast with* **reserve destrengthening**. [11]

reserve valuation method. An approach for calculating reserve amounts. *See also* **modified reserve valuation method**, **net reserve valuation method**, **gross reserve valuation method**, **prospective reserve valuation method**, **retrospective reserve valuation method**, **Commissioners' Annuity Reserve Valuation Method (CARVM)**, and **policy premium method (PPM)**. [11]

retrospective reserve valuation method. A method of computing reserves that sets a value for a reserve liability by looking at a contract's past cash flows—its past premiums and benefits. For most individual deferred annuities, the retrospective reserve is equal to the present value of accumulated net premiums. *Contrast with* **prospective reserve valuation method**. [11]

return. In investing, the reward an investor hopes to receive for taking a risk. [3]

return on investment (ROI). *See* **internal rate of return (IRR)**.

risk. In investing, the possibility that an investor will fail to earn an expected return or will lose all or part of an investment. [3]

risk management. In insurance, the practice of identifying, assessing, and dealing with financial risk in order to eliminate or reduce exposure to it; for insurers, the four options for dealing with risk are avoiding it, controlling it, accepting it, and transferring it. [4]

risk-return tradeoff. The relationship between risk and return that can be summarized in the following manner: as the level of risk increases, the level of return increases; as the level of risk decreases, the level of return decreases. [4]

Ss

sales revenue. The total dollar volume of sales. [1]

sales volume. The number of units of product sold. [1]

scenario analysis. A quantitative modeling process that involves changing data entered into a model and then determining how the changed data affected the model's results. [7]

security. Financial agreement representing evidence of the right to collect repayment of a loan, ownership of an asset, or the legal right to purchase or sell ownership of an asset. [3]

self-administered plan. *See* **trusteed pension plan.**

sensitivity analysis. A technique for using mathematical models for the purpose of measuring the responsiveness of the outcome produced by changing the value of one of a model's user-defined assumptions. [8]

separate account. For insurers, a portfolio set apart from the general account and used to support contracts such as variable annuities, in which the consumer shares or assumes the investment risk. [3]

separate account pension rider. Generally used as an addition to a deposit administration or an immediate participation guarantee contract, a type of contractual arrangement under which an insurer places pension plan assets in the insurance company's separate account investment portfolios, thereby giving the plan sponsor a wide range of choices in the selection of asset types. The rider usually does not make any guarantees regarding investment returns or preservation of invested principal, and the plan sponsor is permitted but not required to purchase an immediate annuity from the insurer at the time of a plan participant's retirement. [12]

settlement option. *See* **payout option**.

settlement option provision. *See* **payout option provision.**

sex-distinct mortality table. A chart showing different mortality rates for males and females. Insurers sometimes use sex-distinct mortality tables to develop higher premium rates for female annuitants and lower premium rates for male annuitants. Also known as *gender-based mortality table*. *Contrast with* **unisex mortality table**. [10]

shareholder. Any owner of stock shares. Also known as *stockholder*. [3]

short term. In investing, refers to the longevity of an asset. In the United States, short-term investments cover periods of less than 1 year, whereas in Canada short-term investments cover from 0 to 6 years. *Contrast with* **intermediate term** and **long term**. [3]

simple interest. The type of interest that is calculated only on the principal invested. To calculate simple interest, multiply the principal invested for a single period by the interest rate for that period. *Contrast with* **compound interest**. [3]

simulation modeling. The use of mathematical models to represent a complex system in order to study how the system behaves under various circumstances. [8]

single premium annuity. A type of annuity contract that is purchased by the payment of one lump-sum premium. [1]

single premium deferred annuity (SPDA) contract. A contract that is purchased with a lump-sum premium payment and that will begin making periodic income payments more than one period after the contract's issue date. [1]

single premium immediate annuity (SPIA) contract. A contract that is purchased with a lump-sum premium payment and that will begin making periodic income payments one period after the contract's issue date. [1]

SPDA contract. *See* **single premium deferred annuity contract**.

specific risk. *See* **nonsystematic risk**.

SPIA contract. *See* **single premium immediate annuity contract**.

split-funded plan. *See* **combination pension plan**.

spread. *See* **profit**.

spread compression. Phenomenon that occurs during periods of rising interest rates when insurers are forced to take a smaller profit because customers immediately demand the higher market rate while the average rate of return on the insurer's investment portfolio rises only slowly. *Contrast with* **spread expansion**. [4]

spread expansion. The widening of an insurer's spread that occurs when market interest rates fall and the insurer reduces crediting rates to the new market level while it continues to earn a higher overall rate of return on investments. *Contrast with* **spread compression**. [4]

standard cost. A cost estimate that represents the average amount of a given type of expenditure for normal business operations. [9]

Standard Valuation Law. The National Association of Insurance Commissioners' model law that sets annuity reserving standards covering both the accumulation phase and the payout phase. [11]

stated interest rate. *See* **nominal interest rate**.

static mortality table. A chart showing mortality rates that have not been modified by multiplying them by a chosen percentage. *Contrast with* **mortality table with projection**. [10]

static valuation. *See* **closed group valuation**.

statutory accounting records. In the United States, a set of financial records that provide the basis for financial reporting to state insurance regulators, whose primary interest is in evaluating insurance companies' long-term financial stability. *Contrast with* **GAAP accounting records**. [11]

stock. An equity security that represents a share of ownership in a business. [3]

stockholder. *See* **shareholder**.

straight life annuity. A type of annuity contract that pays the promised annuity income for so long as the covered person lives, regardless of how long that is. Once the annuitant dies, no further benefit is payable. [1]

summary plan description. A written disclosure document that pension plan sponsors are required by law to give to pension plan participants. [12]

supplemental reserve. Reserve that is usually noncontractual and often voluntarily established for the purpose of strengthening required reserves. [11]

surplus. *See* **owners' equity**.

surplus strain. For an annuity product, the loss, or negative earnings, for the annuity product's first year. [6]

surrender. The withdrawal of an annuity contract's entire accumulation value, subject to an administrative fee and surrender charges, resulting in the termination of the contract. [11]

surrender charge. For an annuity contract, a fee, usually expressed as a percentage of the annuity account value, charged at the time of a withdrawal from the annuity account. Also known as *back-end load, back load*, or *withdrawal charge*. [2]

surrender provision. *See* **nonforfeiture provision**.

surrender value. For an annuity contract, the accumulation value minus any applicable surrender charges. [2]

systematic risk. A possibility of loss that affects all assets in the economic system. Also known as *nondiversifiable risk. Contrast with* **nonsystematic risk**. [4]

Tt

tabular mortality. *See* **expected mortality**.

tabular mortality rate. Any mortality rate shown in a mortality table. [10]

tangible asset. Generally, a thing of value that has physical form. *Contrast with* **intangible asset**. [3]

tax accounting records. A set of financial documents designed for financial reporting to federal and state or provincial taxing authorities. [11]

technical product design. In the development of individual annuity products, the activity in which the insurer designs a contract form, sets a technical product design, and makes sure that procedures and staffing are available to support all aspects of the product. [1]

temporary life annuity. A type of annuity contract that promises to make benefit payments either until the end of a specified period, or until the death of the annuitant, whichever is first. No benefits are payable after death or after the temporary period expires. [1]

time line. A graphic device that shows, for a particular financial transaction, the following essential elements: the end of each compounding or discounting period, the frequency and amount of each cash flow, and the timing of the valuation date. Also known as *line diagram*. [5]

time value of money. The concept that the value of a sum of money will change over time as the result of the effect of interest. [3]

traceable cost. *See* **direct expense**.

trail commission. Commission amount calculated on the basis of an annuity contract's accumulation value, after an initial commission was paid upon the initial premium at the inception of the contract. [2]

transfer fee. For a variable annuity, the amount charged for the administrative processing of an asset transfer between subaccounts once a customer's number of transfers within a given period has exceeded the contract's maximum. [2]

trust. A legal entity that provides for ownership of property by a trustee for the benefit of a trust beneficiary. [12]

trust agreement. A legal document that specifies the rules to be followed by a trustee in administering the assets of a trust. [12]

trust beneficiary. In a trust, the legal entity for whose benefit the trustee manages the trust property. [12]

trustee. In a trust, the legal entity that serves as the fiduciary, owning and managing the trust property for the benefit of the trust beneficiary. [12]

trusteed pension plan. A type of pension plan that is funded through a trust arrangement. Also known as an *uninsured plan* or a *self-administered plan. Contrast with* **combination pension plan** and **fully insured pension plan**. [12]

Uu

unallocated funding contract. A type of pension plan contract in which some or all of the contributions are held in a pooled account and are not attributed to individuals until the time arrives for the disbursement of benefits. *Contrast with* **allocated funding contract**. [12]

unbundled product structure. Product design in which an insurer explicitly discloses various expense charges to customers and also specifies the rate of investment return begin credited to customers. *Contrast with* **bundled product structure**. [9]

uninsured plan. *See* **trusteed pension plan**.

unisex mortality table. A chart showing a single set of mortality rates to be used for both males and females. *Contrast with* **sex-distinct mortality table**. [10]

unit cost. The incurred expense that can be attributed to a single measured amount of product. [9]

user-defined assumption. In a mathematical model, the assumption for any value or formula that the end user of the model can easily change. User-defined assumptions in models of annuity products generally are either product design elements that represent competitive product features or environmental features that are volatile. *Contrast with* **fixed assumption**. [7]

Vv

validation period. For an annuity product, the time period beginning when a product is issued and ending when the product's asset share grows to equal its reserves. [7]

validation point. In asset-share models of annuity products, the first year in which the asset share grows to equal the reserve and the product breaks even. [7]

valuation actuary. An expert in the mathematics of insurance who specializes in rendering a professional opinion as to proper values for an insurance company's assets and liabilities. [1]

valuation date. The date as of which the value of an asset or a transaction is determined. [5]

valuation mortality table. A chart showing mortality rates that are considered conservative because they have a safety margin built in. Insurers use valuation mortality tables to calculate statutory policy reserves. [10]

variable annuity contract. A type of annuity contract characterized by the general absence of guarantees as to investment results; typically variable annuities offer limited guarantees as to investment return and limited guarantees as to cash value or death benefit. [1]

variable costing. *See* **marginal costing**.

variable payout option. Offered by a variable annuity contract, a type of payout option under which the periodic income benefit payments vary in amount based on the performance of the underlying subaccounts. [2]

vesting. A pension plan participant's right to keep all or part of her accrued pension benefit even if she retires early, leaves her job, or ends her association with the plan sponsor. [12]

Ww

waiver of surrender charge provision. In an annuity contract, a written statement specifying that the insurer will not impose a surrender charge on withdrawals under certain conditions, such as unemployment or disability of the contract owner. [2]

window premium. Additional premium payment accepted by most insurers during the first contract year of an SPDA. [1]

withdrawal. The removal of some, but not all, funds from the accumulation account of a deferred annuity contract. Also known as *partial withdrawal* or *partial surrender*. [11]

withdrawal charge. *See* **surrender charge**.

withdrawal privilege. The right of the owner of a deferred annuity contract to withdraw a portion of the contract's accumulated value at any time during the annuity's accumulation period. [2]

INDEX

Aa

Dd

Ee

Ff

Gg–Hh

Ii

Jj–Kk

Ll

Mm

Nn

Oo

Pp

Qq

Rr

Ss

Tt

Uu

Vv

Ww–Zz

IMPORTANT—READ CAREFULLY BEFORE REMOVING THE CD-ROM FROM ITS JACKET. Use of the software program on the enclosed disk is subject to the terms of the license agreement printed below. By removing the disk from the jacket, you indicate your acceptance of the following LOMA License Agreement.

LOMA LICENSE AGREEMENT

This is a legal agreement between you (individual or company) and LOMA. By removing the disk from its jacket, you are agreeing to be bound by the terms of this agreement.

Grant of License

LOMA grants to you the right to use one copy of the enclosed *ExecuView* CD (hereinafter "the software") on a single computer. The software is in "use" on a computer when it is loaded into temporary memory (RAM) or installed into permanent memory (hard disk, CD-ROM, or other storage device) of that computer.

Copyright

The software is owned by LOMA and is protected by U.S. copyright laws and international treaty provisions. Therefore, you must treat the software like any other copyrighted material (e.g., a book or musical recording) EXCEPT that you may either make one copy of the software solely for backup or archival purposes or transfer the software to a single hard disk provided you keep the original solely for backup or archival purposes. You may not copy the written material accompanying the software. The instructional material (hereinafter "the content") contained in the software is also owned by LOMA and protected by U.S. copyright laws and international treaty provisions. It is illegal to make any copy whatsoever of the content; to install the software on a network, intranet, or web site; to download the content to another computer or device; to print screens or otherwise cause the content to be printed; or to in any other way reproduce the content contained in the software.

Other Restrictions

You may not rent or lease the software. You may not reverse engineer, decompile, or disassemble the software or in any way duplicate the contents of the code and other elements therein.

Warranty

LOMA warrants that all software provided by LOMA has been treated with a virus detection, removal, and prevention system before the LOMA software is shipped to the User. Before installing the software, it is the User's responsibility to re-check the software and verify that it is free from any virus, bug, or any other problem whatsoever that may affect User's hardware, software, network, data, database, or any other equipment, material, or operations whatsoever.

Disclaimer of Warranty

LOMA MAKES NO OTHER WARRANTY EXPRESSED OR IMPLIED INCLUDING, WITHOUT LIMITATION, NO WARRANTY OF MERCHANTABILITY OR FITNESS OR SUITABILITY FOR A PARTICULAR PURPOSE. In the event of LOMA's breach of its warranty above, User's sole remedy shall be replacement of the defective LOMA software or refund of the purchase price thereof, as determined at LOMA's sole option. UNDER NO CIRCUMSTANCES SHALL LOMA BE LIABLE TO THE USER OR ANY THIRD PARTY FOR ANY INCIDENTAL OR CONSEQUENTIAL DAMAGES WHATSOEVER.

Limitation of Liability

User agrees to indemnify and hold harmless LOMA, its employees, its agents, and their successors and assigns against any loss, liability, cost or expense (including reasonable attorneys' fees) asserted against or suffered or incurred by LOMA as a consequence of, or in the defense of, any claim arising from or based upon any alleged negligence, act or failure to act, whatsoever of LOMA, its employees, their successors, agents, heirs, and/or assigns with respect to the aforementioned software.

SYSTEM REQUIREMENTS:

- IBM or IBM-compatible computer
- Windows 3.1, Windows 95, Windows 98, Windows NT 4.0, or Windows 2000